PHP Tutorials:

Programming with PHP and MySQL

A set of tutorials derived from a series of lectures

Paul Gibbs – Devon, England

PHP Tutorials: Programming with PHP and MySQL
written by Paul Gibbs

4th Edition Nov 2019 major review and updates.
First published Nov 2014

Copyright

Amazon ASIN Number: B00CBLZ1U0 (eBook – Kindle)
ISBN Numbers:
978-0-9928697-0-0 (eBook – PDF)
978-0-9928697-1-7 (eBook - ePub)
978-0-9928697-2-4 (eBook – Kindle)
978-0-9928697-4-8 (Paper Back)

Preface

Written from a series of college lectures on PHP and MySQL, this book is a practical look at programming. It starts with an introduction to PHP, then goes on to MySQL and how to use SQL with the PHP language.

It introduces web programming and shows how to display and update data from a database. It looks at issues you encounter in real world situations and provides the basic code from which you can then use for further development.

It would be helpful if you have some HTML knowledge, but the examples should provide you with what you need to know. It would also be helpful to have some experience in programming using one of the more popular languages such as Visual Basic, although this is not necessary.

Many of the chapters consists of a series of examples and tasks that illustrate each point and concentrate on simplified code so that you can see how they are used.

* Introduction – Basic PHP concepts.
* Variables - Variables, programming techniques and so on.
* Forms and PHP - Posting data between forms.
* Arrays – loops and array structures.
* Basic PHP structures – using include files.
* Functions – writing and using your own functions.
* Posting Forms – how forms work.
* Email Forms – an email form.
* JavaScript – posting forms with JavaScript.
* SQL and MySQL - Querying database tables using SQL.
* An Example table – some example data.
* Database Access – how to connect to a database.
* Using PHP and MySQL – an example form.
* Further PHP and MySQL - More PHP and MySQL.
* Error handling and debugging - Simple methods to find errors.
* Cookies and sessions - When and where to use them.
* Modifying Records - editing and updating databases with PHP and SQL.
* Classes - An introduction to object orientated programming.
* File Handling - Reading and writing to text files.
* Regular Expressions and Validation - Some validation methods.
* PHP security - Some methods to overcome this issue.
* jQuery, Ajax and Bootstrap.
* htaccess and php.ini - how to use them.
* WordPress - an introduction to creating a WordPress Plugin.
* Appendix – UniformServer and MySQL Management.

Trademarks

MySQL is a trademark of Oracle Corporation and/or its affiliates. Macintosh and Mac OS X are registered trademarks of Apple Inc. Microsoft and Windows are registered trademarks of Microsoft Corp. Dreamweaver is a registered trademark of Adobe Systems incorporated. The WordPress Foundation owns and oversees the trademarks for the WordPress and WordCamp names and logos. Other product names used in this book may be trademarks of their own respective companies. This book is not affiliated with, or endorsed by any of the products mentioned.

Warning and Disclaimer

Every effort has been made to make this book as complete and as accurate as possible, but no warranty or fitness is implied. The information provided is on an 'as is' basis. The author and publisher shall have no liability or responsibility to any person or entity regarding any loss or damage incurred, or alleged to have incurred, directly or indirectly, by the information contained in this book. You hereby agree to be bound by this disclaimer.

Basic Programming Terms

Variables - Areas of memory set aside by the programmer to store data and assigned a name by the programmer. Variables can then be used for such things as temporary storage during calculations or performing tests for decisions.

Data types - Defines the type of data that a variable can hold. This might be a string of characters such as for the name of 'Paul', or may be a numeric value such as someone's age, e.g. 56, or decimal value for the price of a product, e.g. 23.12

Arrays - These are variables, but instead of holding one value, can hold multiple values with each value identified by a reference name. So, you may have an array of towns such as Trowbridge, Chippenham, Lackham referenced by 0, 1 and 2.

Decision-making with if statements - Decision-making or conditional statements allow you to control the flow of a program. We can test a value after doing a calculation, or when someone enters a value into a form. The result of the test will be either true or false and we can then make the script do something depending on the result.

Programming loops - these are for repeating code a set number of times or until a condition is met. They are often used when we have rows of data in a table, and we loop around the rows performing some action until there are no more rows left.

POST and GET - This is how you send data to another web page where you can then process the data.   POST and GET work with forms where the user enters information.

Cookies - A cookie is a small text file that sits on the user's computer.   It is often used to store data so that the user has a better browsing experience should they return to the web site. For example, a shopping cart system may store the items that the user has selected. When they return to the store, the contents of the cart can be displayed and the user can continue shopping.

Sessions - Another way for the programmer to retain information; however, session data is deleted and lost when the user closes the browser window.

OOP or Object Orientated Programming - A class in OOP programming terms is a definition that represents something using variables (called properties in OOP) and functions (called methods in OOP). Objects are then built from the class definition and it is possible for many objects to be based on the same class.

Websites, Source Code and Feedback

Using the code examples

All the code examples with answers to the exercises may be downloaded to your computer from the web site:
https://www.paulvgibbs.com
or:
https://www.withinweb.com/ebooks

The code examples and exercise are grou

ped together in chapters and are referenced in this book by their filename.

If you have any questions or want to provide feedback then use the following email address:

Email: paul@paulvgibbs.com

How to copy and paste text from Kindle books

You may want to copy and paste programming code examples from Kindle onto your computer so that you don't have to re-type them.

To do this in Kindle, highlight the text you want to copy and click on the "Highlight" button. Now go on the web to your Kindle account (https://kindle.amazon.com) and click on "Your Highlights" link. You'll see all the text you've highlighted in your Kindle books. From there, you can copy the text and paste it into another program.

What's New in This Edition

As time has moved on and the technology has changed and improved, it is important to keep up to date with the latest methods in PHP, MySQL and front-end development with JQuery and associated methods. In this new edition, I have added new examples, expanded code explanations and updated material. In particular:

* The removal of code and descriptions only relevant to PHP versions earlier than PHP 7.
* Expansion of code examples.
* More explanation of code as used for connecting to databases using PDO and mysqli.
* Further details in data validation.
* Best coding principles and practices.
* Plus many other changes.

Contents

1 - Introduction to PHP

What is in this Chapter?

* Requirements for PHP.
* Simple PHP script and a PHP page.
* Language syntax.

PHP is an open source scripting language that is especially suited for web development. The term PHP originally stood for 'Personal Home Page' but now stands for 'PHP: Hypertext Preprocessor'.

Developed first by Rasmus Lerdorf in 1994, it is now under the control of the PHP Group. There have been a number of major updates over the years reaching the present major version of PHP 7 (2015) which this book covers.

So what happened to PHP 6? Well, that was a version that took so long to develop and had so many problems that it did not reach completion, and the decision was taken to jump the numbering to PHP 7 to avoid confusion with books and other materials that had already been published about the un-released PHP 6.

PHP code is embedded within HTML pages and enclosed within the special start and end tags
<?php and ?>

The code executes on the web server and NOT on your local computer; the server generates the resulting HTML and sends it back to the client where you see it in your web browser. It is important to realise it is the remote web server that processes the PHP script and hence you need a web server.

PHP is quite easy for newcomers to learn but has many advanced features particularly when working with databases. Unlike other languages, programming modules that you require will be available to you as standard, and with a wide range of inbuilt functions and its ability to integrate with HTML it has made it a preferred language for web programming applications.

PHP powers many of the world's web sites and there is a large community of forums and groups on the internet. If your program outputs an error message, you can often find the answer by searching on Google where you will probably others who have had the same issue.

What you need

If you want to work with PHP at home, either use a remote web server, in which case you will need to purchase web space and a domain name from a hosting company, or you can create a system on your local computer.

The easiest solution for most people is to purchase web space from a hosting company so that you do not have to worry about installing or updating PHP and other programs on your local computer. Hosting companies are very competitive in pricing, they provide large disc space for your files and provide all the administration tools to create and work with MySQL databases.

We can break down the required elements that you need as follows:

A web server

The web server is the computer system that processes requests and sends web pages back to your browser. Nowadays PHP scripts can run on Mac, Linux and Windows computers with the right software.

Apache is a common web server found on Linux type operating systems, but Microsoft IIS servers are also capable of handling PHP.

PHP and MySQL are usually associated with LAMP (**L**inux, **A**pache, **M**ySQL, **P**HP). However, many PHP developers use Windows when developing the PHP application, which is called WAMP (**W**indows, **A**pache, **M**ySQL, **P**HP).

There are several PHP / MySQL / Apache packaged systems that you can download and install on Windows computers. One of these, which you can use for development, is EasyPHP **http://www.easyphp.org/**

PHP

If you are using a hosting company then you don't have to do anything other than check that you are working with the latest version. Some hosts enable you to change the PHP version number for defined folders, which can be useful if you are using outdated functions.

MySQL

Ensure that you have a way to administer your MySQL databases, this is often using the web-based application called **phpMyAdmin**.

Web browsers

It is useful to have a selection of web browsers on your computer so you can test your displays and make sure they work in different environments. The browser you choose depends on personal choice although some have better web development tools than others do. My personal choice for general use is Chrome as it does have very good development displays where you can show html source code and debug JavaScript amongst other things.

A Text Editor

You obviously need an editor to write your PHP scripts. As PHP and HTML are just text files, you can use any text editor such as NotePad or NotePad++. However, there are a number of commercial products such as Dreamweaver. My personal favourite now is Brackets, which is free to download from **http://brackets.io/**. Sublime Text is another free to download editor from **https://www.sublimetext.com/**

FTP Program

An FTP program (such as FileZilla) is needed if you are using a remote Server although some editors such as Dreamweaver have FTP built in.

The processing of PHP

When you use a browser to display a web page on your computer, the remote web server reads the PHP and processes it according to the code. The PHP processor then sends the generated HTML to your web browser.

So, PHP creates an HTML page on the fly based on the coding that you have created in the PHP page.

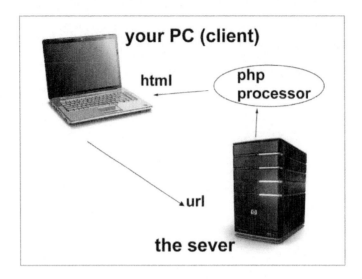

The Client is your local computer, while the Server is the remote computer and will be a web server.

The figure above demonstrates how the process works between a **Client**, the PHP processing module and the **Server** to send HTML back to the browser. All server-side technologies (PHP, for example) use some sort of processing module on the server to process the data and send it back to the client.

If you have a site that consists only of HTML web pages, the server merely sends the HTML data to the web browser as shown in the figure below.

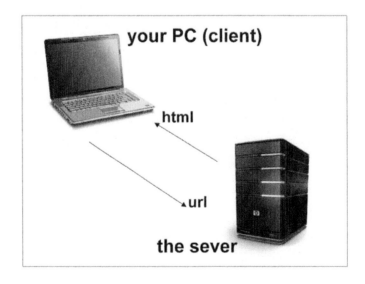

This is why you can view the HTML pages on your local web browser since they do not need to be "served". Whereas you access dynamically generated pages such as those created from PHP through a server that handles the processing.

To the end user, there will not be any obvious difference between a page delivered through PHP and one delivered as just HTML.

PHP allows the creation of dynamic web pages that can display different data on a web page depending on the programming of the PHP script. You often use it in conjunction with a database, enabling you to write programs for e-commerce shopping systems, content management systems and discussion forums.

A simple PHP script

We start with a simple web page that should be a standard XHTML document but can actually be just a blank page without any HTML code at all. The following is an example of an HTML page that you should be familiar with if you have done some web design. The **.php** file extension identifies it to the server as PHP.

```
1.  <!DOCTYPE html>
2.  <html>
3.  <head>
4.  <meta charset="UTF-8" />
5.  <title>Untitled Document</title>
6.  </head>
7.
8.  <body>
9.  Your main body of text goes here
10. </body>
11.
12. </html>
```

PHP is an HTML embedded scripting language. This means you can combine PHP and HTML code within the same script. So it is helpful to have some knowledge of HTML when you do PHP programming.

To place PHP code within a document, you surround the code within PHP tags as shown below. These need to be placed inside the **<body> ... </body>** tags of the HTML page.

```
1.  <?php
2.
3.  ?>
```

The web server treats anything that you place within these tags as PHP code.

NOTE: *Some programmers use <? ?> for the PHP tags. This is bad practice and may not work at all on web servers.*

Error reporting

When an error occurs in a PHP script, it will display that error to the browser. Most web servers work in this way. However, you may find that your server is not displaying errors especially if you are running PHP on a Microsoft IIS server. To overcome this, you can try the following code at the top of each **PHP** script and just after the <?php tag.

```
1.  ini_set('display_errors','On');
2.  error_reporting( E_ALL | E_STRICT | E_DEPRECATED );//Show all errors
```

TASK 1 - A PHP page

You may want to start your programming by creating a folder called **php_tutorials** and then another folder called **tutorials01**. As you progress through the chapters, you can then place your files into these folders.

(1) Create a new document in your text editor. If you are using Dreamweaver, create a web page that will look similar to the following:

```
1.  <!DOCTYPE html>
2.  <html>
3.  <head>
4.  <meta charset="UTF-8" />
5.  <title>Untitled Document</title>
6.  </head>
7.
8.  <body>
9.  Your main body of text goes here
10. </body>
11.
12. </html>
```

(2) Add the opening and closing PHP tags in between the start and end body tags lines 7 and 8.

(3) Save the file as **example1.php**

Code File: 01_introduction/example1.php

(4) Inside the opening and closing tags enter the following:

echo("PHP programming");

```
1.  <!DOCTYPE html>
2.  <html>
3.  <head>
4.  <meta charset="UTF-8" />
5.  <title>A PHP Web Page</title>
6.  </head>
7.
8.  <body>
9.
10. <?php
11.     echo("PHP programming");
12. ?>
13.
14. </body>
15. </html>
```

(5) Save and upload your file to a PHP compatible web server.

(6) Open file in a web browser. To display the page in the browser you will need the URL of the web page on your web server, so this will be something like http://www.yourserver.com/tutorials/file.php

NOTE: You must save the page with a .php extension to tell the server what type of processing it has to do.

This first script simply displays some text on the page using the PHP echo function. This page does little but it does test that your web server and ftp are working.

Note the following:

* PHP is case sensitive so you must enter echo as all lowercase.
* The text to be displayed requires quote marks at the start and quote marks at the end.
* The line of code must be ended by a semicolon (;)

TASK 2 - echo and print

To display information on your web browser we use **echo()** and **print()** statements. There are no real differences between the echo and print statement so most programmers use **echo().**

(There is actually a special version of print that is **printf().** This is to allow formatting of data such as dates and times).

Some examples of **echo()**:

```
1.  echo 'There was an error connecting to the database';
2.
3.  echo "Thank you for your submission to our forum";
```

You may use single or double quotation marks with either function and each line must end with a semicolon **(;)**.

Notice also that you can use the echo statement without brackets ( ).

One issue is displaying single and double quotation marks on the web page, so the following will generate an error:

```
1.  echo "He asked, "What is your name?"";
```

The above line generates an error message similar to the following:

```
Parse error: syntax error, unexpected T_STRING, expecting ',' or ';'
in /mnt/sw/22180/web/tutorial_docs/php/escape.php on line 1
```

```
1.  echo 'Paul's house.';
```

This generates an error message similar to the following:

```
Parse error: syntax error, unexpected T_STRING in
/mnt/sw/22180/web/tutorial_docs/php/escape.php on line 1
```

There are two solutions to this problem.

First, use single quotation marks when printing a double quotation mark and vice versa.

```
1.  echo "Paul's house.";
```

Alternatively, you can *escape* the character by preceding it with a backslash like this:

```
1.  echo 'Paul\'s house.';
```

The following is a further example of the **echo** statement using the built in **date** function.

1. Open the previous page **example1.php** in your text editor.

2. Between the PHP tags add a simple message.

echo date("d m y H:i:s ");

3. Open the file in your Web Browser to test the script is working properly.

If you do a search on the internet for 'PHP date' you should get a detailed description of the way this function works and the different formatting that it can display.

Try modifying the format elements to display the date in different ways such as **Tuesday 10th January 2019**

In **example1.php** you can add your new PHP commands into the same **<?php .. ?>** area as previously or you can create another **<?php ... ?>** start and end tags within the same document.

PHP documentation

The main source of documentation on the web is the PHP manual. It is important to understand how you write functions in PHP documentation because you will be continuously coming across it.

http://php.net/manual/en/index.php

If you do an internet search for 'PHP date' you should get to this page:

http://php.net/manual/en/function.date.php

It tells you the function name, which PHP versions it is available in, a description and the function in a descriptive notation:

string date (string $format [, int $timestamp = time()])

string means that it returns a string,

date is the function name

$format refers to a set of parameters that are listed further down

Anything in [ ] brackets are optional parameters.

PHP syntax

* Variables

All variables should begin with a $ symbol. e.g. $myName

* Variables are case sensitive

PHP in built functions and user defined variables are case insensitive, although variables are case sensitive, so $myName is different to $myname.

* PHP is white space insensitive

PHP will ignore white space characters, tabs etc. in the same way as HTML pages do. This means you can space out your PHP code using tabs and spaces and on different lines to make it easier to read.

* Statements and expressions are terminated by a semicolon character

A statement is any expression followed by a semicolon (;)

* Comments can be single or multi line comments

The multiline comment is the same as in the C language and is:

```
1.  /* this is
2.  a comment
3.  */
```

To comment a single line use # or //

```
1.  # This is a comment
```

The second uses two slashes.

```
1.  //This is also a comment
```

Summary

This Chapter introduced PHP and gave some simple examples of a PHP page. It looked at the echo statement and how to use it to display the current date and time. We also looked at where to find documentation for all PHP functions. In the next Chapter, we look at how to use variables and take a detailed look at PHP functions.

Topics for Review

[1] What file extension should you use for files that are to run on a PHP enabled web server?

[2] List the different ways you can enter comments into a PHP script

[3] What application would you use to administer MySQL databases?

[4] In the PHP echo statement, how do you print out a single quotation mark (') ?

2 - Variables in PHP

What is in this Chapter?

* Understanding variables and variable data types.
* PHP built in server variables.
* Functions for manipulating strings.
* Using PHP on a HTML page.
* Formatting data outputs.

You use variables to store data during the processing of the web page. You then display the data or perform other calculations on it using mathematical expressions like multiplication and division. A variable is simply an area of memory to store information that the programmer assigns to a particular identifier.

Some examples of variables might be:

45 - a whole number representing someone's age
Peter - a string representing a person's name
2013-01-28 - a string representing a date
22.40 - a decimal number representing the cost of an item

Variables and Data Types

A variable name, also called its identifier, must start with a dollar sign ($), for example: $address.

* Variable names are case sensitive so $address and $Address are two different variables.

* The first character after the $ must be a letter or underscore, followed by any number of letters, numbers, or underscores.

Assign values to variables using the equals sign (=) like the following:

$address = "London";

There are eight data types as follows:

* **Integers** – whole numbers
* **Doubles** – floating point numbers
* **Booleans** – true or false
* **Null** – a special type with just the value of NULL
* **Strings** – sequences of characters
* **Arrays** – indexed collections
* **Objects** – instances of classes
* **Resources** – references for database connections or files

In PHP, you do not require to declare variables or give them data types as you may have to do with other programming languages like Visual Basic. PHP automatically converts the variable to the correct data type, depending on its value.   Therefore, a PHP variable does not know in advance whether it will store a number or a string. This is termed 'loosely typed'.

There are advantages and disadvantages with a loosely typed language. Coding is simpler as you do not have to worry about data types, but it can cause potential problems when you may use a variable expecting one data type and it actually holds a different data type.

Some examples of variables and their use in PHP would be:

```
1.  $name = "Paul";
2.  $age = 27;
3.  $isStudent = true;
4.  $cost = 1.99;
5.  $currentDate = "2014-01-05";
```

NOTE: *You enclose strings and dates with quote marks while numbers do not have the quote marks.*

There is no specification on the way to define a variable name, but we quite often use something called the **Camel Notation**.

An example of this is:

$firstName = "Paul";

The **Camel Notation** is where the first word starts with a lower case, and the following words start with an upper case.

Another approach is to prefix the name with the data type, so we might use the following:

```
1.  intAge = "47";
2.  strFirstName = "Paul";
```

This helps us to identify the purpose of a particular variable.

Whatever system you choose, make sure that you are consistent throughout your script.

TASK 1 - Some examples of variables

To demonstrate the use of variables we will do a simple calculation.

(1) Create a new PHP document in your text editor. If you are using Dreamweaver, it will automatically create some HTML code for you.

(2) Save the file with the name **variables.php**

(3) Within the <body> tags of the html page, add your PHP tags.

```
1.  <?php
2.
3.  ?>
```

* Create a variable with your name and echo it to the web page.
* Create a variable called TAX and set it to 0.2 (20%)
* Create a variable called productcost and set it to 34.20
* Calculate the TAX, display the TAX and display the new price of the item.

```
1.  //-----------
2.  $name = "Paul";
3.  echo("My name is $name<br/>");
4.  //-----------
5.  $tax = 0.2;
6.  $productcost = 34.20;
7.  $taxcost = $productcost * $tax;
8.  $cost = $taxcost + $productcost;
9.  //-----------
10. echo("TAX is $taxcost<br/>");
11. echo("Total cost is $cost<br/>");
12. //-----------
```

(4) Upload the page to the web server, run it in the browser and check the results.

TASK 2 - Pre-defined variables

PHP includes a number of pre-defined variables for use in displaying information about the system. We can use these to work with, or to display such things as your IP address, the name of the file that you are working on and so on.

These pre-defined variables are accessed using the **$_SERVER** array.

(1) Open the **variables.php** file in the editor.

(2) Within the <body> tags, add another set of PHP tags.

```
1.  <?php
2.  //Your code goes here
3.  ?>
```

(3) Create the following variables using **$_SERVER** as follows:

```
1.  $file = $_SERVER['PHP_SELF'];
2.  $user = $_SERVER['HTTP_USER_AGENT'];
3.  $address = $_SERVER['REMOTE_ADDR'];
```

This above script uses three variables that come from the **$_SERVER** array.

PHP_SELF returns the name of the script being run:

$_SERVER['PHP_SELF'];

HTTP_USER_AGENT returns the capabilities of the web browser and other details of the system accessing the script:

$_SERVER['HTTP_USER_AGENT'];

The IP address of the user accessing the script is accessed using REMOTE_ADDR:

$_SERVER['REMOTE_ADDR'];

(4) Enter the following code in the page.

```
1.  echo "<p>The current filename is: <strong>$file</strong>.</p>";
2.  echo "<p>The user details are: <strong>$user</strong> <br/>with
        address: <strong>$address</strong></p>";
```

(5) Upload the file to the web server and open the file in the Web Browser to test the script is working properly.

TASK 3 - Strings and string manipulation

Strings hold text information as words and sentences and are enclosed in quote marks. Anything stored in quote marks becomes a string.

The following are examples of strings:

'Paul'

"My name is Paul"

'July 5, 2020'

We assign a string variable to a variable name in the following way:

```
1.  $first_name = 'Paul';
2.  $today = 'July 5, 2020';
```

In order to print out the value of a string, use either **echo()** or **print()**:

```
1.  $first_name = 'Paul';
2.  $today = 'July 5, 2020';
3.  echo $first_name;
4.  echo "Hello, $first_name";
```

Another example of a string is:

```
1.  $age = "25";
```

As it is enclosed by quote marks, it becomes a string.

Doing mathematical operations on this value may give unexpected results, as you should normally use:

```
1.  $age = 25;
```

Or convert the string to a numerical value:

```
1.  $age = "25";
2.  $intAge = (int)$age;
```

Whenever you do any numerical calculations, make sure you have not defined the numbers as strings.

(1) To illustrate the use of strings, using the same PHP file **variables.php** and within the PHP tags, create three variables by adding the code below inside the PHP tags.

```
1.  //Create the variables
2.  $first_name = 'Paul';
3.  $last_name = 'Gibbs';
4.  $work = 'Super Software Company';
```

(2) Add the echo statement below, on one line and test the script in your Web browser.

```
5.  echo "<p>$first_name $lastname works at $work</p>";
```

TASK 4 - Some string functions

One of the most common string functions is the **Concatenation** operator, which is **(.)** and has the effect of adding two strings together:

```
1.  $town = 'Trowbridge';
2.  $county = 'Wiltshire';
3.  $address = $town . ', ' . $county;
```

The **$address** variable now has the value **Trowbridge, Wiltshire**

So that a comma and a space are added to the line.

Concatenation works with strings or numbers.

```
4. $address = $town .  ',  ' . $county . 'BA14 OES';
```

(1) To test the concatenation of strings we can use the same PHP file **variables.php** and within the PHP tags add the following code:

```
5.  $myname = $first_name . ' ' . $last_name;
6.  echo "$myname works at $work.";
```

(2) Open and test in your Web browsers.

If you enter a search in Google for **PHP string functions** it should return the page http://php.net/manual/en/ref.strings.php that lists all the functions available.

Here are a few of the more common ones:

Trimming Strings functions	
trim()	Removes whitespace at the beginning and end of a string.
ltrim()	Removes whitespace at the beginning of a string.
rtrim()	Removes whitespace at the end of a string.

Presentation functions	
htmlentities()	Escapes all HTML entities.
strtoupper()	Converts a string to uppercase
strtolower()	Converts a string to lowercase.
ucfirst()	Converts the first character of a string to uppercase.
ucwords()	Converts the first character of each word in a string to uppercase.

Converting Strings and Arrays functions	
explode()	Splits a string into an array on a specified character or group of characters.
implode()	Converts an array into a string, placing a specified character or group of characters between each array element.
join()	Same as implode().

Substrings functions	
substr(str,pos)	Returns the substring from the character in position pos to the end of the string
substr(str,-len)	Returns the substring from len characters from the end of the string to the end of the string
substr(str,pos,len)	Returns a len length substring beginning with the

	character in position pos.
substr(str,pos,-len)	Returns a substring beginning with the character in position pos and chopping off the last len characters of the string.
strstr(haystack,needle, before_needle)	If the third argument (before_needle) is false (default), then it returns the part of the haystack from the needle onwards. If the third argument (before_needle) is true, then it returns the part of the haystack before the needle. The needle can be a string or an integer (or a number that can be converted to an integer).
stristr(haystack,needle, before_needle)	Same as strstr(), but case insensitive
strpos(haystack,needle)	Finds the position of the first occurrence of a specified needle in a haystack (string). The needle can be a string or an integer (or a number that can be converted to an integer).
strrpos(haystack,needle)	Finds the position of the last occurrence of a specified needle in a haystack (string). The needle can be a string or an integer (or a number that can be converted to an integer).
str_replace()	Replaces all occurrences of one string with another string.

Comparing Strings functions	
strcmp()	Compares two strings. Returns < 0 if str1 is less than str2, > 0 if str1 is greater than str2, and a 0 if they are equal.
strcasecmp()	As above but case sensitive.
strlen()	Returns the length of a string.

Exercise 2.1

This exercise is to try out the function **str_replace**

Use the string:

```
1.  $mystring = "This script is written by name";
```

Look up **str_replace** on the web and use it to substitute the text of **name** in the string **$mystring** with your name, and display the result on the web page.

Exercise 2.2

This exercise is to try out **strpos**

If we have a string that is 'http://www.wwithinweb.com' and we want to check that http has been entered in the string, we can use strpos to test for this.

Look up **strpos** on the web and use it to check for the occurrence of http in a string.

TASK 5 - Numeric date types

PHP has both INTEGER and DOUBLE (floating-point decimal number) types, so valid numbers would be:

```
1.  $an_integer = 27;
2.  $a_double = 2.3456;
3.  $e_notation = 2.3e2;
```

You do not place quotes around Numbers. If you did it would make them strings, nor do you include commas to indicate thousands.

PHP has fewer data types than other programming languages so making it easier to work with.

Use the following list of math operators to perform calculations:

Simple mathematical operators

+   Addition, for example $result = $a + $b
-    Subtraction, for example $result = $a - $b
*   Multiplication, for example $result = $a * $b
/   Division, for example $result = $a / %b

%   Modulus, for example $result = $a % $b
++   Increment, for example $result = ++$a
--   Decrement, for example $result = --$a

PHP has the standard arithmetic operators and many other functions to deal with numbers. Two that we will look at here are **round()** and **number_format().** The former rounds a decimal either to the nearest integer.

```
1.  $n = 2. 3456;
2.  $n = round($n);    //will return 2
```

Or:

```
1.  $n = 2.183645;
2.  $n = round($n, 3);       //will return 2.183
```

Round also has an optional parameter to define the type of rounding of

PHP_ROUND_HALF_UP
PHP_ROUND_HALF_DOWN
PHP_ROUND_HALF_EVEN
PHP_ROUND_HALF_ODD

The **number_format()** function turns a number into the more commonly written version, grouped into thousands using commas.   For example:

```
1.  $n = 493849;
2.  $n = number_format ($n);     //will return 493,849
```

Exercise 2.3

As a simple exercise, we want to do a calculation on a salary to calculate tax and to display the result in our web browser

Assume the salary is £25,000 and the tax rate is 20%

First, calculate the tax on the salary, and then calculate the salary less tax.

Display the two values to the web browser.

TASK 6 - Constants

Constants are values that cannot change during the execution of the script. Assign constants any single value, a number or a string of characters.

To create a constant, you use the **define()** function as follows:

```
1.  define ('NAME', 'value');
```

By convention, the name of a constant is all capital letters. In addition, constants do not use the initial dollar sign (**$**) as with variables.

An example of displaying a constant is:

```
1.  define ('USERNAME' , 'gibbpv');
2.  echo "Hello, " . USERNAME;
```

Constants are often used for configuration settings, so you may see it used with setting database username / passwords and similar situations.

TASK 7 - Single and double quoted strings

We can use single and double quote marks in **echo()** and **print()** statements, however, there is a difference in how they behave.

In PHP, values enclosed in single quote marks are **not** interpreted and are displayed 'as is'. However, values that are enclosed in double quote marks are interpreted.

If we want to display certain characters within double quote marks we have to **escape** those characters, that is place the \ character before it.

Escaped Characters Code

\"	Double quotation mark
\'	Single quotation mark
\\	Backslash
\n	Newline
\r	Carriage return
\t	Tab
\$	Dollar sign

As an example, assume you have:

```
1.  $var = "Paul";
2.  echo "\$var is equal to $var";
```

Will display:

```
$var is equal to Paul
```

While:

```
1.  echo '\$var is equal to $var';
2.  \$var is equal to $var.
```

Will display:

```
\$var is equal to $var.
```

You can see in the above examples, that double quote marks will display the value of $var, while single quote marks will display $var exactly as it is.

TASK 8 - PHP and HTML

It is common in PHP to output HTML code. The easy way to do this is to use single quote marks when printing HTML within PHP.

```
1.  echo '<table width="80%" border ="0" cellspacing ="2" cellpadding ="
    3" align= "center" >';
```

If you were to print out this HTML using double quotation marks, you would have to escape all the double quotation marks in the string as follows:

```
1.  echo "<table width=\"80%\" border =\"0\" cellspacing =\"2\"
    cellpadding =\"3\" align= \"center\">";
```

Another way of printing out HTML is to do the following:

```
1.  <?php
2.  // ..... some code ......
3.  ?>
4.     <img src="delete.gif" width="10" height="10" />
5.  <?php
6.  // ..... some code ......
7.  ?>
```

In the above example, we use <?php ... ?> tags to go from PHP and HTML instead of writing the HTML in the PHP code.

TASK 9 – Data type casting and formatting the outputs

As a recap, PHP does not require you to declare variables or give them data types, as you may have to do with other programming languages like Java or C#. PHP automatically converts the variable to the correct data type, depending on its value.

So $name = "fred"; works by just assigning a value to the variable name and it understands it as a string.

To forcibly convert a variable to a certain type, either cast the variable or use the **settype()** function on it.

Casting is the process where we explicitly convert the data. This may sometimes be required to improve security for example, where we take user input and convert to an integer. The process of casting is placing the required data type in brackets in front of the data for example:

(int) or (integer) - cast to integer
(bool) or (boolean) - cast to Boolean
(float) or, (double) or (real) - cast to float
(string) - cast to string
(array) - cast to array
(object) - cast to object

```
1.  $float_num = 10.9;
2.  echo (int)$float_num;
```

The above code converts 10.9 to integer resulting in the value of 10.

The **settype** function can also convert the data type as in the following example:

```
1.  //----------------------------
2.  $value = "1";
3.  settype($value, "bool");
4.  var_dump($value); // Outputs: bool(true)
5.  //----------------------------
6.  $value = "0";
7.  settype($value, "bool");
8.  var_dump($value); // Outputs: bool(false)
9.  //----------------------------
```

The **printf()** function can be used to output to a particular format to make them look more presentable. So for example:

```
1.  printf("%d", "17,999");
```

Will display **17**.

The general form of printf is:

printf(type specifier, value);

NOTE: printf returns an integer value of the length of the string while sprintf returns a string.

The example above uses the **%d** format specifier. This formats the value as a signed decimal integer. The 'd' is known as a type specifier to say what type the output data should be. **printf()** supports a wide range as follows:

b   Format the argument as a binary integer (e.g. 11000110).
c   Format the argument as a character with the argument's ASCII value.
d   Format the argument as a signed decimal integer.
e   Format the argument in scientific notation (e.g. 9.344e+3).
f   Format the argument as a floating-point number using the current locale settings (e.g. in France a comma is used for the decimal point).
F   As above, but ignore the locale settings.
o   Format the argument as an octal integer.
s   Format the argument as a string.
u   Format the argument as an unsigned decimal integer.
x   Format the argument as a lowercase hexadecimal integer (e.g. 2faf47).
X   Format the argument as an uppercase hexadecimal integer (e.g. 2FAF47).

Exercise 2.4

If Australia has 6 states and 10 territories print this out using a **printf** statement:

Example: **printf(** "Australia comprises %d states and %d territories", 6, 10);

Exercise 2.5

Write a program to convert 20 degrees Fahrenheit to Centigrade and display the results as a floating-point number:

Temperature in Centigrade = (5 / 9) * ($Tf - 32)

Exercise 2.6

Write a script that has three variables $a, $b and $c. Assign some numerical values to each of these three variables and then calculate the average. Display the result using an echo statement and display as a floating point number to two decimal places – you will need to use the number_format function.

Summary

This Chapter looked at the handling of variables in PHP, which is a loosely typed language. This means that you do not have to define the data type of a variable because PHP will convert it to the correct data type. Sometimes you may have to convert to a required data type, in which case you use the cast technique. The Chapter then looked at the built in variables using the **$_SERVER** array that is often used to find out about the system.

String functions are very important, and PHP seems to have an endless number of built in string manipulation functions some of which you use with formatting and outputting to HTML.

This Chapter provides many of the basic concepts of the PHP language that we will go on to use in later Chapters.

Topics for Review

[1] List the eight data types that are used for variables.

[2] What is the difference in using a single quotation mark (') and a double quotation mark (") in an echo statement?

[3] Look up the built in variable $_SERVER in the PHP documentation on the web and list as many uses of uses as you can.

[4] What does escaping a character mean and how would you use this method to display HTML such as a table on a web page?

[5] How do you use the printf statement to format a decimal number?

3 - Forms and PHP

What is in this Chapter?

* HTTP **GET** and **POST** concepts.
* HTML form basics and PHP handler.
* Some simple data validation.
* Conditional processing with **if** and **switch** statements.

Web forms are an important concept in web programming, allowing the user to input data and to submit it to the server where the PHP script processes it. The script might store the data in a database or might process it further or send an email.

To do this we first look at creating an HTML form and how we reference input values such as text boxes, drop down lists and so on. We post these values to the web server where we have a PHP script that acts as the form handler. The PHP script usually validates and checks data before it takes any further action such as saving to a database.

POST and GET methods in web forms

A form consists of HTML code containing input boxes, dropdown elements and other places where you can set or choose values. We then submit the form data to the PHP code to handle and process the data.

We do this using the **GET** and **POST** methods in HTTP.

The **GET** method passes arguments from one page to another using the URL query string. You will have seen this used in your web browser quite a bit as you surf through pages on the internet.

So a URL would append the data on to the URL as follows:

* A question mark (?)
* A variable name and equal sign and the value.
* An ampersand (&), a variable name and equal sign and the value.

We would then read the data in PHP using **$_GET["variablename"]**

The problem with **GET** is that you are limited in the number of characters that you can send in a URL and so most forms use the **POST** method. In addition, you can see the data being sent so it is considered not to be secure. However, we use **GET** a great deal, particularly for moving between pages, and we will come across examples in later Chapters.

The **POST** method is described below and that uses the **$_POST["variablename"]** function to read the data.

Name / value pairs

The following illustrates the **GET** method of submitting data:

```
http://www.sitename.com/index.php?category=media&subcategory=music
```

In this example, there is a name of 'category' with a value of media, and a name of subcategory and a name of music.

To read this you would use:

```
1.  $value1 = $_GET["category"];
2.  $value2 = $_GET["subcategory"];
```

In the example, **$value1** will be media and **$value2** will be music.

These are called **name / value** pairs.

HTML Forms

TASK 1 - Create an HTML Form
When working with forms, we normally create them by first creating our HTML with user input text boxes or whatever is required, and then create the PHP code to process the data that was entered into the form. We can create separate pages for the HTML page and PHP page, or we can create just one page, where the HTML code and PHP are on the same page. Usually, it is better to have the HTML and PHP

on the same page and most examples will use this technique.

Here are the standard opening and closing form tags.

```
1.  <form name = "formhandler" action = "formhandler.php" method ="post"
    >
2.
3.  </form>
```

action - which page the data will be sent to

method – either post or get

post is the most common method as it is able to send more data then get. **get** appends the data onto the URL of the page and is limited to just over 2000 characters.

The following task creates an HTML form looking similar to the following:

(1) Create a new HTML document in your text editor.

(2) Save the file as **loanenquire.html** in your **php_tutorial** folder.

Code File: 03_forms_and_php/loanenquire.html

(3) Insert the form opening and closing tags under the **<body>** tag as shown below.

```
1.  <form name="loan" method="post" action="loan_handler.php">
2.
3.  </form>
```

(4) Begin to write the HTML form as shown below, starting just after the opening <form tag.

```
1.  <h1>Enter your details:</h1>
```

(5) Add two text box inputs:

```
1.  <p><strong>Your Full Name</strong> <input type = "text"
    name = "fullname" size="30" maxlength="30" /></p>
2.  <p><strong>Your Email Address</strong> <input type="text"
    name = "emailaddress" size="30" maxlength="30" /></p>
```

(6) Add a pair of radio buttons:

```
3.  <p><strong>I am</strong> <input type="radio" name="employment"
    value="unemployed" /> unemployed <input type="radio"
    name="employment" value="employed" /> employed</p>
```

(7) Add a drop down box:

```
1.  <p><strong>Your Age</strong>
2.  <select name="age">
3.     <option value="">Make a selection</option>
4.            <option value="18-29">18 - 29</option>
5.            <option value="30-60">30 - 59</option>
6.            <option value="60+">Over 60</option>
7.  </select></p>
```

(8) Finally complete the form with a submit button as shown below.

```
1.  <p><input type="submit" name="Submit" value="Submit" /></p>
```

(9) Upload the page onto the web server and test it looks correct your Web browser. At this point, clicking on the submit button will have no effect because there is no PHP code to process the data.

TASK 2 - Handling HTML form data

Now that we have an HTML form (loanenquire.html), we now write a PHP script to handle the data that was posted from the form. In this example, we create a separate PHP file but we will see later on that we can add all the code into just one file. We can make the PHP script do all kinds of functions, such as interacting with a database, sending an email and so on. We look at these techniques in later chapters.

To transfer data from a form to a PHP script we can add in form elements into out HTML form like the following:

```
1.  <form .....
2.
3.  <input type="text" name="first_name" size="20" />
4.
5.  </form>
```

The PHP page that receives the form data will assign what the user entered into this form element to a variable called **$_POST['first_name'].**

NOTE: "first_name" much exactly match the name in the text box.

$_POST['first_name'] can then be used like any other variable; printed, used in mathematical calculations etc.

The following tasks creates the PHP page that is used by the formhandler.html page.

(1) Create a new PHP document in your text editor. If you are using Dreamweaver, you may have to delete all the automatically generated HTML code before you continue. In the <title></title> tags give the page the title.

```
1.  <title>Loan Enquiry</title>
```

(2) Save the file with the name **loan_handler.php**

Code File: 03_forms_and_php/loan_handler.php

(3) Within the body tags, add your opening and closing **PHP** tags.

```
1.  <?php
2.
3.  ?>
```

(4) Create data variables for the required POST variables:

```
1.  $name = $_POST['fullname'];
2.  $email = $_POST['emailaddress'];
3.  $employment = $_POST['employment'];
4.  $age = $_POST['age'];
```

The data entered into the fullname form input that has a 'name' value of fullname, will be accessible through the variable **$_POST['fullname'].**

The data entered in the emailaddress form input that has a 'name' value of emailaddress, will be accessible through the variable **$_POST['emailaddress'],** and the same applies to the remainder of the data.

(5) Using echo, display the received name, email and comments values by adding the script below.

```
1.  echo "<p>Thank you, <b>$name</b>, for your enquiry</p>
2.  <p>We will reply to you at your email address: <strong>$email</stron
    g>.</p>";
3.  echo( "<p>You are $employment $age years old</p>" );
```

(6) Load the script to your web server and test it works by filling in the form and submitting the data.

Exercise 3.1

Improve the layout of the form on loanenquire.html. Wrap the form fields around table elements so that the display is nicely structured.

Other FORM input types

Other than the form input types mentioned above, there are a few other form inputs we might use:

hidden field type – used when we want to take information from a web page without the user entering the data, and then passing the information to another web page.

password field type – these are really text boxes but where the text is replaced by * characters.

TASK 3 - Handling Magic Quotes

Magic quotes is an old PHP concept that is no longer relevant in PHP 7. However, you may come across it and it is worth mentioning as a historical aside.

The developers of PHP introduced magic quotes to make working with database data more secure.

When we work with databases we use SQL, however, single quote marks in SQL have a special meaning that may cause the SQL statement to fail or might be part of a SQL injection attack. To overcome this we might 'escape' single quote marks with a backslash to make it a correct SQL statement.

Magic quotes would automatically add a backslash to single quotes so that it would be just ordinary text in a SQL statement.

So the word Paul's becomes Paul\'s and will be handled correctly in SQL.

Unfortunately, this caused endless problems, as it did not account for the context of the data and it became necessary to check if magic quotes were on or not in the particular installation of PHP.

Nowadays, we use other methods of handling SQL injection; in particular, we use the PDO method of database access that is described in later Chapters.

The function **stripslashes** was often used with magic quote processing. **stripslashes** returns a string with backslashes removed so Paul\'s becomes Paul's and so on. There may be situations where you need to use stripslashes.

In our example, we can strip the slashes before we display the text on our web page.

(1) Open **loan_handler.php**

(2) Modify the code to use the following:

```
1.  $name    = stripslashes($_POST['fullname']);
2.  $email   = stripslashes($_POST['emailaddress']);
```

(3) Test this works in your Web browser.

Now the **$name** and **$email** variables will have any backslashes removed.

TASK 4 - Conditional processing

Use conditionals to change the processing of a script according to criteria. In PHP we have the following statements **if, else** and **elseif** (this can also be written as two words **else if**).

```
1.  if (condition) {
2.
3.  // Do some processing here when the condition is true
4.
5.  }
```

If the condition is **true**, the code in the curly brackets { } will be executed. If the condition is not true, the PHP will just continue.

We can then add the else statement:

```
1.  if (condition) {
2.
3.  // Do some processing here when the condition is true
4.
5.  } else {
6.
7.  // Do some processing here when the condition is false
8.
9.  }
```

In this case, if the condition is **true**, the code in the curly brackets { } will be executed as before but now if the condition is not true, the code in the else statement will be executed.

We can extend the statements to multiple conditions as shown below.

```
1.  if (condition 1) {
2.
3.  // Do some processing here when condition 1 is true
4.
5.  } elseif (condition 2) {
6.
7.  // Do some processing here when condition 2 is true
8.
9.  } else {
10.
11. // Do some processing here when neither condition 1 or
        condition 2 is true
12.
13. }
```

If condition 1 is **true**, the code in the curly brackets { } will be executed. If the condition is not true, the next elseif condition will test if condition 2 is true. The process will continue with as many elseif statements as you want. If all the conditions are false, then the last else statement will be executed. However, the last else statement is optional.

You should note that the condition is **true** if:

* The value is other than 0, is an empty string or is null.
* The value is a Boolean value of **true**.

A condition statement can be true for many reasons and we can do all kinds of processing to calculate the condition using the operators listed below:

Comparative and logical operators:

Symbol	Represents	Example
==	is equal to	$x == $y
!=	is not equal to	$x != $y
<	less than	$x < $y
>	greater than	$x > $y
<=	less than or equal to	$x <= $y
>=	greater than or equal to	$x >= $y
!	Not	!$x
&&	And	$x && $y
!!	Or	$x || $y
XOR	and not	$x XOR $y

For those who are more familiar with Visual Basic language, note the use of double symbols as in the example of == rather than one symbol.

So, for example we can use:

```
1.  if ( $name == 'paul')
2.  {
3.
4.  }
```

TASK 5 - Adding Conditionals to our script

We can add a conditional statement to our **loan_handler.php** script to read the value of the radio button.

(1).Open **loan_handler.php**.

Code File: 03_forms_and_php/load_handler1.php

(2) Add the new **$employment** variable as shown below.

Insert the following in place of the line $employment = $_POST['employment'];

```
1.  // Create the $employment variable
2.  if (isset($_POST['employment'])) {
3.      $employment = $_POST['employment'];
4.  } else {
5.      echo( "<p>You forgot to select your employment state</p>" );
6.      $employment = NULL;
7.  }
```

The **isset** is a simple way of checking that the user has made a selection. If the user has made a selection then the **$_POST['employment']** will have a value, meaning the condition
if (isset($_POST['employment'])) is true. If the user has not made a selection at all, then the variable **$_POST['employment']** will not be set.

(3) If the user did not select an employment option, we can print out a message.

(4) Save the file and upload to your Web server. Open in your Web browsers and test all the conditionals work correctly.

TASK 6 - Validating Form Data

All data entered into forms should be validated. This will include:

* Check for correct expected characters, for example, a person's name would not have a $ in it.
* Check data types where applicable, so a person's age would be a positive numerical integer value within some limit on the maximum and minimum age.
* Put limits on text length, so you might set the maximum characters for a person's name to 50.

All of these data validation are to help stop unwanted security issues particularly with SQL injection. Validation should happen using PHP scripts on the server before the data is used. You can also do validation on the local client computer using JavaScript in the browser. However, this form of validation can be by-passed so you should always have validation in the PHP script.

At this stage, we have not covered enough code methods to be able to show validating all the data. However, we can check if values have been entered into a text box or other selected fields in a form by using the empty function as follows:

```
1.  if (!emptyempty($_POST['fullname'])) {
2.      $name = stripslashes($_POST['fullname']);
3.  } else {
4.      $name = NULL;
5.    echo '<p><font color="red"> Please enter in your name</font></p>';
6.  }
```

TASK 7 - The switch statement

The other conditional that we have not covered is the **switch** statement and is really a replacement for a multiple if else series of statements.

The switch statement simplifies complicated if statements.

```
1.  switch ( $i ) {
2.      case 0:
3.          echo "i equals 0";
4.          break;
5.      case 1:
6.          echo "i equals 1";
7.          break;
8.      case 2:
9.          echo "i equals 2";
10.         break;
11.     default:
12.         echo "No value was entered";
13. }
```

The **switch** statement makes coding of multiple **if..elseif** statements much easier to read and easier to maintain.

If you leave out the **break;** statement, it will just drop through to the next statement and what happens will depend on the values being checked.

NOTE: *Use of the **default** value to catch any values of $i that do not fit into the other values.*

Summary

This Chapter describes one of the most important uses of the web – posting and processing of data from a form. The data from a form is sent to a PHP script on the server as **name / value** pairs were we manipulate and use as we wish. In later Chapters, we will show how to use this data to interact with a database.

Topics for Review

[1] Explain the difference between POST and GET.

[2] Explain the difference between using = and ==

[3] In a <form> element, what is the purpose of the action entry?

[4] How would you test if the contents of a string were empty?

[5] What should you look out for when you are doing data validation?

 - Arrays and Loops

What is in this Chapter?

* Creating indexed and associative arrays.
* Accessing and traversing arrays.
* Multidimensional arrays.
* for and while loop.

If you have used other programming languages then you will have come across the concept of arrays. Python for example, has a list data structure that is similar to arrays. An array is a variable that can hold more than one value at a time and where each value is accessed using a key. The value stored can be a string, a number or another array.

We can think of an array as a list of **key / value** pairs where the key is an index that uniquely identifies the values in the list. Values in arrays are often referred to as **elements**. We use the key to access these elements and we can retrieve all elements by using **loops**.

The big advantage with an array is that we can easily access all elements using quite simple programming and we can extract a specific element using a particular key.

There are three types of arrays: **indexed** where the key is a number, **associative** where the key is a string value, and **multi-dimensional** that is an array containing one or more arrays.

Arrays are an important concept in PHP because it is how data is held after being retrieved from a database. We can access the elements in the array using loops and display the values onto our web pages thus creating dynamic web sites.

Creating Arrays

Indexed arrays

An example of an array might be a list of employees like this:

Key	Value (or element)
0	Bob
1	Sally
2	Charlie
3	Clair

We can represent it as a table:

Key	0	1	2	3
Value	Bob	Sally	Charlie	Clair

To initialise the elements an array of employees we can use:

```
1.  $employees[0] = "Bob";
2.  $employees[1] = "Sally";
3.  $employees[2] = "Charlie";
4.  $employees[3] = "Clare";
```

Notice that the unique key is in square brackets [ ].

Or we can do the following:

```
1.  $employees[] = "Bob";
2.  $employees[] = "Sally";
3.  $employees[] = "Charlie";
4.  $employees[] = "Clare";
```

In the above case, PHP knows that it has to increment the key value each time and we don't have to put anything into the square brackets. This makes programming with arrays very easy and is a particular feature of PHP.

Another way of initialising is:

```
1.  $employees = array ("Bob", "Sally", "Charlie", "Clair");
```

Or another way is:

```
1.  $employees = array(1=>"Bob", 2=>"Sally", 3=>"Charlie", 4=>"Clair");
```

In the above example, we use the special symbol => to separate the index from the value.

It is also valid to do:

```
1.  $employees[10] = "Bob";
2.  $employees[34] = "Sally";
3.  $employees[45] = "Charlie";
4.  $employees[99] = "Clare";
```

The above shows that you do not have to use consecutive numbers for the array key although the array keys have to be unique.

Associative arrays

Associative arrays use string values to identify the index rather than numbers meaning we can use meaningful values for the keys.

An example of an associative array might be:

Key	Value
WI	Wiltshire
SO	Somerset
CO	Cornwall
O	Dorset
DE	Devon
GL	Gloucestershire

Initialisation of this array would be:

```
1.  $counties["WI"] = "Wiltshire";
2.  $counties["SO"] = "Somerset";
3.  $counties["CO"] = "Cornwall";
4.  $counties["DO"] = "Dorset";
5.  $counties["DE"] = "Devon";
6.  $counties["GL"] = "Gloucestershire";
```

Or another way to initialise would be:

```
1.  $counties = array ( "WI" =>"Wiltshire", "SO" =>"Somerset",
    "CO"=>"Cornwall", "DO"=>"Dorset", "DE" => "Devon",
    "GL" => "Gloucestershire");
```

Assigning a range of values

Another way to create an array is to use the **range()** function to return an array of elements like this:

```
1.  $numbers = range (3, 6);
```

The above is the same as making an array of numbers 3, 4, 5 and 6.

```
1.  $letters = range( "a", "z");
```

The above is the same as making an array of all letters of the alphabet from a to z.

```
1.  $reversed_numbers = range(5, 2);
```

The above is the same as making an array of numbers for 5, 4, 3 and 2

Getting the Size of an Array

The **count( )** and **sizeof( )** functions are used to return the number of elements in the array. Both are identical in function and there is no advantage in using one over the other.

Both return a number value representing the number of elements in the array. So for our counties array, we can display the number of elements as:

```
1.  echo ( count( $counties ) );
```

This should return 6 in our example.

Accessing arrays

Accessing individual elements of an array

Individual elements of an array can be accessed using the following method:

```
1.   echo $employees[1];      //will display Sally
```

NOTE: *With indexed arrays, the index value has no quote marks around it because it is a number and not a string.*

For associative arrays, we can use the following method:

```
1.   echo $counties["DO"];       //will display Dorset
```

NOTE: *The index is a string we put it into quote marks.*

With associative arrays, we can also do the following:

```
1.   echo $counties[4];      //will display Dorset
```

So if we want to display the value, then we can do something like the following:

```
1.   echo "DO represents the county : $counties["DO"] ");
```

The foreach loop and traversing through an array

The main function to traverse all elements in an array is the **foreach** loop that is used in the following way:

```
1.   foreach ($array as $key => $value) {
2.      echo("The value is $value<br/>");
3.   }
```

The **foreach** loop repeats for each element in the array **$array**, assigning each element to **$value**. The loop continues for all elements in the array.

The **foreach** loop provides an easy way to traverse all elements of an array.

NOTE: *The **foreach** loop only works for arrays and objects and note the use of the => symbol to reference the key / value.*

To access both the keys and values we use:

```
1.   foreach ($array as $key => $value) {
2.      echo ("The array value at $key is $value.<br/>");
3.   }
```

Another form of the **foreach** loop is:

```
1.   foreach ( $array as $value ) {
2.      echo("The value is $value<br/>");
3.   }
```

As you can see, this does not reference the key of the array.

Sorting Arrays

If we take the counties array we created earlier:

```
1.   $counties = array ( "WI"=>"Wiltshire", "SO"=>"Somerset",
     "CO"=>"Cornwall", "DO"=>"Dorset", "DE"=>"Devon",
     "GL"=>"Gloucestershire");
```

We can sort it very easily using:

```
2.   sort($counties);
```

NOTE: The **sort()** function resets the keys, so the **key-value** relationship is lost.

However, you can sort an array by value while maintaining the keys, using **asort()**.

Another sort which you may find useful is **ksort()** that sorts the array by the key.

You can also reverse sort arrays using:

rsort() – this is like sort() but reverses the order
arsort() – this is like asort() but reverses the order
krsort() – this is like ksort() but reverses the order

Some array examples

TASK 1 – Illustrating an associative array

This task illustrates retrieving elements from an associative array.

(1) Create a new PHP page called **county.php**

Code File: 04_array/county.php

(2) In between the **<body>** tags of the web page, create the PHP start and end tags **<?php ?>**

```
1.  <?php
2.
3.  ?>
```

(3) Inside the PHP start and end tags, create a variable called $countries and initialise it with counties.

```
1.  $counties = array ( "WI" =>"Wiltshire", "SO"=>"Somerset",
    "CO"=>"Cornwall", "DO"=>"Dorset", "DE"=>"Devon",
    "GL"=>"Gloucestershire");
```

(4) Use echo statements to display some of the values, for example:

```
1.  echo($counties["SO"]);
```

(5) Test the script on the web server.

TASK 2 – Illustrating the foreach loop

(1) To show how the **foreach** loop works, create a new PHP page called **beatles.php**

Code File: 04_array/beatles.php

(2) In between the **<body>** tags of the web page, create the start and end tags **<?php ?>**

(3) Create an associative array.

```
1.  $beatles[] = "John";
2.  $beatles[] = "George";
3.  $beatles[] = "Ringo";
4.  $beatles[] = "Paul";
```

(4) Display the results using a foreach loop.

```
1.  foreach ( $beatles as $key => $value)
2.  {
3.      echo("The Beatles : $value<br/>");
4.  }
```

(5) Upload the PHP file to the web server and test it.

TASK 3 - HTML and an associative array

This task illustrates using HTML with the results of an associated array and creates HTML on the fly.

(1) Create a new PHP page called **months.php**

Code File: 04_array/months.php

(2) In between the **<body>** tags of the web page create the PHP end and start tags **<?php ?>**

```
1.  <?php
2.
3.  ?>
```

(3) Inside the PHP start and end tags, create a new array called months as shown below:

```
1.  //Make the months array
2.  $months = array (1=>'January', 2=>'February', 3=>'March', 4=>'April'
    , 5=>'May', 6=>'June', 7=>'July', 8=>'August', 9=>'September', 10=>'
    October', 11=>'November', 12=>'December');
```

(4) Use a **foreach** loop to create a drop down selector list as shown below. **Note** the use of single quote marks and double quote marks:

```
1.  echo "<select name='month'>\n";
2.  foreach ( $months as $key => $value ) {
3.    echo "<option value='$key'> $value</option>\n";
4.  }
5.  echo "</select>\n";
```

(5) Save and load the file to your Web server. Open the file in your Web browsers and test the array driven drop down selector.

(6) View the source of you page to view the HTML - you should see the select HTML.

In the example above, we are creating HTML dynamically, and it will look something like this if you view the source code of the page in your browser.

```
1.  <select name='month'>
2.    <option value='January'>January</option>
3.    <option value='February'>February</option>
4.    <option value='March'>March</option>
5.    <option value='April'>April</option>
6.    <option value='May'>May</option>
7.    <option value='June'>June</option>
8.    <option value='July'>July</option>
9.    <option value='August'>August</option>
10.   <option value='September'>September</option>
11.   <option value='October'>October</option>
12.   <option value='November'>November</option>
13.   <option value='December'>December</option>
14. </select>
```

TASK 4 - Using arrays

We will now use arrays to create an HTML drop down selector and show how to use it in a form.

(1) Create a new PHP web page and in the HTML, give the page the title:

```
1.  <title>Dates</title>
```

(2) Save the file with the name **dates.php**

Code File: 04_array/dates.php

(3) Add the form opening tag as shown below and find the script under the opening body **<body>** tag.

```
1.  <form action="dates.php" method="post">
2.
3.  </form>
```

(4) Add your opening and closing PHP tags between the form tags.

```
1.  <?php
2.
3.  ?>
```

(5) Create an array for the months as shown below and insert it within the opening and closing PHP tags.

```
1.  //Make the months array
2.  $months = array (1=> 'January', 2=>'February', 3=>'March', 4=>'April
    ', 5=>'May', 6=>'June', 7=>'July', 8=>'August', 9=>'September',
    10=>'October', 11=>'November', 12=>'December')
```

(6) Create the arrays for the days of the month and the years as shown below.

```
1.  //Make the days array
2.  $days = range(1,31);
3.  //------------
4.  //Make the years array
5.  $years = range(1999,2015);
```

(7) Generate the **month's** drop down selector as shown below.

```
1.  echo "<select name='month'>\n";
2.  foreach ($months as $key => $value) {
3.      echo "<option value='$key'> $value</option>\n";
4.  }
5.  echo"</select>\n";
```

NOTE: The \n is the new line character so that when you view the HTML source code it will look more presentable.

With each **foreach** loop, we can generate the HTML code for the month pull-down menu. Each part of the loop will create a line of code like the following:

<option value="1">January</option>

(8) Generate the **day's** drop down selector as shown below.

```
1.  echo "<select name='day'>\n";
2.  foreach ($days as $key => $value) {
3.      echo "<option value='$value'> $value</option>\n";
4.  }
5.  echo "</select>\n";
```

(9) Generate the **year's** drop down selector as shown below.

```
1.  echo "<select name='year'>\n";
2.  foreach ($years as $key => $value) {
3.      echo "<option value='$value'> $value</option>\n";
4.  }
5.  echo "</select>\n";
```

Notice that we are using the $value as both the option value and as the label.

(10) Save and load the file to your Web server. Open the file in your Web browser and test the page works. The drop down menus should display the months, days and years.

(11) View the source of you page to view the HTML. The source code should look exactly the same as though you had created it all in HTML.

Exercise 4.1

Code File: 04_array/array_exercise_answers.php

(1) Create an associative array of some EU countries and display those countries in a drop down list using a **foreach** loop. So uk is the United Kingdom, fr is France and so on.

(2) Create an associative array of some HTML colour names with the name and its equivalent hexadecimal value and display them as a set of radio buttons using a foreach loop. e.g. $colours = {'red' => '#ff0000', 'green' => '#00ff00'};

The for and while Loops

We have already looked at **foreach** loops and this section looks at the other types of loops which are the **for** and **while** loops.

The while loop looks like this:

```
1.  while (condition) {
2.  //Do some processing
3.  }
```

As long as the condition statement is **true**, the loop will continue to execute. Once it becomes **false**, the loop stops.

For example:

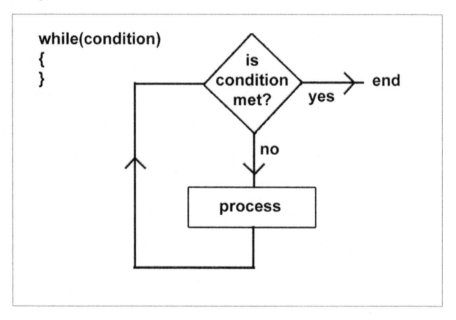

NOTE: *If the condition is never true, the loop will never be executed and conversely, if the condition is never false, the loop could carry on forever and will never end.*

The **while** loop is often used when working with results from a database. In this case, we just loop around all rows of the array until there are no more rows to process. We will see examples of this in later Chapters on databases.

The other form of the while loop is the **do..while** loop. The **do..while** loop looks like this:

```
1.  do
2.  {
3.  //Do some processing
4.  } while (condition)
```

In this situation, the process always takes place before the condition is tested.

For example:

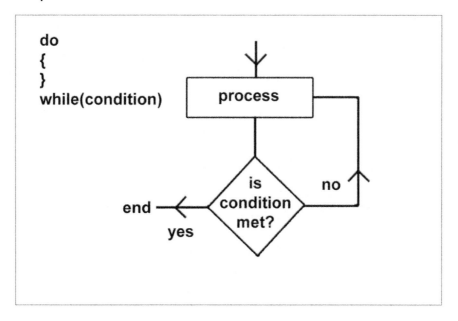

The **for** loop is more complicated and looks like this:

```
1.  for (expr1; expr2; expr3) {
2.  //Do some processing
3.  }
```

For example:

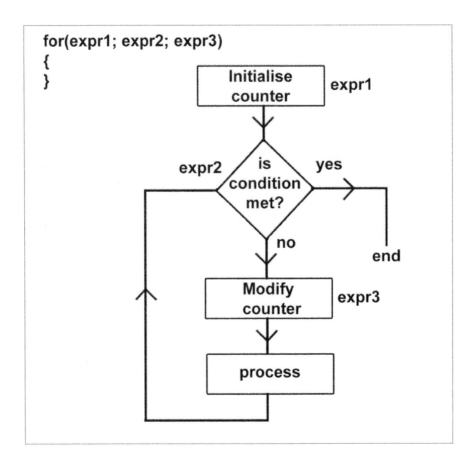

```
for(expr1; expr2; expr3)
{
}
```

expr1 is the initial expression that defines the start condition.

expr2 is the condition expression. If true, the contents of the loop are executed, if false, the loop ends.

expr3 is the closing expression that is executed after expr2 is executed.

An example will help to explain it:

```
1.  for ($i = 0; $i <=10; $i++) {
2.      echo $i;
3.  }
```

The first time this loop is run, the **$i** variable is set to a value of 0. The condition is then checked to see if it is less or equal to 10? Since this is true, 0 is printed out. Then **$i** is incremented to 1 by the closing expression (**$i++**).

The condition expression is then checked again and so on until the condition expression is false, that is when **$i** is equal to 10.

The result of this script will be the numbers 0 to 10 printed out.

TASK 5 - Using loops and if statements

Exercise 4.2

We are now going to return to **dates.php** and rewrite it using **while** and **for loops** in place of **foreach** loops. Copy **dates.php** and create a new file **dates1.php**.

Code File: 04_array/dates1.php

We do not need the **$days** array or the **$years** array as we are going to loop around, so we can remove the lines

$days = range(1, 31);

and

$years = range(1999, 2015);

Now rewrite the **$days foreach** loop with a **for** loop and re-write the **$years foreach** loop with a **while** loop.

Exercise 4.3

(1) Use an **if** statement to print the string "youth message" to the browser if an integer variable **$age** is between 18 and 35. If **$age** is any other value then the string "Generic Message" should be printed to the browser.

(2) Extend the code to print the string "Child Message" if the **$age** is between 1 and 17.

(3) Create a **while** statement that prints every odd number between 1 and 49

(4) Convert the **while** statement of (3) to a **for** statement.

Code File: 04_array/flow_and_loops_exercise_answers.php

Multi-dimensional Arrays

The arrays that we have looked at so far are single arrays with key and the equivalent values. However, we can create arrays where the array element contains another array and so on. This is a multi-dimensional array.

The example that we looked at earlier was the **$counties** array as shown below:

```
1.  $counties = array ('WI' => 'Wiltshire', 'SO' => 'Somerset', …);
```

If you create another array created in a similar way for the USA.

```
1.  $states = array ('AL' => 'Alabama', 'AK' => 'Alaska', …);
```

We can combine these two arrays into a multidimensional array as shown below:

```
1.  $region = array ('UK' => '$counties', 'USA' => '$states');
```

$region is a multidimensional array. To access the **$counties** array, you refer to **$region['UK']**. To access **Wiltshire**, use **$region ['UK'] ['WI']**. You use the name of the multidimensional array, and reference the first array in square brackets followed by the second inner array in square brackets. **$region['US']['AK']** will retrieve **Alaska**.

So we can access an element of the array as follows:

```
1.  echo "The UK county whose abbreviation is WI is : " .
        $region['UK']['WI'];
```

You can still access multidimensional arrays using the **foreach** loop, but you may have to place one **foreach** loop inside another.

An example of where you would use a multidimensional array is with data extracted from a database because a table consists of rows and columns as follows:

	Rowid	Firstname	Lastname
Row 0	1	Paul	Gibbs
Row 1	2	Fred	Blogs
Row 2	3	Joe	Soap

So $table[1]['firstname'] is **Fred**

The print_r function

print_r is a special function for displaying all the contents of an array. You would use **print_r** during debugging:

print_r($region);

Actually, the **print_r()** function can be used to print out human-readable information about any variable but it is particularly useful for arrays.

So the following array $states will look like:

```
1.  <?php
2.  $states = array ('AL' => 'Alabama', 'AK' => 'Alaska');
3.  print_r($states);
4.  ?>
```

Results in the output:

Array ([AL] => Alabama [AK] => Alaska)

Summary

From this Chapter you should see how to work with the different types of arrays that are available in PHP – indexed and associative array. The Chapter also looked at **for, while** and **do** loops that you use to process the data from arrays. The manipulation of arrays is a basic requirement of PHP particularly when working with rows extracted from databases.

Topics for Review

[1] Explain the difference between indexed and associative arrays.

[2] Indexed arrays begin with what numerical position?

[3] Consider the code required to access elements of an array using the for loop and the foreach loop.

[4] Look at how you use a foreach loop to echo to the page the html required to create a dropdown list.

5 - Basic PHP Structures

What is in this Chapter?

* Types of include files
* Uses of include files

As you develop larger web sites, you may find an issue of maintenance. You may have a menu that you copy onto each of your HTML web pages, but if you have to make changes to your menu, you then have to modify each web page.

include files give you a way to create one version of the menu that you reference in each web page. This method can then be applied to other common elements of your web site, such as the header, footer etc.

We use **include** files to separate out common elements to make our web pages easier to maintain.

In some documentation, you may see the term **SSI** or **Server Side Includes** that refers to this technique.

Using include Files

PHP has four functions for using external files:

* include()
* include_once()
* require()
* require_once()

There are used in the following way:

```
1.  include ("includes/header.php");
```

This places the contents of the file includes/header.php into the main file.

The main difference between **include()** and **require()** when using them is that the **include()** function will print a warning if there is an error but will continue to process the script. The **require()** function will print an error and halt the processing of the script. Otherwise, both functions work exactly the same when the script is working properly.

Both functions also have a _once version. This ensures that the file in question is only included once regardless of how many times the script may try to include it.

TASK 1 - Including Multiple Files

In this task we will use include files to construct a template layout to separate the elements of an HTML page that we then add to all files using the **includes** keyword to give a consistent look.

(1) In your folder for this Chapter, create a new folder with two sub folders called **includes** and **images**.

I would recommend that all folder names should be in lower case as using upper case might cause issues on servers that are case sensitive.

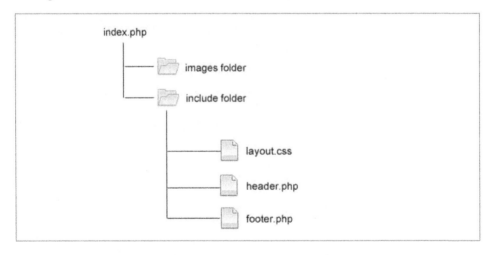

The above figure shows what we are trying to achieve for this structure. We are going to put all our common include files into the **includes** folder with the main PHP page at the root of the folder structure. The main PHP page will then include all the required files.

(2) Copy the style sheet below, save it in your new includes **folder** with the filename **layout.css**.

```
1.  body {
2.      font: 100% Verdana, Arial, Helvetica, sans-serif;
3.      background:#E6E6E6;
4.      margin: 0;
5.      padding: 0;
6.      text-align: center;
7.      color: #000000;
8.  }
9.  .oneCol #container {
10.     width: 46em;
11.     background: #FFFFFF;
12.     margin: 0 auto;
13.     border: 1px solid #000000;
14.     text-align: left;
15. }
16. .oneCol #mainContent {
17.     padding: 0 20px;
18. }
```

Code File: 05_basic_php_structures/script01/includes/layout.css

The above is just a standard style sheet to position column elements on the page.

(3) Copy the HTML script below, save it in your new includes **folder** with the filename **header.php**.

```
1.  <!DOCTYPE html>
2.  <html>
3.  <head>
4.  <meta charset="UTF-8" />
5.  <title><?php echo($pagetitle); ?></title>
6.  <link rel="stylesheet" href="includes/layout.css" type="text/css"
       media="screen" />
7.  </head>
8.  <body class="oneCol">
9.  <div id="container">
10.    <div id="mainContent">
```

Code File: 05_basic_php_structures/script01/includes/header.php

Notice the use of the title variable that we have placed in the <title> tag line 5 as follows:

```
5.  <title><?php echo $pagetitle; ?></title>
```

We want to set the title of the page that appears in the <title> tag to be changeable for each page. To do this we create a variable **$pagetitle** that will be printed out by the PHP. We can use this method for other page properties if we want, such as the meta description tags.

(4) Copy the HTML script below, save it in your new **includes** folder with the filename **footer.php**

```
1.  <!-- MAIN CONTENT ENDS HERE -->
2.  </div>
3.    Copyright &copy; <?php echo (date("Y")); ?>
4.    <strong>|</strong>  Page updated
5.    <?php echo( date ("F Y", getlastmod())); ?>
6.  <!-- end #container --></div>
7.  </body>
8.  </html>
```

Code File: 05_basic_php_structures/script01/includes/footer.php

(5) Create a new PHP document in your text editor. If you are using a text editor such as Dreamweaver, delete all HTML leaving a blank page. Save the page into your **pages** folder with the file name **index.php**.

(6) Add your opening and closing PHP tags.

```
1.  <?php # Script - index.php
2.
3.  ?>
```

(7) Insert the page title variable and include the HTML header. Insert these between the opening and closing PHP tags.

```
1.  $pagetitle = "Home page";
2.  include ("includes/header.php");
```

(8) Insert the HTML script below, **AFTER** the closing PHP tag.

```
1.  <h1> Main Content</h1>
2.  <p>This is the main content. This is the main content. This is the
    main content. This is the main content.</p>
3.  <p>This is the main content. This is the main content. This is the
    main content. This is the main content.</p>
4.  <p>This is the main content. This is the main content. This is the
    main content. This is the main content.</p>
5.  <p>This is the main content. This is the main content. This is the
    main content. This is the main content.</p>
6.  <p>This is the main content. This is the main content. This is the
    main content. This is the main content.</p>
7.  <h2>H2 level heading</h2>
8.  <p>This is sub content. This is sub content. This is sub content.
    This is sub content.</p>
9.  <p>This is sub content. This is sub content. This is sub content.
    This is sub content.</p>
10. <p>This is sub content. This is sub content. This is sub content.
    This is sub content.</p>
11. <p>This is sub content. This is sub content. This is sub content.
    This is sub content.</p>
12. <p>This is sub content. This is sub content. This is sub content.
    This is sub content.</p>
```

(9) Insert the final PHP section and include the footer file.

```
1.  <?php
2.  include ('includes/footer.php');
3.  ?>
```

Code File: 05_basic_php_structures/script01/index.php

(10) Upload all the new folders and files to your Web server and open index.php in your Web browsers to test everything is working correctly.

NOTE: *The reference to the file that you are including can be a relative path in the form of include('includes/footer.php ') in which case the footer.php file is in a folder below the current file, or it may be include('../include/footer.php') if the footer.php file is in a folder above the current file. The two dots denote 'move up one level'. You can also reference to the root of your web site by something like include('/include/footer.php')*

Summary

This Chapter introduced the relatively simple concept of include files that has important uses in large web sites. Without include files we would not be able to construct sites that have consistent layout.

Topics for Review

[1] What is the difference between require() and require_once() ?

[2] What advantage to you gain by using require_once() instead of require() ?

[3] Consider the use of referencing the file with a relative path or with a path based on the root of your web site for example: require('includes/footer.php') and require('/includes/footer.php')

6 - Functions

What is in this Chapter?

* Using arguments in functions.
* Writing a function.
* Variables and their scope.
* Common date and time functions.

PHP has many built in functions for all aspects of programming. As with other programming languages, PHP allows you to define and use your own functions. In PHP, we often call these User Defined Functions.

A function is a block of code that we can use many times. Functions allow you to follow the **DRY** concept in programming – **D**on't **R**epeat **Y**ourself. You specify functionality or behaviour in a function and then use it in your application to reduce the amount of code you write and the amount of maintenance that is required. You can then place your functions into common include files that you can use in all your web pages.

Functions are defined as follows:

```
1.  function function_name() {
2.  //function code here
3.
4.  //---------------------
5.  //optional return value for function
6.  return a value
7.  }
```

The name of the function can consists of a combination of letters, numbers and underscore characters. The main restriction is that you cannot use a PHP built in function name for your function such as **echo**, **date**, **time** etc.

A peculiarity of PHP is that function names are case insensitive, even though other aspects of PHP are case sensitive. It is unclear why this is so, but the recommendation is that you use the same case when you call the function as you do when you declare the function.

The function can perform particular operations or calculations. It can also return a value that you have calculated by using the keyword **return**.

Functions that take arguments

We can pass values into a function so that it can perform calculations or operations on those values. So for example, the following function takes two arguments, **$first_name** and **$last_name**:

```
1.  function display_myname ($first_name, $last_name) {
2.      echo($first_name . ' ' . $last_name);
3.  }
```

We can then call the function as you would any other function in PHP, sending values or other variables to it:

display_myname ('Paul', 'Gibbs');

Or

$last_name='Gibbs';

display_myname ('Paul', '$last_name');

As with any PHP function, if you don't enter the correct number of arguments, you will get a fatal error.

The arguments must also be in the correct order as defined by the function definition.

Setting default argument values in a function

We do not have to pass in all values into a function. We can set a default value for an argument as follows:

```
1.  function display_myname ($name, $greeting = 'Hello' ) {
2.      echo "$greeting, $name!";
3.  }
```

If a value is passed in, the passed value is used; otherwise, the default value is used.

We can set default values for as many arguments as we want providing that the default arguments **come last** in the function definition. In other words, the required arguments should always be first.

Examples of User Defined Functions

TASK 1 - A User Defined Function

We can illustrate the techniques of user-defined functions by writing a simple function.

(1) Create a new document in your text editor and remove any HTML if the editor has created it. Save this as **functions.php**

Code File: 06_functions/functions.php

Copy in the following text, upload it to the web server and check that it is working.

```
1.  <?php
2.
3.  $name = "Paul";
4.  echo("Hello $name<br/>");
5.
6.  ?>
```

(2) We now modify the script by adding in the function **sayHello()** as follows:

```
1.  <?php
2.  sayHello();
3.  //-----------------------------------------
4.  function sayHello() {
5.
6.          $name = "Paul";
7.          echo("Hello $name<br/>");
8.  }
9.  //-----------------------------------------
10. ?>
```

The above function returns no values and has no arguments, but does the same as the first example.

The line **sayHello();** calls all the code that is defined in the function. We can use this code as many times as we want and if we place the function in an include file then we can use it in other PHP files.

(3) Modify the **sayHello()** function code to include an argument in this case called **$name**

```
1.   <?php
2.   sayHello("Paul");
3.   sayHello("John");
4.   sayHello("George");
5.   sayHello("Ringo");
6.
7.   //-------------------------------------
8.   function sayHello($name) {
9.           echo("Hello $name<br/>");
10. }
11. //-------------------------------------
12. ?>
```

This function allows us to call it **multiple times** and pass in different arguments.

(4) Now modify the code to add in an optional argument, in this case the optional argument is **$greeting.**

```
1.   <?php
2.   sayHello("Paul");
3.   sayHello("Ringo", "Goodby");
4.
5.   //-------------------------------------
6.   function sayHello( $name, $greeting = 'Hello') {
7.           echo("$greeting $name<br/>");
8.   }
9.   //-------------------------------------
10. ?>
```

Running this on the web server will display the optional value if we don't specify it in the function.

(5) Finally, we can return the value from the function as follows:

```
1.   <?php
2.   echo sayHello("Paul");
3.   echo sayHello("Ringo", "Goodby");
4.
5.   //-------------------------------------
6.   function sayHello($name, $greeting = 'Hello') {
7.           $returnvalue = "$greeting $name<br/>";
8.           return $returnvalue;
9.   }
10. //-------------------------------------
11. ?>
```

(6) Now that we have the complete function we can extract that code and place it into a separate include file and reference that include file from within the main page.

The main page now becomes:

```
1.  <?php
2.  include_once("misc.php");
3.
4.  echo sayHello("Paul");
5.  echo sayHello("Ringo", "Goodby");
6.  ?>
```

The function itself is in now in a separate file called **misc.php.**

```
1.  <?php
2.  //---------------------------------------------
3.  function sayHello($name, $greeting = 'Hello') {
4.      $returnvalue = " $greeting $name<br/> ";
5.      return $returnvalue;
6.  }
7.  //---------------------------------------------
8.  ?>
```

Upload both files to the web server and the test the **functions.php** file in the web browser.

TASK 2 - Exercise

Exercise 6.1

Write a function to test if a string is a valid telephone number that has to be between 5 and 10 characters long and contains only numbers. It should return true if the string is OK, false if the string is not. You will need to use the strlen and is_numeric PHP functions to do this.

Code File: 06_functions/istelno.php

Variable Scope

We need to introduce a concept of **variable lifetime**. The lifetime is the time that the variable is available for use in a particular part of the web page. This is often the duration of the web page.

However, variables that are defined inside functions normally only exist within the function itself. Variables defined outside of a function are not available within it. Hence, a variable within a function can have the same name as one outside of it and still be an entirely different variable with a different value.

```
1.  <?php
2.  $var = 1;
3.
4.  //----------------
5.  function doSomething() {
6.      $var = 2;
7.  }
8.
9.  //----------------
10. doSomething();
11.
12. echo($var);
13. ?>
```

In the example above, it will display **1** even though we call the function **doSomething()**

This is the concept of **variable scop**e. The scope of the variable $var used in the function is the function itself.

The global statement

If you want a variable in a function to be global for this web page and so be the same value inside and outside the function, then we place the word **global** in front of the variable in the function as shown below:

```
1.  <?php
2.  $var = 1;
3.
4.  //--------------
5.  function doSomething() {
6.      global $var = 2;
7.  }
8.
9.  //--------------
10. doSomething();
11. echo( $var );
12. ?>
```

Now when this is run in a web browser, it will display the result of **2**.

In the example above, **$var** inside of the function is now the same as **$var** outside of it.

Another option for overcoming variable scope is to make use of the superglobals: **$_GET, $_POST, $_REQUEST**, etc. These variables are accessible within any function (hence they are superglobal).

Date and Time Functions

The date() function

are two **PHP** date/time related functions the **date()** function and the **getdate()** function.

The **date()** function returns a string of text for a certain date and time according to the format you specify.

```
1.  <?php
2.  string date(string format, [int timestamp]);
3.  ?>
```

The timestamp is an optional argument representing the number of seconds since the Unix Epoch (Midnight Jan 1st 1970). It allows you to get information, like the day of the week for a particular date. PHP will use the current time on the server if you do not specify the timestamp.

The following is a list of some of the **format** codes for the **date()** function. For a complete list, refer to the online PHP documentation.

Character	Meaning
Y	Year as 4 digits
y	Year as 2 digits
n	Month as 1 or 2 digits
m	Month as 2 digits
F	Month as name
M	Month as 3 letters
j	Day of the month as 1 or 2 digits
d	Day of the month as 2 digits
l(lowercase L)	Day of the week as name
D	Day of the week as 3 letters
g	Hour, 12-hour format as 1 or 2 digits
G	Hour, 24-hour format as 1 or 2 digits

h	Hour, 12-hour format as 2 digits
H	Hour, 24-hour format as 2 digits
i	Minutes
s	Seconds
a	am or pm
A	AM or PM

The **date()** function can take any combination of these parameters to determine its returned results

For example:

```
1.  <?php
2.
3.  echo date( 'F j, Y'); // Will display the current date in the
        form July 12, 2013
4.
5.  echo date('H:I'); //Will display the current time in the form 17:02
6.
7.  echo date('Today is D');    //Will display the current day in the
        form Today is Tuesday
8.
9.  ?>
```

The second argument to the **date()** function is a **UNIX timestamp**.

You can find the timestamp for a particular date using the **mktime()** function that returns an integer value in seconds for the UNIX timestamp.

For example:

```
1.  <?php
2.  $stamp = mktime (hour, minute, second, month, day, year);
3.  ?>
```

We can find the current date time stamp using the **time()** function.

So:

```
1. <?php
2. $nowunix = time(); //is unix timestamp for current time in seconds
3. ?>
```

We can use this time stamp for calculations, so for example, say we want the date in 7 days' time, we can calculate the number of seconds for 7 days then add it on to the current time, and then display it using the date() function.

Exercise 6.2

(1) Create a new web page called **datefunction.php**

Code File: 06_functions/datefunction.php

(2) Use the **date()** function to display the current date / time in the format similar to the following:

Tuesday 19 July 2002 14:09

(3) Use the **time()** function to display the UNIX time in seconds.

(4) Calculate the number of seconds in 7 days and then use the **date()** function to display the date and time in 7 days' time.

The getdate() function

```
1. array getdate([int timestamp]);
```

The **getdate()** function can be used to return an associative array representing the parts of the date and time as follows:

Key	Value
year	Year, 4-digits numeric
mon	Month, numeric
month	Month name
mday	Day of the month, numeric

wday	Day of the week, numeric
yday	Day of the year, numeric
weekday	Day of the week name
hours	Hours, numeric
minutes	Minutes, numeric
seconds	Seconds, numeric
0	Seconds since last Epoch

For example:

```
1.  $dates = getdate();
2.  echo $dates['month'];    //July
```

This function also has an optional timestamp argument. If that argument is not used, **getdate()** returns the information for the current date and time.

TASK 3 - Selecting dates

We are going to create a drop down list of months with the current month pre-selected. This is similar to previous exercise that we did on dates, except that the script will automatically select the current month.

(1) Create a new web page and call it **displaydates.php**

Code File: 06_functions/displaydate.php

(2) Copy the following code into the page.

```php
1.  <?php
2.
3.  $mon = array (1 => "Jan", 2 => "Feb", 3 => "Mar", 4 => "Apr", 5 =>
    "May", 6 => "Jun", 7 => "Jul", 8 => "Aug", 9 => "Sep", 10 => "Oct",
    11 => "Nov", 12 => "Dec", );
4.
5.  $currentdate = getdate();
6.  $month = $currentdate["mon"];
7.  ?>
8.  <select name="month">
9.
10. <?php
11.     for ( $m = 1; $m<=12; $m++)
12.     {
13.      ?>
14.      <option value="<?php echo($m); ?>" <?php if ($month == $m)
            {echo"selected";} ?> >
15.      <?php echo($mon[$m]); ?></option>
16.      <?php
17.     }
18. ?>
19. </select>
```

(3) Upload the code to your web area and test it.

We are using a select drop down list to display a list of months but we are calculating what month it is and then pre-selecting the drop down list with the current month.

NOTE: *This code uses the for loop rather than the foreach loop. There is no advantage using one method over another but this example illustrates a different approach.*

Exercise 6.3

Now modify the above code to include a day drop down list for days from 1 to 31 and a year drop down list for years from 2010 to 2020. The current day and the current year should all be pre-selected in the drop down lists.

Code File: 06_functions/displaydate1.php

TASK 4 - Handling dates between mySQL and PHP

We have not looked at mySQL yet, but when programming with mySQL we often need to present the date / time in a way that mySQL can accept.

The best way is to use the format of **YYYY-mm-dd** for inserting and updating dates as this is a universal format.   Dates would then look like 2020-03-05 to represent the 5th March 2020.

Summary

Functions are where we begin to construct more sophisticated programs allowing us to write code in reusable blocks making maintenance much easier. It is this principle that enables us to create large complex robust programs. Functions can optionally return values and we can optionally pass values into them adding flexibility to our code.

Topics for Review

[1] Do you always have to use the return keyword in a function?

[2] Consider the issues of using the global statement on a web page. For instance, a function is meant to be a self-contained block of code. If you use a global variable then you may be introducing unwanted side effects making the code difficult to debug.

[3] Format a date to appear in different ways. How would you use it to display the date in the form of 2020-02-03 to represent year-month-day?

7 - Posting Forms

What is in this Chapter?

* Using a more complicated HTML form handler.
* Posting a form back to itself.
* Retaining data in a posted form.

In a previous Chapter, we saw how to use two separate files to handle HTML forms: one that displays the form and another that receives and processes it. However, we can have the complete process in one script to make maintenance easier.

Handling HTML Forms in one script

To do this we use a simple **if** statement as follows:

```
1.  if (   check if this page has been submitted   ) {
2.
3.  // Process the form data here, e.g. do some calculation, save data to database.
4.
5.  } else {
6.
7.  // Display the HTML form to allow the user to enter data.
8.
9.  }
```

To determine whether the form has been submitted, we normally check that a **$_POST** variable is set (assuming the POST method is being used). For example, you can check **$_POST["Submit"],** assuming that the submit button has a value of Submit.

So, if we want a page to display a form and then to do some processing when the submit button is pressed, such as adding a record to a database, we can use something like this:

```
1.  if (isset($_POST['Submit'])) {
2.
3.  //Process the form data here, e.g. do some calculation, save
       data to database...
4.
5.  } else {
6.
7.  //Display the HTML form to allow the user to enter data.
8.
9.  }
```

The above code will process the form data when the submit button is pressed, or it will display the form itself when the page is first loaded.

TASK 1 - Posting to itself

In order to demonstrate this, we will create a product calculator form. First, we will create a form that posts data to itself.

(1) Create a new web page in your text editor. This will be a PHP page called **products.php** and consists of three input text boxes and a submit button. Either you can copy the text from below, or if you are using Dreamweaver, you can insert the controls into Dreamweaver from the Insert -> Form menu or type in the code by hand.

(2) Save this file as **products.php.**

```
1.  <!DOCTYPE html>
2.  <html>
3.  <head>
4.  <meta charset="UTF-8" />
5.  <title>Product item details</title>
6.  </head>
7.
8.  <body>
9.
10. <form name="product" method="post" action="products.php">
11.
12.
    <p>Product item name <input type="text" name="item" size="20" /></p>
13.  <p>Product cost <input type="text" name="cost" size="10" /></p>
14.  <p>Tax value <input type="text" name="tax" size="10" /> %</p>
15.  <p><input type="submit" name="Submit" value="Submit" /></p>
16.
17. </form>
18.
19. </body>
20. </html>
```

(3) Upload this file to the web server and check that it displays correctly. If you press the submit button, the form is posted to the server but nothing will happen at this point as there is no PHP code.

Note that the action in the <form> tag is to **products.php** file.

Code File: 07_posting_forms/products.php

(4) The next step is to add in the following conditional statement under the **<body>** tag.

```php
1.  <?php
2.  //------------------------
3.  if (isset($_POST["Submit"]))
4.  {
5.     $item = $_POST["item"];
6.     $cost = $_POST["cost"];
7.     $tax = $_POST["tax"];
8.     //-----------
9.     $tax = ($tax / 100) * $cost;
10.    $totalcost = $tax + $cost;
11.    //-----------
12.    echo("The cost of the item $item is $totalcost including
           tax of $tax");
13. }
14. ?>
```

This uses the **isset** function to test if the **POST** value is present. If it is present, then it retrieves all the values, does the calculations, and displays the results. It then displays the form again.

Therefore, the complete file now looks like this:

```php
1.  <!DOCTYPE html>
2.  <html>
3.  <head>
4.  <meta charset="UTF-8" />
5.  <title>Product item details</title>
6.  </head>
7.
8.  <body>
9.
10. <?php
11. if (isset($_POST["Submit"]))
12. {
13.    $item = $_POST["item"];
14.    $cost = $_POST["cost"];
15.    $tax = $_POST["tax"];
16.    //--------
17.    $tax = ($tax / 100) * $cost;
18.    $totalcost = $tax + $cost;
```

```
19.   //--------
20.     echo("The cost of the item $item is $totalcost including tax
            of $tax");
21. }
22. ?>
23. <form name="product" method="post" action="product1.php">
24.
25.   <p>Product item name <input type="text" name="item" size="20"/></p>
26.   <p>Product cost <input type="text" name="cost" size="10" /></p>
27.   <p>Tax value <input type="text" name="tax" size="10" /> %</p>
28.   <p><input type="submit" name="Submit" value="Submit" /></p>
29.
30. </form>
31.
32. </body>
33. </html>
```

Code File: 07_posting_forms/products1.php

Upload this file to the server, and this time when you fill in the text boxes and press submit it will display the results.

(5) The next step is to change the action in the form:

action="product.php"

to:

action="<?php echo $_SERVER['PHP_SELF']; ?>"

$_SERVER['PHP_SELF']; is a PHP server variable identifying this file. This means that we can change the file name and it will still correctly post back to itself.

(6) We can now extract the calculation code and place it into a function as follows:

```
1.  function calctax($cost, $tax)
2.  {
3.      $tax = ($tax / 100) * $cost;
4.      $totalcost = $tax + $cost;
5.      return $totalcost;
6.  }
```

So the code now becomes:

```
1.  <!DOCTYPE html>
2.  <html>
3.  <head>
4.  <meta charset="UTF-8" />
5.  <title>Product item details</title>
6.  </head>
```

```
7.
8.  <body>
9.  <?php
10. //--------------
11. if ( isset($_POST["Submit"]))
12. {
13.     $item = $_POST["item"];
14.     $cost = $_POST["cost"];
15.     $tax = $_POST["tax"];
16.     $totalcost = calctax($cost, $tax);
17.     echo("The cost of the item $item is $totalcost");
18. }
19. ?>
20. <form name="product" method="post" action
          = "<?php echo $_SERVER['PHP_SELF']; ?>" >
21.
22.   <p>Product item name <input type="text" name="item" size="20"/></p>
23.   <p>Product cost <input type="text" name="cost" size="10" /></p>
24.   <p>Tax value <input type="text" name="tax" size="10" /> %</p>
25.   <p><input type="submit" name="Submit" value="Submit" /></p>
26.
27. </form>
28.
29. </body>
30. </html>
31. <?php
32.
33. //--------------
34. function calctax($cost, $tax)
35. {
36.     $tax = ($tax / 100) * $cost;
37.     $totalcost = $tax + $cost;
38.     return $totalcost;
39. }
40. ?>
```

Code File: 07_posting_forms/products2.php

(7) To make this into a useful application we need to test the inputs particularly for the cost and the tax values. If these are not entered as numeric values, the script will fail in the calculation.

```
1.  <!DOCTYPE html>
2.  <html>
3.  <head>
4.  <meta charset="UTF-8" />
5.  <title>Product item details</title>
6.  </head>
7.
8.  <body>
9.  <?php
10. //--------------
11. if (isset($_POST["Submit"]))
```

```
12. {
13.    $item = $_POST["item"];
14.    $cost = $_POST["cost"];
15.    $tax = $_POST["tax"];
16.    //--------------
17.    if ( isset($_POST["item"]) && is_numeric($_POST["cost"]) &&
18.         is_numeric($_POST["tax"]) )
19.    {
20.    $totalcost = calctax($cost, $tax);
21.    echo("The cost of the item $item is " .
           number_format($totalcost, 2));
22.    }
23.    else
24.    {
25.        echo("Re-enter data");
26.    }
27. }
28. ?>
29. <form name="product" method="post" action
        ="<?php echo $_SERVER['PHP_SELF']; ?>">
30.    <p>Product item name <input type="text" name="item" size="20"/></p>
31.    <p>Product cost <input type="text" name="cost" size="10" /></p>
32.    <p>Tax value <input type="text" name="tax" size="10" /> %</p>
33.    <p><input type="submit" name="Submit" value="Submit" /></p>
34.
35. </form>
36.
37. </body>
38. </html>
39. <?php
40.
41. //--------------
42. function calctax($cost, $tax)
43. {
44.    $tax = ($tax / 100) * $cost;
45.    $totalcost = $tax + $cost;
46.    return $totalcost;
47. }
48. ?>
```

Code File: 07_posting_forms/products3.php

In this version, we validate the inputs using the **isset** function to check if data has been entered. For the numeric values, we can test using the is_numeric function.

NOTE: The use of the **number_format** function to display the total cost with two decimal places.

Recap on handling PHP and HTML on one page

In the next block of code, we show a more general way of handling PHP and HTML.

Each section of code in the page is split into functions with the first function being called **main()** and being called at the top of the page.

Each function may have parameter inputs and may return values from the functions depending on requirements. Functions provide a more reusable method of programming and neater code.

```
1.  <?php
2.  //----------------------------------------
3.  //The start of the page
4.  main();
5.  //----------------------------------------
6.  //The function that controls which part to got to
7.  function main()
8.  {
9.      if (isset($_POST['Submit'])) {
10.             $submit = $_POST['Submit'];
11.             updatedb();
12.     } else {
13.             $submit = "";
14.             displayform();
15.     }
16. }
17. //----------------------------------------
18. //display the form
19. function displayform()
20. {
21.     ?>
22.     <form name="update" method="post" action
            ="<?php echo $_SERVER['PHP_SELF']; ?>">
23.
24.     </form>
25.     <?php
26. }
27. //----------------------------------------
28. //do something here such as update a database
29. function updatedb()
30. {
31. }
32. ?>
```

NOTE: The use of the **<?php echo $_SERVER['PHP_SELF']; ?>** in the above code for the action of the form. This is used to post back to itself so no matter what the name of the page is, it will still post back to the same page.

Exercise 7.1

One thing we could have done is to enter in a default tax amount. We can do this by using the value field of the tax input box. Modify the script so that the value of the input box is set as a default value of 20.

TASK 2 - Retaining data in forms

Retaining the data in a form after it was posted is useful when you want the form to remember the value that the user entered. You may want this to happen in case the processing failed and you want the user to re-enter or change the data. This can easily be done using the **$_POST** variable.

If we want PHP to display the value that was entered in the form after it was submitted we can do something like the following:

```
1.  <input type="text" name="city" size="30"
        value="<?php echo $city; ?>" />
```

To test if the value was posted, we use the built in PHP function **isset()**:

```
1.  <input type="text" name="city" size="30"
2.  value="<?php
3.  if (isset($_POST['city'])) {
4.      echo $_POST['city'];
5.  }
6.  ?>" />
```

All we are doing is checking if the post value exists and if it does exist then we display the value.

Exercise 7.2

Modify the product.php script to so that the form retains the values for $item, $tax and $cost using the method as shown above.

Code File: 07_posting_forms/products4.php

TASK 2 - Questions

Question 2.1

Write a function to test if a string is a valid telephone number that has to be between 5 and 10 characters long and contains only numbers. It should return true if the string is OK, false if the string is not. You will need to use the strlen and is_numeric **PHP** functions to do this.

Code File: 07_posting_forms/istelno.php

Question 2.2

Write a short web page that uses this function. Create an input box for the telephone number, and a form to go around it. Post the form back to itself and if the value entered is not correct, display an error message.

Code File: 07_posting_forms/istelnoform.php

Summary

This Chapter illustrates coding techniques to post forms to itself. When we add functions to the forms, we can then do our processing on the server, including validating inputs, which is an important requirement when we save the data to a database. Later Chapters will use these techniques to create forms that modify data in a database.

Topics for Review

[1] How can you test if a form has been submitted to itself?

[2] How can you retain data in an input text box after the form was submitted?

[3] How can you test if an input value that has been entered is numeric?

[4] What php code can you use to identify the action so that it posts back to itself?

- An Email Form

What is in this Chapter?

* How to use the **mail()** function.
* An email test script.
* An example register script.

Sending emails from PHP is quite simple and requires the use of the mail() function which we describe in the next part. We only need to know the email address of the sender and the email address to be used as the "from" address. We also need a subject and the body text of the email of course.

However, the web server that you are using must be set up correctly and for most of us that has to be left to the administrators at the hosting company to set up the configuration details that are required.

The **mail()** function is essentially a wrapper that sends the mail message over to the local mail system or to an SMTP server which then actually sends the mail. If your **php.ini** file has not been set up correctly, and emails are not being sent out from your PHP script, then you will have to contact your host because you probably will not be able to access the **php.ini** file.

The mail() function

The only mail function available in **PHP** is **mail()**.

The simplest use of **mail()** is:

```
1.  mail ($to, $subject, $body);
```

The **$to** value should be the destination email address, with multiple addresses separated by commas. The **$subject** value will create the email subject line, and the **$body** value is where you put the contents of the email. We use the \n within the string when creating the body to make the text go over multiple lines.

The **mail()** function takes a fourth optional parameter for additional headers. This is where you could set up the **From**, **Reply-To**, **Cc**, and **Bcc** settings. For example:

```
1.  mail('paulvgibbs@yahoo.co.uk', 'PHP course', $body,
        'From: paulg@hotmail.com');
```

To use multiple headers for cc and bcc in your email, separate each with **\r\n;**

```
1.  $headers = "From: fred@hotmail.com\r\n Cc: pete@hotmail.com,
        Jane@smith.com\r\n";
2.  mail('paulvgibbs@yahoo.co.uk', 'PHP course', $body, $headers);
```

TASK 1 - A Test Email Script

The following shows a simple email test script you might use to see if your emails are being sent from your web server.

```
1.  <?php
2.
3.  //----------------------------
4.  $to = "to@somewhere.com";
5.  $subject = "PHP Course";
6.  $body = "This is a test email\n\nfrom my website";
7.  $headers = "From: from@somewhereelse.com\r\n";
8.
9.  //----------------------------
10. mail($to, $subject, $body, $headers);
11. ?>
```

Code File: 08_email_form/emailtest.php

Create a new **PHP** page called **emailtest.php** with the above code, change the $to variable and $from variable email addresses as appropriate and test it on your web server.

TASK 2 - A basic PHP email form

(1) Create a new PHP document in your text editor. If you are using a text editor such as Dreamweaver, delete all HTML leaving a blank page. Save the page into your folder with the file name **comments.php**.

Code File: 08_email_form/comments.php

(2) Insert the script below.

(3) Save the script and publish to your Web server, then test in your Web Browsers. The full code is shown below:

```php
1.   <?php
2.
3.   // A simple email form - Check the form has been submitted
4.   if(isset($_POST['submitted'])) {
5.       $errors = array(); //initialise an error array.
6.       //Check for a name
7.       if(emptyempty($_POST['name'])) {
8.           $errors[] = "Enter your name.";
9.       }
10.
11.      //Check for an email address
12.      if(emptyempty($_POST['email'])) {
13.          $errors[] = "Enter your email address.";
14.      }
15.
16.      //Check for comments
17.      if(emptyempty($_POST['comments'])) {
18.          $errors[] = "Enter your comments.";
19.      }
20.
21.      if(emptyempty($errors)) {// If there are no errors
22.      // send the comments
23.      $to = "me@mysite.com";   //your email address
24.      $body="The following comments were entered on the
             web site\n\n" . $_POST['name'] . "\n\n" . $_POST['email'] .
             "\n\n" . $_POST['comments'];
25.      mail($to, 'Comments from website', $body, 'From: admin@site.com');
26.      echo '<h1>Thank you</h1>
27.      <p>Thank you for your comments. We will contact you as soon
             as possible.</p><p><br /></p>';
28.
29.      } else { //Report the errors.
30.
31.          ?>
32.          <h2>Error</h2>
33.          <p>The following error(s) occurred:</p>
34.          <?php
35.          echo("<p>");
36.          foreach ($errors as $msg) {
37.              echo " - $msg<br />\n";
38.          }
39.          echo("</p>");
40.          echo "<p>Correct your error and try again</p><br/><br/>";
41.          unset($errors);
42.      }
43.
44.  } else {
45.
46.      //Display the form
47.      ?>
48.      <h2>Register</h2>
```

```
49.
50.    <form action="comments.php" method="post">
51.       <p>Name: <input type="text" name="name" size="20"
                maxlength="40"/></p>
52.       <p>Email Address: <input type="text" name="email" size="20"
                maxlength="40"/></p>
53.       <p>Comments: <textarea name="comments"
                cols="60" rows="8"></textarea></p>
54.       <p><input type="submit" name="submit" value="register"/></p>
55.       <p><input type="hidden" name="submitted" value="TRUE"/></p>
56.    </form>
57.
58.       <?php
59. }
60. ?>
```

You will need to modify the script for the **$to** value located on line 23 in the above display. Change **me@myswbsite.com** to your destination email address.

Register

Name:

Email Address:

Comments:

register

This is quite a basic example and you would not use in a working system because you need to add in code to check the validity of the characters for the name, email address and comments.

For information on validating email fields, refer to the Chapter on Regular Expression Validation.

The script uses the method of setting an error array that is populated if there is an error. The error array can then just be checked and the messages displayed if there is an error.

NOTE: *The PHP **mail()** function does not actually send the email. It is the server that sends the email and so you must have a correctly set up system.*

If you are using a hosted web server then there should not be any problems, but if you are working on a local computer, you will not be able to send out the emails.

Email settings are in the **php.ini** file and could be set up to use an external SMTP email service.

Send email further development

The email register form above will work; however, to use it in a real situation we should make a number of improvements:

* Fully validate all inputs into the form.
* Test the name and comments fields for dubious content.
* Restrict the number of characters that a user can enter into the input fields.
* Use a **CAPTCHA** script to make sure that the submission is from a person and not from an automated program.

Summary

Many web sites incorporate a form for the visitor to ask questions and then the form sends the results to a site administrator by email. The basic code is straightforward; however, there are many pitfalls in web forms particularly when validating the data entered. This Chapter illustrates the bare bones of a feedback form.

Topics for Review

[1] If you have a website with a control panel, check out the email features that you have. You should be able to redirect emails from your hosting system to a different email address such as gmail, which you may find more convenient.

[2] Using the test email script in this Chapter, try a test to see if it will send an email to one of your email accounts. Make sure you check your spam box if you don't see the email.

[3] To overcome problems with emails going into the spam box, you can try sending emails to an SMTP email account but you will need to use a PHP script such as PHPMailer.

9 - JavaScript Submit

What is in this Chapter?

* Using JavaScript to submit a form.
* Some validation techniques using JavaScript.

This Chapter illustrates the technique of submitting a form with JavaScript with some basic checks on the data input. JavaScript is client side coding (that is on the PC, tablet or mobile device) and so checking the data on the client before it is submitted to the server gives a better user experience. However, you must also validate the data on the server using PHP as well, because JavaScript may not be enabled on the browser.

Submit a form with JavaScript

The following form consists of the input text fields, and a **button**. Note that it is not a **submit** button.

The form name is **'frmCreate'** so in JavaScript the submission of the form is **frmCreate.submit(frmCreate)**.

Also note that JavaScript is case sensitive, so to refer to the contents of a text box in JavaScript you use **frmCreate.txtItem_Number.value**

```
1.   <!DOCTYPE html>
2.   <html>
3.   <head>
4.   <meta charset="UTF-8" />
5.   <title>Submit a form using JavaScript</title>
6.
7.      <script language="javascript" type="text/javascript">
8.      //----------------------------------------------
9.      //Javascript that will submit the form when all entries are valid
10.     function button_onclick(frmCreate) {
11.        var themessage = "Error in entries : ";
12.        var isOK = true;
13.        if ( frmCreate.txtItem_Number.value == "" ) {
```

```
14.           themessagethemessage = themessage + "\n" + "* Enter PayPal
          item code";
15.           isOK = false;
16.         }
17.         if ( frmCreate.txtItem_Name.value == "" ) {
18.           themessagethemessage = themessage + "\n" + "* Enter
            PayPal item name";
19.           isOK = false;
20.         }
21.         if ( isOK == false ) {
22.            window.alert(themessage);
23.         } else {
24.            frmCreate.submit(frmCreate);
25.         }
26.       }
27.       </script>
28.
29.  </head>
30.  <body>
31.
32.  <!-- START OF MAIN FORM -->
33.  <form name="frmCreate" method="post" action="test.html">
34.  <input type="button" name="Create" value="Create"
     language="javascript" onClick="return button_onclick(frmCreate)" />
35.  <br/><br/>
36.  <table>
37.  <tr>
38.  <td>
39.      <strong>Product Item Reference</strong>
40.  </td>
41.  <td>
42.      <input type="text" name="txtItem_Number" />
43.  </td>
44.  </tr>
45.
46.  <tr>
47.  <td>
48.      <strong>Product Item Name</strong>
49.  </td>
50.  <td>
51.      <input type="text" name="txtItem_Name" size="50" /><br/>
52.  </td>
53.  </tr>
54.  </table>
55.
56.  </form>
57.  <!-- END OF MAIN FORM -->
58.
59.  </body>
60.  </html>
```

Code File: 09_javascript_submit/javascript_submit_01.php

Submit a form with JavaScript input validation

The following script extends the above script to include some more data validation so that the values of the inputs are checked using JavaScript before submission.

To do this we have added in a couple of JavaScript functions and use an OnBlur JavaScript function on one of the text boxes so that the value is tested when the cursor moves out of the text box.

```
1.   <!DOCTYPE html>
2.   <html>
3.   <head>
4.   <meta charset="UTF-8" />
5.   <title>Submit a form using Javascript with input validation</title>
6.       <script language="javascript" type="text/javascript">
7.       //---------------------------------------------
8.       //Javascript will submit the form when all entries are valid
9.       function button_onclick(frmCreate) {
10.        var themessage = "Error in entries : ";
11.        var isOK = true;
12.        if ( frmCreate.txtItem_Number.value == "" ) {
13.            themessagethemessage = themessage + "\n" + "* Enter
           PayPal item code";
14.            isOK = false;
15.        }
16.        if ( frmCreate.txtItem_Name.value == "" ) {
17.            themessagethemessage = themessage + "\n" + "* Enter
           PayPal item name";
18.            isOK = false;
19.        }
20.        if ( isOK == false ) {
21.            window.alert(themessage);
22.        } else {
23.            frmCreate.submit(frmCreate);
24.        }
25.      }
26.      //---------------------------------------------
27.      //Checks if the entry is numeric
28.      function isNumeric(inputVal) {
29.          numeric = true;
30.          inputStr = inputVal.toString();
31.          for (var i = 0; i< inputStr.length; i++) {
32.              var oneChar = inputStr.charAt(i);
33.              if (oneChar < "0" || oneChar > "9") {
34.                  return false;
35.              }
36.      }
37.      if (numeric == false) {
38.          return false; }
39.          else {
40.          return true; }
41.      }
42.      //---------------------------------------------
```

```
43.        function LowerLimit_onblur(frmCreate) {
44.           if ( !isNumeric( frmCreate.txtLowerLimit.value ) ) {
45.               window.alert("Enter a integer number");
46.               frmCreate.txtLowerLimit.value = "";
47.                  frmCreate.txtLowerLimit.focus();
48.           }
49.       }
50.    </script>
51. </head>
52. <body>
53. <!-- START OF MAIN FORM -->
54. <form name="frmCreate" method="post" action="test.html">
55. <input type="button" name="Create" value="Create"

    language="javascript" onClick="return button_onclick(frmCreate)" />
56. <br/><br/>
57. <table>
58. <tr>
59. <td>
60.    <strong>Product Item Reference</strong>
61. </td>
62. <td>
63.    <input type="text" name="txtItem_Number" />
64. </td>
65. </tr>
66.
67. <tr>
68. <td>
69.    <strong>Product Item Name</strong>
70. </td>
71. <td>
72.   <input type="text" name="txtItem_Name" size="50" /><br/>
73. </td>
74. </tr>
75.
76. <tr>
77. <td>
78.    <strong>Enter lower limit</strong>
79. </td>
80. <td>
81.   <input type="text" name="txtLowerLimit" class="inputbox" value="5"
        size="3" LANGUAGE="javascript"
        onBlur="return LowerLimit_onblur(frmCreate)" />
82. </td>
83. </tr>
84. </table>
85. </form>
86. <!-- END OF MAIN FORM -->
87.
88. </body>
89. </html>
```

Code File: 09_javascript_submit/javascript_submit_02.php

Summary

JavaScript, HTML web pages and PHP are often designed to work together to give a good user experience. This Chapter illustrates some methods of validating data on the client computer using JavaScript before it is posted to the server.

Topics for Review

[1] If you are using JavaScript or jQuery on a form to validate user input, why should you also have to validate the user input using PHP on the server?

[2] Have a look at jQuery to validate user data. We look at the use of jQuery in a later Chapter of this book.

10 - SQL and MySQL

What is in this Chapter?

* Creating a database in MySQL.
* Creating tables in MySQL.
* SQL statement examples.

This Chapter looks at the MySQL database system, creating databases, creating and managing tables through the web interface phpMyAdmin, and using some SQL queries. Later Chapters will look at how PHP and SQL queries are used together to display information on web pages.

MySQL database and phpMyAdmin

PHP commonly uses MySQL as the database system. Web hosts do provide other types of databases, but normally you will use MySQL.

Another database system that you may come across is PostgreSQL. So what is the difference between PostgreSQL and MySQL? Well, MySQL is considered a good choice for web-based systems where you require straightforward data access. Whereas PostgreSQL does have advantages when working with larger data sets and can be faster. If you are interested, there are many resources available on the internet that discuss the differences.

However, you should be aware that if you intend to use the PHP **mysqli** functions as shown in later Chapters of this book, then you have to use a MySQL database.

Most web hosting packages will have a control panel that will allow you to create databases and users, and this will include **phpMyAdmin**.

phpMyAdmin is web-based software used for creating and maintaining MySQL databases. You usually access **phpMyAdmin** through your web hosting control panel where you just click on an icon or link and it will load up **phpMyAdmin** in your browser.

There are a number of different versions of **phpMyAdmin** reflecting the different versions of MySQL that are available, but they are essentially the same, although the latest versions have rather more fancy displays and improve the user experience.

Creating a database in MySQL

The way in which you create a database will depend on the system that you are using. With a commercial web-hosting package, you will access a control panel that will often have a special wizard for creating databases and users. This is how you normally work with the database.

However, you can quite easily create databases in **phpMyAdmin**.

(1) Login to **phpMyAdmin**

(2) Click on the **Databases** tab. This will display a list of current databases and a box to allow you to enter a new database name. This may not be available on a commerical hosted system.

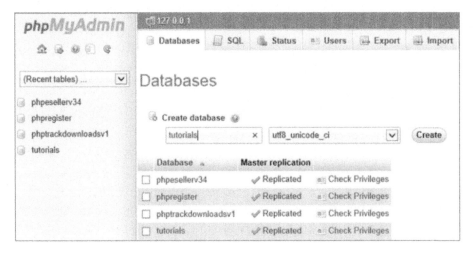

Quite often within the database name, you will see your login id followed by an underscore (12345_). All the databases you create must be pre labelled with your login id. This keeps your databases distinct from other databases that are using the same base system.

For example, your login id might be 12345 so the identity of a database called tutorials is:

```
12345_tutorials
```

(3) Give your database a new name of **tutorials.**   In the **Collation** drop down list, choose **utf8_unicode_ci**, and then click on **Create**.

Collation defines the character set and sort order for the database and a good choice is **utf8_unicode_ci**.

Your database has now been created.

Database user permissions

To perform actions on a database with PHP, you require a database user with the required permissions and you place those user details in the PHP connection script.

How you set up the database user and permissions will depend on your hosting system and the facilities that you have with your control panel.

It is normal to define a database user with just **SELECT, UPDATE, INSERT** and **DELETE** privileges. If read only access is required, then only **SELECT** privileges are needed.

Creating a database user with SQL

Creating a user for the database means defining the username and password and then applying privileges so the user can perform certain operations on the database. Not all users will have full privileges. Some will not be able to create or delete tables; others will just have the ability to read data and not update data.

This section shows how to create a user using a SQL script that you may want to do when you are using an installation on your local computer using **phpMyAdmin**.

Basic method

Enter the following SQL scripts into the SQL tab of **phpMyAdmin**. The basic method of creating a user is as follows:

```
1.   CREATE USER 'newuser@localhost' IDENTIFIED BY 'password';
```

At this point, the user has no privileges to do anything so now we have to grant privileges to this user:

```
2.   GRANT SELECT ON databasename . * TO 'newuser@localhost';
```

This will grant SELECT permissions on all tables of the database called databasename.

Follow this with:

```
3. FLUSH PRIVILEGES;
```

This tells the server to reload the grant tables. If you do not do this, you will not be able to connect to **MySQL** using the new user account.

A more concise way of creating a user

```
1. GRANT SELECT, INSERT, UPDATE, DELETE ON TUTORIALS.* TO
   'paul@localhost' IDENTIFIED BY 'paul123';
2. FLUSH PRIVILEGES;
```

This creates a user called **paul** with password of **paul123** and with those specified permissions.

If the user needs to CREATE tables, then add CREATE to the list.

To create a new root account with full admin rights:

```
1. GRANT ALL PRIVILEGES ON *.* TO 'ADMIN'@LOCALHOST IDENTIFIED
   BY 'password';
```

This gives all privileges to all databases for the given user.

Creating tables in MySQL

There are really two ways in which we can create tables in MySQL

{1) Use the facilities in **phpMyAdmin** where you create the tables using the web interface. Table name, column names, column data type are all listed within the web interface making it a straightforward process.

(2) Create the table from an existing SQL script.

When you define a database table, you need to consider the following basic points:

* Identify the name of the columns in the table. For this, we normally follow a naming convention of no spaces and the use of standard characters a-z and 0-9. Some designers like to prefix their table name with a code; so for example, they may define a table name as ipn_password. Putting ipn as a prefix helps to separate out tables in a large database.

* Identify the **primary key** made from one or more columns. All tables must have a primary key; this uniquely identifies each row in a column. A primary key is often an auto incremented field, but can be more than one column to provide the unique record.

* Identify the **data types** for the columns to create the correct field types and to restrict the range of data.

* Identify any **indexes** for the table to help speed up sorting and place constraints on the data.

* Identify if the column should allow nulls (no value) or not.

* Identify the **character set** for the field - normally the same as the database collation, which could be for example **utf8_unicode_ci**

MySQL data types

The main types of data that are stored in a database are:

* Text or string types
* Numbers
* Dates and Times

In practice, the data types that you will use are **VARCHAR**, **FLOAT**, **TEXT**, **INT** and **DATE.** The following table lists most of the data types that are available.

Numerical Data Types:

INT - An integer that can be signed or unsigned. Signed range from -2147483648 to 2147483647, unsigned range is from 0 to 4294967295. It can be up to 11 digits long.

TINYINT - A small integer that can be signed or unsigned. Signed range is from -128 to 127, unsigned range is from 0 to 255. It can be up to 4 digits long.

SMALLINT - A small integer that can be signed or unsigned. Signed range is from -32768 to 32767, unsigned range is from 0 to 65535. It can be up to 5 digits long.

MEDIUMINT - A medium-sized integer that can be signed or unsigned. Signed range is from -8388608 to 8388607, unsigned range is from 0 to 16777215. It can be up to 9 digits long.

BIGINT - A large integer that can be signed or unsigned. Signed range is from -9223372036854775808 to 9223372036854775807, unsigned range is from 0 to 18446744073709551615. It can be up to 20 digits long.

FLOAT(M,D) - A floating-point number that cannot be unsigned. The display length (M) and the number of decimals (D) can be optionally defined.   The default values are 10,2. Decimal precision can be up to 24 places for a FLOAT.

DOUBLE(M,D) - A double precision floating-point number that cannot be unsigned. The display length (M) and the number of decimals (D) can be optionally defined. The default values are 16,4. Decimal precision can be up to 53 places for a DOUBLE. REAL is a synonym for DOUBLE.

DECIMAL(M,D) - An unpacked floating-point number that cannot be unsigned. Each decimal corresponds to one byte. Both the display length (M) and the number of decimals (D) are required. NUMERIC is a synonym for DECIMAL.

Date and Time Types:

DATE - A date in YYYY-MM-DD format that is between 1000-01-01 and 9999-12-31.

DATETIME - A date and time in YYYY-MM-DD HH:MM:SS format which is between 1000-01-01 00:00:00 and 9999-12-31 23:59:59.

TIMESTAMP - A timestamp starting from midnight, January 1, 1970 up to 2037. This looks like the previous DATETIME format but without the hyphens, that is YYYYMMDDHHMMSS.

TIME - Stores in HH:MM:SS format.

YEAR(M) - Stores a year in 2 or 4-digit format. So YEAR(2) is a year between 1970 to 2069 (70 to 69), while YEAR(4) can be 1901 to 2155. The default length is 4.

String Data Types:

CHAR(M) - A fixed length string between 1 and 255 characters. M is optional and defaults to 1.

VARCHAR(M) - A variable length string between 1 and 255 characters. Defining M is mandatory.

BLOB or TEXT - A field with a maximum length of 65535 characters. BLOBs are 'Binary Large Objects' and store binary data, such as images or other types of files. The difference between BLOB and TEXT is to do with how data is sorted and compared. BLOBs are case sensitive but TEXT fields are not case sensitive.

TINYBLOB or TINYTEXT - A BLOB or TEXT column with a maximum length of 255 characters.

MEDIUMBLOB or MEDIUMTEXT - A BLOB or TEXT column with a maximum length of 16777215 characters.

LONGBLOB or LONGTEXT - A BLOB or TEXT column with a maximum length of 4294967295 characters.

ENUM - An enumeration is a list from which the value must be selected (or it can be NULL). For example, an ENUM field might be 'male' or 'female' so ENUM would be defined as ('male', 'female') and only those values (or NULL) could be used.

Exercise 10.1

As a simple exercise in creating a table, we will use **phpMyAdmin**

Create a new table with the following details using **phpMyAdmin**.

Suggested table name: sales

Suggested fields names: RecID, CompanyName, DateOfPurchase, Quantity, Cost

Define a primary key and define data types as appropriate.

RecID	INT	Auto-Number	Primary key
CompanyName	VARCHAR		
DateOfPurchase	DATE		
Quantity	INT		
Cost	FLOAT		

Each table has to have a primary key that is unique to identify a row. Other columns can also have unique values such as CompanyName.

Exercise 10.2

We will create a set of tables, which we will use in later exercises, by running a SQL script.

Open the file **sql_scripts_for_courses_database.txt** in notepad. You can find this file as part of the download code associated with the book.

Copy all the contents of the file by pressing Control-A.

In **phpMyAdmin**, select the required database, and then select the SQL tab. Paste the text into the text box using Control-V.

Run the script by pressing the Go button.

A number of tables should have been created with each table populated with the test data.

Do the same for **sql_script_for_staff_table.txt** if you have not already done so, in the same database. This will create a staff table.

Code File: 10_sql_and_mysql/ sql_scripts_for_courses_database.txt

Code File: 10_sql_and_mysql/ sql_script_for_staff_table.txt

MySQL Documentation

The official MySQL web site is http://dev.mysql.com/doc/ with SQL syntax located at http://dev.mysql.com/doc/refman/5.6/en/sql-syntax.html

There is another site http://www.w3schools.com/sql/default.asp that has a good listing of SQL examples.

Creating Tables Using an SQL Script

An easy way to create database tables is to use a SQL script that you can paste into the SQL box of the **phpMyAdmin** interface. This will use the CREATE TABLE statement. You will often come across this when you install an application that you purchased or downloaded.

An example of such a script is shown below:

```
1.  CREATE TABLE IF NOT EXISTS staff (
2.      recid MEDIUMINT UNSIGNED NOT NULL AUTO_INCREMENT,
3.      loginid VARCHAR(6) NOT NULL,
4.      first_name VARCHAR(15) NOT NULL,
5.      last_name VARCHAR(30) NOT NULL,
6.      email VARCHAR(40) NOT NULL,
7.      start_date DATE NULL,
8.      department VARCHAR(20) NULL,
9.      contractor INT default '0' NOT NULL,
10.     salary DECIMAL(19,4) NULL,
11.     PRIMARY KEY (recid)
12. );
```

The first line **CREATE TABLE IF NOT EXISTS** staff creates the table called 'staff' if the table does not already exist

The second line, **recid MEDIUMINT UNSIGNED NOT NULL AUTO_INCREMENT**, defines the first column called 'recid' as an integer value that cannot be NULL. It is also defined as an auto increment field meaning that when a record is created the value of this field is incremented by 1 from the previous row. You do not have to give this field a value because it is automatically created whenever a new row is created. recid values are never duplicated, even if a row is deleted. This field is also a primary key as defined in the last line of the CREATE TABLE statement.

What this means is that each row will have a unique value for recid, which is an important requirement for modification statements: insert, update and delete.

It is recommended that all tables have such a field even if you do not intent to use modification statements on it.

All the following lines are the various columns, each with a data definition type and size and a NULL or NOT NULL requirement. For those with a NOT NULL requirement it is usual to have a default value.

The following image shows the SQL tab in **phpMyAdmin** interface.

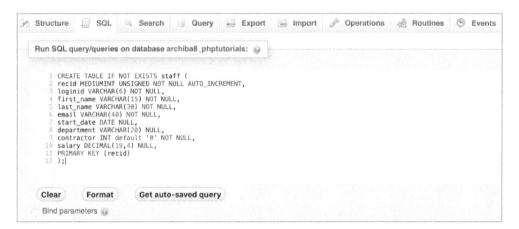

SELECT SQL statements

The **SELECT** statement is used to retrieve data from a table or tables. The basic form of the **SELECT** statement is:

```
1.  SELECT column_names FROM table_name;
```

The simplest SELECT query is:

```
1.  SELECT * FROM table_name;
```

The asterisk means you want to return every column from the table. You can specify particular columns if you wish by separating the name of each column by a comma like the following:

```
1.  SELECT last_name, email FROM staff;
```

NOTE: *That SQL is case in-sensitive, but I tend to use upper case for keywords and lower case for columns making the SQL easier to read.*

In addition, we can call a column name using an **alias** such as:

```
1.  SELECT first_name, last_name as name FROM staff;
```

If you run this SQL statement in the database, you will see that the column last_name is now displaying as "name".

Exercise 10.3

In **phpMyAdmin**, click on the SQL tab and enter the following SQL query:

```
1.  SELECT * FROM staff;
```

This will retrieve all the rows.

Modify the SQL query to

```
1.  SELECT * FROM staff ORDER BY last_name DESC;
```

This will sort the display by last_name.

Conditional SQL statements

The above SQL statements return all the rows in the table. To return only rows that we want, we use the **WHERE** clause in a SQL statement to filter out the rows.

The basic form of the where clause is:

```
1.  SELECT * FROM table_name WHERE column_name = 'value';
```

The table below is a list of the most common operators.

MYSQL Operators

Operation	Meaning
=	Equals
<	less than
>	greater than
<=	less than or equal to
>=	greater than or equal to
!=	not equal to
IS NOT NULL	has a value
IS NULL	does not have a value
BETWEEN	within a range
NOT BETWEEN	outside a range
OR (also | |)	where one or two conditionals is true
AND (also &&)	where both conditionals is true
NOT (also !)	where the condition is not true

We can use these operators together, along with parentheses, to create more complex expressions, for example:

```
1.  SELECT * FROM Person WHERE (personid >= 10 AND personid <= 20) OR
    (FirstName = 'paul');
```

NOTE: *If you copy and paste the above code into **phpMyAdmin**, sometimes you will see an error because the quote marks are not copied over correctly. If you see an error, first edit the SQL statement in **phpMyAdmin** by re-typing the quote marks and re-run the query.*

We can display entries where certain fields are empty using the **NULL** operator:

```
1.  SELECT * FROM StudentGrade WHERE grade IS NULL;
```

Or:

```
2.  SELECT * FROM Person WHERE HireDate IS NULL;
```

The Like and Not Like operators

We can check for equality with the **WHERE** clause using the = operator together with other types of operators as listed above. However, with strings, we often want to be less specific. For this, we can use the **LIKE** and **NOT LIKE** operators.

We use the **LIKE** operator with the wild card characters:

* The underscore (_) to match a single character.
* The percentage sign (%) to match zero or more characters'.

```
3.  SELECT * FROM staff WHERE last_name LIKE 'Star%';
```

Would display all staff names that start with the characters 'star'

Note that the statement is not case sensitive.

Other examples of the **LIKE** statement including combining two statements together:

```
4.  SELECT * FROM staff WHERE email LIKE '%beatles.com';
```

Will return all email addresses that end in beatles.com

```
5.  SELECT * FROM staff WHERE email LIKE '%beatles.com' AND
    first_name = 'paul';
```

As the previous statement but the first name must also be 'paul'.

The underscore character represents any single character. Therefore, an example of this is:

```
1.  SELECT * FROM staff WHERE first_name LIKE 'p___';
```

Would display the rows from the person table where the first name has four characters with the first character is a p. Therefore, this would match Pete and Paul in our staff table.

We can also select from a group using square brackets [ ]. So the following example:

```
2.  SELECT * FROM staff WHERE Last_Name LIKE '[kg]ete';
```

Would match the words **kete** and **gete** because the first word can be either **k** or **g**

Exercise 10.4

Using the person table in the course database:

(1) From the person table, display all the persons with a first name of roger:

(2) From the person table, display all the persons with a Hire Date greater than 2003-12-01

NOTE: *The best way to represent dates in PHP and storing them in a database is to use the format of yyyy-mm-dd This format is a universal format.*

(3) From the person table, display all the persons with no hiredate.

(4) From the person table, display all the persons whose last name starts with a letter "a".

INSERT SQL statements

The **INSERT** statement is used to create a new row in the table with data.

The general form of the **INSERT** statement is:

```
1.  INSERT INTO table_name (column1, column2 …) VALUES
    ('value1', 'value2' …);
```

In the above version, we are defining the column names; however there is another version of the INSERT statement where we do not identify the column names only the values, in this case you must include all values in the table, even those values that are NULL.

An example of this would be:

```
1.  INSERT INTO table_name VALUES ('value1', 'value2' ..);
```

Note the use of quote marks as follows:

* String names (for CHAR, VARCHAR and TEXT column types) must be quoted.
* Date and time values must be quoted.

However:

* Numeric values should **NOT** be quoted.
* SQL functions are **NOT** quoted.
* The word NULL is **NOT** quoted.

An example of an **INSERT** statement would be:

```
1.  INSERT INTO staff (loginid, first_name, last_name, email) VALUES
    ('GIBBPV', 'Paul', 'Gibbs', 'paulvgibbs@yahoo.co.uk');
```

NOTE: *In the staff table there is a field called recid that is an auto incremented field. We do not have to insert any data into this field, as MySQL will automatically create its value for us.*

Exercise 10.5

Create an **INSERT** statement similar to the above for the table staff, with your first name and last name and run the SQL in **phpMyAdmin**.

After you have run the statement, you can check if the data is in the user table and see that there is a new recid.

UPDATE SQL statements

We use the **UPDATE** statement to modify an existing record or records in the table.

The general form of the **UPDATE** statement is:

```
1.  UPDATE table_name SET column1='value1', column2='value2'
    WHERE column3='value3';
```

The above example updates two columns - you can add more by separating the name-value with a comma. Most **UPDATE** statements use a **WHERE** clause often based on the primary key to define the unique record. Without a **WHERE** clause, all records would be updated.

An example of an **UPDATE** statement is:

```
1.  UPDATE staff SET start_date = NOW() WHERE recid = 35;
```

This will update the start_date for the record with the recid of 35, assuming that there is a recid of 35.

Note that if you just do:

```
1.  UPDATE staff SET start_date = NOW();
```

It will update all the rows in the table rather than the one row.

NOTE: *The column names in the update statement are quoted for strings and date/time but are **NOT** quoted for numbers or for the **NULL** value.*

Exercise 10.6

The previous **INSERT** statement that you used to insert a new person in the staff table created a new record with a unique recid. Look up the recid that was created and then write an **UPDATE** statement to update the column first_name for that recid.

Run the statement in **phpMyAdmin** and check that it worked.

DELETE SQL statements

The **DELETE** statement is used to delete a record or records depending on the **WHERE** clause.

The general form of the **DELETE** statement is:

```
1.  DELETE FROM table_name WHERE column = 'value';
```

Note that the statement:

```
1.  DELETE FROM table_name;
```

This will delete all records from the table and cannot be undone.

NOTE: *Whenever you use a **DELETE** statement, you would normally have a **WHERE** clause, otherwise you could delete all your date from the table.*

An example of a **DELETE** statement is:

```
1.  DELETE FROM staff WHERE recid = 35;
```

Exercise 10.7

The previous **INSERT** statement that you used to insert a new person in the staff table created a new record with a unique recid. Using that recid write a SQL **DELETE** statement similar to the one above.

Run the statement in **phpMyAdmin** and check that it worked.

Join tables

Databases normally consist of a number of tables with each table holding specific data. This is the principle of relational databases to ensure there is no duplication of data.

So for example, the course table has a column called DepartmentID. This column contains ID references to the department table - this column is called a **foreign key**. The department table consists of a list of DepartmentID and department names.

It is the foreign key that provides the link between the two tables and enables us to look up the department name from a DepartmentID. The advantage with this method is that the data is not duplicated in the tables; it is only a reference that is included in the other table.

We can use the key fields to link together two tables.

There are several types of joins available to SQL. We will use the two most basic joins, which are the **inner join** and the **outer** or **left join**.

The Inner Join

The inner join returns all records from two tables where the two keys match, for example with the courses database:

```
1.  SELECT * FROM Person INNER JOIN StudentGrade ON
    Person.PersonID = StudentGrade.StudentID;
```

Another example of an inner join is:

```
1.  SELECT concat(firstname, '  ' , lastname) AS name,grade, courseid
    FROM Person INNER JOIN StudentGrade ON Person.personid
    = StudentGrade.studentid ORDER BY name;
```

This should return about 40 rows.

Another way to do an inner join, which you may come across, is as follows:

```
1.  SELECT concat(firstname, '  ' , lastname) AS name,grade, courseid
    FROM Person, StudentGrade WHERE Person.personid =
    StudentGrade.studentid ORDER BY name;
```

The first method is the standard way of depicting JOINs although you will see the second method used in some older textbooks.

Therefore, a join is the way that that you retrieve all of the information from both the Person and StudentGrade tables wherever a Person.PersonID is the same as the StudentGrade.StudentID.

NOTE: *When selecting from multiple tables and columns, you use the **dot syntax** in the form of **table_name.column_name** when there are columns with the same name in different tables. This is quite common because column names in different tables can often be the same, particularly the primary key and foreign key. If you try to run a SQL query where you do not do this, and the column names are the same, you will get an error message and the SQL will not run.*

The Outer Join

The outer or left join returns all records from the left table even if there is no matching key value in the right table.

An example of this join is:

```
1.  SELECT concat(firstname, '  ' , lastname) AS name,
    grade, courseid FROM Person LEFT JOIN StudentGrade ON
    Person.personid = StudentGrade.studentid ORDER BY name;
```

This returns about 49 rows because there are some students who are not on any courses.

NOTE: *With LEFT JOINs, the order in which the tables are named is important. So in this example all the person records will be returned along with all the student grade information if a match is made.   If no match exists for a studentid row, then NULL values will be returned instead.*

Some further points about joins

* You can perform joins across databases using the database name in the SQL statement providing the databases are on the same server. It is even possible to

join tables across different servers but this is an advanced subject.
* Joins can include **WHERE** clauses to filter out the data returned.
* You can make a join using any column, not just the primary and foreign keys, although you usually make the join with the primary and foreign keys.
* We can make joins with more than two tables.
* We can join tables to itself to create a self-join.

Exercise 10.8

Display a list of courses against departments ordered by the department name

To do this, create a SQL statement that INNER JOINs the course table and the department table using the departmentid as the joining key.

A more complex join

If we want to combine three tables together, one way is to do a query of a query like the following:

```
1.  SELECT * FROM
    (
         SELECT ….. FROM ….. INNER JOIN … ON ….
    ) AS x
    INNER JOIN ON ….
```

Note the x which is an alias.

Therefore, this would look something like:

```
1.  SELECT firstname, lastname, title FROM
    (
    SELECT firstname, lastname, personid, courseid FROM
    StudentGrade INNER JOIN Person ON Person.PersonID =
    StudentGrade.StudentID )
    AS x INNER JOIN Course ON x.CourseID = Course.CourseID;
```

A query of a query is a useful way of making a complex query more manageable and easier to understand.

GROUP BY and HAVING

Use the SQL **GROUP BY** Clause to retrieve data grouped according to one or more columns.

We often use this when calculating fields with **SUM** or **COUNT**.

For Example: Say we have a table of employees, their departments, and the salary of each employee. If you want to know the total amount of salary spent on each department, the query would be:

```
1.  SELECT department, SUM(salary) FROM staff GROUP BY department;
```

The output will look something like the following:

department	Sum(salary)
Art	202999
Music	236185

NOTE: *The GROUP BY clause should contain all the columns in the select list except those used with the group functions.*

The **HAVING** clause is analogous to the **WHERE** clause in a SQL statement and is used to filter and limit the **GROUP BY** query in the same way.

So in the department table, we might use this as follows:

```
1.  SELECT department, SUM(salary) FROM staff GROUP BY department
    HAVING department = 'TV';
```

This would calculate the salaries per department for employees in department TV.

Exercise 10.9

Using our example tables in the course database, display the count of the number of students for each courseid using a GROUP BY clause.

To do this, create a SQL statement using an INNER JOIN using the person and StudentGrade tables.

Then modify the query by adding in the GROUP BY courseid.

To work out the number of persons, use the COUNT keyword.

The BETWEEN operator

The **BETWEEN** operator is used in a **WHERE** statement to filter the output between two values.

```
1.  SELECT column_name(s) FROM table_name WHERE column_name
    BETWEEN value1 AND value2;
```

This is particularly useful for returning data between dates for example:

```
2.  SELECT * FROM Person WHERE hiredate
    BETWEEN '2000-12-01' AND '2003-12-01';
```

Will return all rows where the hiredate is between the two dates.

NOTE: *the use of the date in yyyy-mm-dd format to overcome issues with countries that use different data formats.*

The IN operator

The **IN** operator is another useful operator to select multiple values in a **WHERE** clause.

```
1.  SELECT column_names(s) FROM table_name WHERE column_name
    IN (value1, value2, value3,  ......);
```

As an example in our database tables:

```
1.  SELECT * FROM StudentGrade WHERE CourseID IN (2021, 2030);
```

This will return all rows where the CourseID is 2021 or2030.

Sub queries

A sub query, or inner query, or nested query, is a query in a query. A sub query is usually added in the **WHERE** clause of the SQL statement. Most of the time, a sub query is used when you know how to search for a value using a **SELECT** statement, but do not know the exact value.

An example of a sub query:

```
1.  SELECT * FROM StudentGrade WHERE studentid IN
    (SELECT personid FROM Person WHERE enrolmentdate >= '2003-01-01');
```

In the above example, the WHERE clause is a separate select query which is then part of an IN statement.

Views

In Version 5 of MySQL databases, you can create **views**, which are virtual tables or queries made up of SQL queries and joins.

An example of a view using our database tables would be:

```
1.  CREATE VIEW person_grades
    AS
    SELECT * FROM StudentGrade WHERE enrolmentid IN
    (SELECT personid FROM Person WHERE enrolmentdate >= '2003-01-01');
```

Running the above SQL will create the view, which will appear in the listing of tables in **phpMyAdmin**.

You can then query the view in the same way as you can query any other tables, even joining the view as part of other queries.   Note that a view does not physically store the data and hence is often referred to as a virtual table.

Therefore, the following is a valid query:

```
1.  SELECT * FROM person_grades;
```

If you have to create a very complex query, one way to do it may be to split the problem into a view or views, which you can then include in other queries. The underlying complexity of the view is hidden and it can be queried using simple SQL statements.

Views can include computed fields, which again helps to simplify complex problems.

However, views can slow down your SQL processing especially if the view is based on other views. Another issue with views is that if you change the underlying structure of the tables that the view is based on, you have to change the view as well.

Not only can you create views that can be queried using SQL SELECT statements, you can also create views that can perform updates on the underlying data. That means you can INSERT, DELETE and UPDATE the underlying tables that the views are based on. However, there are certain rules and restrictions for this to work.

The SELECT statement that defines the view must not include the following:

DISTINCT, GROUP BY, HAVING, UNION, LEFT JOIN or OUTER JOIN and aggregate functions such as MIN, MAX SUM and so on. You can look up the MySQL documentation if you are interested in other restrictions.

Advantages of Views

Views can simplify a complex query - you can simplify very complex sql query into a view so that you can refer to it using a single SELECT statement.

Views can make your business login more consistent – if you have to use the same formula in a sql expression a number of times, you can create a single view for consistency.

Views can add extra security - you can restrict sensitive data to certain users by creating a view to show the non-sensitive data, giving them permissions for the view but restricting their permissions to the underlying tables.

Views can help with backward compatibility - sometimes you may want to make modifications that result in removing a table. You could then create a view with the same name as the table that was removed and hence maintain backward compatibility.

Transactions

Transactions are an advanced subject and for most situations would not be something that you would need to use in your systems.

A transaction is a collection of SQL statements. So a task may for example, consist of a number of update statements. If one of these should fail, you may end up with some tables correctly updated but others not correctly updated, particularly if one update has data from a previous update.

To overcome this you define the SQL statements as a transaction. If one SQL statement should fail, you roll back the data to its initial state. Only when all the statements are successful would you commit the transaction.

When you are entering SQL statements into MySQL you may use the begin / commit / rollback transaction commands.

So, say we are working with our **person** table and do an **INSERT** statement, we can either commit or rollback the transaction.

The problem with **phpMyAdmin** is that all the lines have to be one command so it is not easy to demonstrate.

However, we can demonstrate it using the following SQL statements and check the results for each.

Copy the following lines into the SQL editor in **phpMyAdmin**:

```
1.  begin;
2.  INSERT INTO Person (firstname, lastname) VALUES ('fred', 'blogs');
3.  commit;
```

Examine the person table. We should see that a new record has been created.

Now copy the following lines into the SQL editor in **phpMyAdmin**:

```
1.  begin;
2.  INSERT INTO Person (firstname, lastname) VALUES ('fred', 'blogs');
3.  rollback;
```

In this case, the transaction has been rolled back and the record has not been created.

Summary

If you are going to use PHP to work with databases then you need to know at least some SQL. Database development and design is a complete subject in itself but you should have learnt enough from this Chapter to understand how to extract and manipulate table rows. As you work with PHP and databases, you can gradually pick up how to do specific things.

We started by looking at how to create databases and tables. The Chapter then looked at how to select, insert, update and delete rows. Joining tables together from a relational database is an important concept to understand.

The following Chapters will look at the PHP code required to connect to a database and then display data.

Topics for Review

[1] If you have web hosting, try creating a database and then create a few tables within that database. Make sure that you also create a user that has permissions to access the database if you are going to connect to it with PHP.

[2] You may want to investigate different web hosting packages. Some only give you one MySQL database. Others give you the ability to create an unlimited number of databases providing you do not exceed a size limit.

11 - The Staff Table

What is in this Chapter?

This Chapter provides further exercises in SQL using a test table called staff and working with the phpMyAdmin interface.

Creating The Staff table

We first need to create the table and populate it with test data.

(1) Log on to your web server and access **phpMyAdmin.**

(2) In **phpMyAdmin** open a database or create a new database if you do not have one set up. We have called our database "tutorials".

(3) Open the text file **sql_script_for_staff_table.txt** in NotePad and copy the text from NotePad.

```
1.  CREATE TABLE staff (
2.  recid MEDIUMINT UNSIGNED NOT NULL AUTO_INCREMENT,
3.  loginid VARCHAR(6) NOT NULL,
4.  first_name VARCHAR(15) NOT NULL,
5.  last_name VARCHAR(30) NOT NULL,
6.  email VARCHAR(40) NOT NULL,
7.  start_date DATE NULL,
8.  department VARCHAR(20) NULL,
9.  contractor INT default '0' NOT NULL,
10. salary DECIMAL(19,4) NULL,
11. PRIMARY KEY (recid)
12. );
13.
14. INSERT INTO staff (loginid, first_name, last_name, email, start_date
    , department, salary) VALUES
15. ('FERMEN','Enrico','Fermi', 'enrico@science.com', '2010-03-
    10', 'Development', 24348.00),
16. ('ZUSEKO','Konrad','Zuse', 'konrad@science.com', '2006-11-
    09', 'Development', 25837.40),
```

```
17. ('BORNMA','Max','Born', 'maxborn@science.com', '1999-08-
    25', 'Development', 28384.20),
18. ('LEEXHA','Harper', 'Lee', 'harper@authors.com', '1999-03-
    04', 'Art', 15398.00),
19. ('SIMPHO','Homer','Simpson', 'homer@simpson.com', '2008-03-
    09', 'TV', 34938.50),
20. ('JOBSST','Steve', 'Jobs', 'steve@science.com', '2005-10-
    10', 'Development', 26387.00),
21. ('SIMPLI','Lisa', 'Simpson', 'lisa@simpson.com', '2004-09-
    27', 'TV', 35987.50),
22. ('HARRGE','George', 'Harrison', 'george@beatles.com', '1989-04-
    05', 'Music', 30989.50),
23. ('LENNJO','John', 'Lennon', 'john@beatles.com', '2000-10-
    02', 'Music', 29378.50),
24. ('BANKIA','Ian', 'Banks', 'ian@authors.com', '2002-03-
    09', 'Art', 16390.50),
25. ('MCCAPA','Paul', 'McCartney', 'paul@beatles.com', '2012-01-
    03', 'Music', 31839.50),
26. ('WALTRO','Roger', 'Walters', 'roger@pinkfloyd.com', '2003-10-
    02', 'Music', 31983.00),
27. ('MASONI','Nick', 'Mason', 'nick@monkees.com', '1998-02-
    10', 'Music', 29290.50),
28. ('JENNED','Edward','Jenner','edward@science.com', '2007-12-
    27', 'Development', 27387.00),
29. ('FORSEM','E.M.', 'Forster', 'edwardforster@authors.com', '1999-05-
    22', 'Art', 16398.50),
30. ('PULLPH','Phillip', 'Pullman', 'phillip@authors.com', '2001-03-
    04', 'Art', 17239.00),
31. ('PLANMA','Max','Planck', 'maxplanck@science.com', '2001-09-
    25', 'Development', 23938.50),
32. ('HORNNI','Nick', 'Hornby', 'nick@authors.com', '2002-02-
    04', 'Art', 18398.90),
33. ('BANKME','Melissa', 'Bank', 'melissa@authors.com', '2000-12-
    02', 'Art', 15290.00),
34. ('GILMDA','David', 'Gilmour', 'david@pinkfloyd.com', '2004-10-
    04', 'Music', 18398.00),
35. ('JORDRO','Robert', 'Jordan',   'bob@authors.com', '2002-04-
    03', 'Art', 17398.00),
36. ('SIMPMA','Marge', 'Simpson', 'marge@simpson.com', '2000-10-
    03', 'TV', 36938.98),
37. ('RUTHER','Ernst','Rutherford', 'ernst@science.com', '1997-11-
    13', 'Development',  28298.00),
38. ('MCGUUR','Ursula', 'McGuin', 'ursula@authors.com', '2003-03-
    03', 'Art', 16009.50),
39. ('GREEGR','Graham', 'Greene', 'graham@authors.com', '2012-04-
    04', 'Art', 18398.90),
40. ('STARRI','Ringo', 'Starr', 'ringo@beatles.com', '1999-11-
    23', 'Music', 32908.60),
41. ('CORNWB','Bernard', 'Cornwell', 'bernard@authors.com', '1998-02-
    04', 'Art', 17390.00),
42. ('WYNDJO','John', 'Wyndham', 'john@authors.com', '2009-03-
    09', 'Art', 18290.00),
43. ('BABBCH','Charles','Babbage', 'charles@science.com', '1988-06-
    20', 'Development', 24987.50),
```

```
44. ('BARRSY','Syd', 'Barrett', 'syd@pinkfloyd.com ', '2004-04-
    20', 'Music', 31398.00),
45. ('ELIOTS','T.S.', 'Eliot', 'thomas@authors.com', '2000-01-
    06', 'Art', 16398.00),
46. ('SIMPBA','Bart', 'Simpson', 'bart@simpson.com', '2001-09-
    03', 'TV', 32989.90),
47. ('FARAMI','Michael', 'Faraday','michael@science.com', '2005-12-
    22', 'Development', 24389.00),
48. ('SIMPMA','Maggie', 'Simpson', 'maggie@simpson.com', '2005-04-
    08', 'TV', 36343.00),
49. ('SIMPAB','Abe', 'Simpson', 'abe@simpson.com', '1986-03-
    09', 'TV', 37983.00);
```

Code File: 11_staff_table/ sql_script_for_staff_table.txt

(4) In **phpMyAdmin** click on the top bar SQL link that opens the SQL editor box, and paste the text then click on **Go** to execute the code.

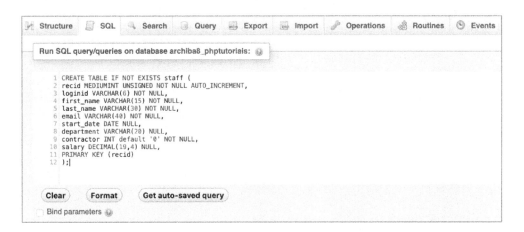

(5) Check that the **staff** table was created by looking at the list of tables in the database - you may have to refresh the display to load the current list of tables. Then browse the data in the table and check that the data was inserted.

SQL Exercises based on the staff table

The following questions are based on the staff table that you have just created. You can find the answers in Chapter 11 of the files associated with the book.

(1) Display all staff with a beatles.com email address from the staff table. This will require the use of the **LIKE** statement. .

(2) Count the staff with an authors.com email address from the staff table. You may need to look up on the internet the use of the **COUNT** statement as used in SQL.

(3) Display the staff who have a **registration_date** before the start of the year 2000

(4) Display the staff who have a **registration_date** between the start of the year 2001 and the end of the year 2008. You may need to look up on the internet the use of the **BETWEEN** statement as used in SQL.

Code File: 11_staff_table/sql_exercises_answers.txt

Creating the Course tables

We can create the tables that are associated with 'courses' in the same way by running the SQL script **sql_scripts_for_courses_database.txt** in the **phpMyAdmin** interface. This script will actually create a set of tables one after another.

Code File: 11_staff_table/sql_scripts_for_courses_database.txt

SQL Exercises based on the Courses database tables

The following questions are based on the course database tables that you should have created in the previous Chapter or using the above script. You can find the answers in Chapter 11 of the files associated with the book.

(1) Display all the courses from the course table that have credits of 4.

(2) Display all the courses from the course table that have credits of either 3, 4 or 5. This will require the use of the **IN** statement.

(3) Display the department name from the department table with a budget **greater** than 20000.

(4) Display the course title that each department is running. You will need to combine the two tables together using an **INNER JOIN.**

Code File: 11_staff_table/sql_exercises_answers.txt

Summary

After completing these exercises, you should have a good introduction to using SQL on the test tables. The exercise illustrate the simple SQL statements that you need to work with when analysing data in a set of tables.

Topics for Review

[1] Take the opportunity to go through phpMyAdmin and check out its features. The appendix of this book includes a section on using **phpMyAdmin** that you may find useful.

12 - Database Access

What is in this Chapter?

* Using PHP to connect to a database.
* Reading and modifying data using **mysqli**.
* Using PHP Data Objects (PDO) to read and modify data.

The following examples show the basic code needed for connecting and linking to a database. To use them in your applications you will probably want to extract the connection details and place those into a separate 'include' file, which is the technique that we use in later sections.

SQL Selecting and Updating – mysqli

A note about mysqli functions

To make our connections and read information from the database we will be using the PHP **mysqli** functions as opposed to the **mysql** functions. The **mysqli** functions are available in PHP version 5 onwards. The original **mysql** functions were depreciated from PHP version 5.5 and removed from PHP 7. There are probably gazillions of web sites that use **mysql** functions, and these will eventually stop working as the servers are upgraded to PHP 7, so you can use your knowledge to update old scripts.

The "I" in **mysqli** refers to improved, provides better more efficient database access, and is slightly simpler to use. They also have object oriented versions as well as procedural versions. Note that **mysqli** only works with MySQL databases.

TASK 1 - Create table data

First, we need to create our sample database table and data to use in our examples. If you have not already done so in previous Chapters, use the following SQL script in your MySQL database to create the table and data.

```
1.  CREATE TABLE IF NOT EXISTS staff (
2.  recid MEDIUMINT UNSIGNED NOT NULL AUTO_INCREMENT,
3.  loginid VARCHAR(6) NOT NULL,
4.  first_name VARCHAR(15) NOT NULL,
5.  last_name VARCHAR(30) NOT NULL,
6.  email VARCHAR(40) NOT NULL,
7.  start_date DATE NULL,
8.  department VARCHAR(20) NULL,
9.  contractor INT default '0' NOT NULL,
10. salary DECIMAL(19,4) NULL,
11. PRIMARY KEY (recid)
12. );
13.
14. INSERT INTO staff (loginid, first_name, last_name, email, start_date
    , department, salary) VALUES
15. ('FERMEN','Enrico','Fermi', 'enrico@science.com', '2010-03-
    10', 'Development', 24348.00),
16. ('ZUSEKO','Konrad','Zuse', 'konrad@science.com', '2006-11-
    09', 'Development', 25837.40),
17. ('BORNMA','Max','Born', 'maxborn@science.com', '1999-08-
    25', 'Development', 28384.20),
18. ('LEEXHA','Harper', 'Lee', 'harper@authors.com', '1999-03-
    04', 'Art', 15398.00),
19. ('SIMPHO','Homer', 'Simpson', 'homer@simpson.com', '2008-03-
    09', 'TV', 34938.50),
20. ('JOBSST','Steve', 'Jobs', 'steve@science.com', '2005-10-
    10', 'Development', 26387.00),
21. ('SIMPLI','Lisa', 'Simpson', 'lisa@simpson.com', '2004-09-
    27', 'TV', 35987.50),
22. ('HARRGE','George', 'Harrison', 'george@beatles.com', '1989-04-
    05', 'Music', 30989.50),
23. ('LENNJO','John', 'Lennon', 'john@beatles.com', '2000-10-
    02', 'Music', 29378.50),
24. ('BANKIA','Ian', 'Banks', 'ian@authors.com', '2002-03-
    09', 'Art', 16390.50),
25. ('MCCAPA','Paul', 'McCartney', 'paul@beatles.com', '2012-01-
    03', 'Music', 31839.50),
26. ('WALTRO','Roger', 'Walters', 'roger@pinkfloyd.com', '2003-10-
    02', 'Music', 31983.00),
27. ('MASONI','Nick', 'Mason', 'nick@monkees.com', '1998-02-
    10', 'Music', 29290.50),
28. ('JENNED','Edward','Jenner','edward@science.com', '2007-12-
    27', 'Development', 27387.00),
29. ('FORSEM','E.M.', 'Forster', 'edwardforster@authors.com', '1999-05-
    22', 'Art', 16398.50),
30. ('PULLPH','Phillip', 'Pullman', 'phillip@authors.com', '2001-03-
    04', 'Art', 17239.00),
31. ('PLANMA','Max','Planck', 'maxplanck@science.com', '2001-09-
    25', 'Development', 23938.50),
32. ('HORNNI','Nick', 'Hornby', 'nick@authors.com', '2002-02-
    04', 'Art', 18398.90),
33. ('BANKME','Melissa', 'Bank', 'melissa@authors.com', '2000-12-
    02', 'Art', 15290.00),
34. ('GILMDA','David', 'Gilmour', 'david@pinkfloyd.com', '2004-10-
    04', 'Music', 18398.00),
```

```
35. ('JORDRO','Robert', 'Jordan',   'bob@authors.com', '2002-04-
    03', 'Art', 17398.00),
36. ('SIMPMA','Marge', 'Simpson', 'marge@simpson.com', '2000-10-
    03', 'TV', 36938.98),
37. ('RUTHER','Ernst','Rutherford', 'ernst@science.com', '1997-11-
    13', 'Development',  28298.00),
38. ('MCGUUR','Ursula', 'McGuin', 'ursula@authors.com', '2003-03-
    03', 'Art', 16009.50),
39. ('GREEGR','Graham', 'Greene', 'graham@authors.com', '2012-04-
    04', 'Art', 18398.90),
40. ('STARRI','Ringo', 'Starr', 'ringo@beatles.com', '1999-11-
    23', 'Music', 32908.60),
41. ('CORNWB','Bernard', 'Cornwell', 'bernard@authors.com', '1998-02-
    04', 'Art', 17390.00),
42. ('WYNDJO','John', 'Wyndham', 'john@authors.com', '2009-03-
    09', 'Art', 18290.00),
43. ('BABBCH','Charles','Babbage', 'charles@science.com', '1988-06-
    20', 'Development', 24987.50),
44. ('BARRSY','Syd', 'Barrett', 'syd@pinkfloyd.com ', '2004-04-
    20', 'Music', 31398.00),
45. ('ELIOTS','T.S.', 'Eliot', 'thomas@authors.com', '2000-01-
    06', 'Art', 16398.00),
46. ('SIMPBA','Bart', 'Simpson', 'bart@simpson.com', '2001-09-
    03', 'TV', 32989.90),
47. ('FARAMI','Michael', 'Faraday','michael@science.com', '2005-12-
    22', 'Development', 24389.00),
48. ('SIMPMA','Maggie', 'Simpson', 'maggie@simpson.com', '2005-04-
    08', 'TV', 36343.00),
49. ('SIMPAB','Abe', 'Simpson', 'abe@simpson.com', '1986-03-
    09', 'TV', 37983.00);
```

Code File: 12_database_access/sql_script_for_staff_table.txt

TASK 2 - Reading database using mysqli_fetch_assoc

This example is used for SELECT statements.

Create a new web page called **php_fetch.php** and enter the following:

```php
1.  <?php
2.
3.  //Example of fetching data from a database using mysqli_connect
4.
5.  //Make a connection to the database
6.  $link = mysqli_connect("databasehostname", "databaseusername",
        "databasepassword", "databasename");
7.
8.  //Check the connection
9.  if (!$link) {
10.     printf("Could not connect to database: %s\n",
            mysqli_connect_error());
```

```
11.    exit();
12. }
13.
14. //Create the sql query
15. $query = "SELECT * FROM staff ";
16.
17. //Execute the query against the database
18. $result = mysqli_query( $link, $query );
19.
20. //---------------
21. if (!$result) { //Display any error message
22.    printf("Error in connection: %s\n", mysqli_error($link));
23.    exit();
24. }
25.
26. //---------------
27. //Fetch the result into an associative array
28. while ( $row = mysqli_fetch_assoc( $result ) ) {
29.    $table[] = $row;  //add each row into the table array
30. }
31.
32. //---------------
33. //Display the rows
34. if ($table) { //Check if there are any rows to be displayed
35.    //Retrieve each element of the array
36.    foreach($table as $d_row) {
37.     echo($d_row["first_name"] . " " . $d_row["last_name"] . "<br/>");
38.    }
39. }
40. else
41. {
42.     echo("No rows to be displayed");
43. }
44.
45. //---------------
46. //Close the connection
47. mysqli_close($link);
48. ?>
```

Code File: 12_database_access/php_fetch.php

You must enter the details for **databasehostname, databaseusenname, databasepassword** and **databasename** that depends on your particular set up. **databasehostname** will probably be localhost.

Run the web page and review the output

The process that this script uses is:

* Connect to database
* Create the SQL
* Run the query

* Fill the array
* Output the array to the page

Exercise 12.1

Modify the SQL SELECT statement in **php_fetch.php** to sort the order of the output by first_name.

Exercise 12.2

Modify **php_fetch.php** to display the email as well as the first name and last name.

Exercise 12.3

Format the output of **php_fetch.php** to display it within a table similar to the following:

```php
1.  <?php
2.  if ($table) { //Check if there are any rows to be displayed
3.  ?>
4.  <table>
5.  <tr>
6.      <td>First Name</td>
7.      <td>Last Name</td>
8.      <td>Email</td>
9.  </tr>
10. <?php
11.
12.     //-----------
13.     //Retrieve each element of the array
14.     foreach($table as $d_row) {
15.     ?>
16.        <tr>
17.           <td><?php echo($d_row["first_name"]); ?></td>
18.           <td><?php echo($d_row["last_name"]); ?></td>
19.           <td><?php echo($d_row["email"]); ?></td>
20.        </tr>
21.        <?php
22.
23.     }
24. ?>
25. </table>
26. <?php
27. }
28. ?>
```

Code File: 12_database_access/php_fetch1.php

TASK 3 - Creating a function to return a table as an array

How can we modify our code to make it reusable?

We can easily do this using a function as follows:

```php
1.  <?php
2.  //-------------------/*
3.  * Returns an array
4.  */
5.  function user_array()
6.  {
7.      //Make a connection to the database
8.      $link = mysqli_connect("databasehostname", "databaseusername",
            "databasepassword", "databasename");
9.
10.     //------------
11.     //Check the connection
12.     if (!$link) {
13.         printf("Could not connect to database: %s\n",
                mysqli_connect_error());
14.         exit();
15.     }
16.     //Create the sql query
17.     $query = "SELECT * FROM staff ";
18.
19.     //Execute the query against the database
20.     $result = mysqli_query( $link, $query);
21.     if (!$result) {
22.         printf("Error in connection: %s\n",
                mysqli_error($link));
23.         exit();
24.     }
25.
26.     //Fetch the result into an associative array
27.     while ( $row = mysqli_fetch_assoc( $result ) ) {
28.         $table[] = $row;     //add each row into the table array
29.     }
30.
31.     //Close the connection
32.     mysqli_close($link);
33.     //Return an array
34.     return $table;
35. }
36. //-------------------
37. ?>
```

What the above code does is it uses a function called **user_array()** to return a table. We can then use this function in the following way:

```php
1.  $users = user_array();
2.
3.  //-------------------
```

```
4.  if ($users) {    //Check if there are any rows to be displayed
5.    //Retrieve each element of the array
6.    foreach($users as $d_row) {
7.      echo($d_row["first_name"] . " " . $d_row["last_name"] . "<br/>");
8.    }
9.  }
```

We call the **users_array()** function and then access the elements of the array in a **foreach** loop. The elements of the array are simply accessed using: $d_row["first_name"]. This method is very useful when working with database access scripts. In the above script, you will have to supply the **databasehostname**, **databaseusername**, **databasepassword** and **databasename** values of course, but you could do that through an include file.

Code File: 12_database_access/return_array.php

TASK 4 - Modifying database using mysqli_query

Used for insert, update and delete statements.

Create a new web page called **php_updates.php** and enter the text as below:

```
1.  <?php
2.
3.  //--------------
4.  //Example of manipulating data in a database
5.  //Use for INSERT, UPDATE OR DELETE SQL queries
6.
7.  //--------------
8.  //Make a connection to the database
9.  $link = mysqli_connect("databasehostname", "databaseusername",
            "databasepassword", "databasename");
10.
11. //--------------
12. //Check the connection
13. if (!$link) {
14.    printf("Could not connect to database: %s\n",
            mysqli_connect_error());
15.    exit();
16. }
17.
18. //--------------
19. //Make the sql query
20. $query = " INSERT INTO staff (loginid, first_name, last_name,
    email, start_date) VALUES ('blogsf', 'Fred', 'Blogs',
    'fred@mysite.com', '2012-04-03') ";
21.
22. //--------------
23. //Execute the query against the database
24. $result = mysqli_query( $link, $query );
```

```
25.
26. //--------------
27. if (!$result) { //Display any error message
28.     printf("Error in connection: %s\n", mysqli_error($link));
29.     exit();
30. }
31.
32. //--------------
33. //Get the number of rows affected
34. $num_rows = mysqli_affected_rows($link);
35. echo("<p>Number of rows affected : $num_rows</p>");
36.
37. //--------------
38. //Return the number of the automatically incremented field
    after the insert statement
39. $recid = mysqli_insert_id($link);
40.
41. //--------------
42. echo("<p>Record id of new row : $recid</p>");
43.
44. //--------------
45. //Close the connection
46. mysqli_close($link);
47. ?>
```

Code File: 12_database_access/php_updates.php

Run the web page and review the output that is displayed.

Go into **phpMyAdmin** and check the data was inserted.

Exercise 12.4

Modify the above script so that it uses a delete statement to delete the newly inserted row.

Exercise 12.5

We want to modify **php_updates.php** to add in a form to allow the user to enter data.

To do this you need to do the following changes to the **php_updates.php** file.

(1) Modify the SQL statement so that the values that are entered into the INSERT statement are replaced with variables for first_name, last_name, email and start_date.

(2) At the bottom of the page, add in a form and a set of text boxes where a user can enter those variables. The form should post back to itself.

(3) At the top of the page add in the code that is used to collect the data from the form using **$_POST**.

(4) Check that the page is working by entering values into the form and submitting. This creates a new record in the database.

(5) If you have time look at validating the input data.

SQL Selecting and Updating – PHP Data Objects (PDO)

This section shows some of the basic syntax for using PDO (PDO = PHP Data Objects). PDO is only available in PHP 5.1 and above.

The advantage of PDO is that you pass your variables into the SQL function using **prepared statements**.

To be exact, **mysqli** can also use prepared statements but the advantage with PDO is when you want to switch to use a different database type such as PostgreSQL instead of MySQL, you do not have to modify your queries. Whereas **mysqli** only works with MySQL databases.

As you are not creating your SQL by adding strings together, they are **more secure** but the programming is a little more involved. The bind parameter is a way of stopping most SQL injection problems and they do not have a problem with quote marks.

Prepared statements are termed "parameterized queries" when working with programming languages like Microsoft dot.net, and provide a way to prevent SQL injection into databases.

You do not have to worry about quote marks when using PDO because they are used 'as is' in the data.

You can define the data types and the length of the data for the PDO object. This means that you have more control over the data types than when you use SQL statements.

The other advantage with PDO is that it has a 'data-access abstraction layer' meaning you can use the same function calls to access different databases. This may be important if you are considering developing an application to work with different database platforms.

PDO statements also have their own try / catch exception handling features that we explain later in this Chapter. You should always include these in your production code to control errors.

TASK 5 - Simple SQL Fetch and PDO

The example below is probably the simplest method of retrieving data from a database using PDO. This method is termed the **lazy method**.

```php
1.  <?php
2.
3.  //------------------------
4.  //Simple SQL fetch with PDO
5.  error_reporting( E_ALL | E_STRICT | E_DEPRECIATED );
6.
7.  //------------------------
8.  $dbname = 'databasename';
9.  $user = 'databseusername';
10. $pass = 'databasepassword';
11.
12. //------------------------
13. $first_name = "paul";
14.
15. //------------------------
16. $dbh = new PDO("mysql:host=localhost;dbname=$dbname", $user, $pass);

17. $stmt = $dbh->prepare("SELECT * FROM staff where first_name = ?");
18. if ($stmt->execute(array($first_name))) {
19.    while ($row = $stmt->fetch()) {
20.       print_r($row);
21.    }
22. }
23. ?>
```

Code File: 12_database_access/php_pdo_objects_basic.php

(1) Create the above file and then add in your database name, username and password to access the staff table.

(2) As PDO are objects, we have to create a new object using the **new** keyword.

(3) We then access the **prepare** method.

In the SQL statement, notice the use of the question mark (?) used as a **placeholder** for the parameter variable that we are passing in. This is how we separate the **data** from the **instructions** and hence the data will not be wrongly interpreted as an instruction and we illuminate the SQL injection problem.

This means that we can get rid of all any **mysql_real_escape_string** and similar statements to sanitise the data. (**mysql_real_escape_string** is not in PHP 7 but you may come across it in older code).

In fact, there are two ways to pass variables to the prepared statement. We show the second method in later examples that use **named placeholders** and is useful when you want to use the same data in several locations.

(4) We then call the **execute** method, passing in the variable that we are using in the SQL statement.

(5) In the above example, the results are displayed using **print_r**.

*NOTE: The above method is termed the **lazy method** and there are a couple of limitations, first the execute statement always expects an array and the data type of the value **MUST BE A STRING**.*

TASK 6 – SQL Fetch using bindValue or bindParam

The following example illustrates the regular method of working with PDO to fetch data and pass parameters into the prepared statement.

Using bindValue and named placeholders

```php
1.  <?php
2.  //-------------------
3.  //SQL fetch using bindValue
4.  error_reporting( E_ALL | E_STRICT | E_DEPRECIATED );
5.
6.  //-------------------
7.  $dbname = 'databasename';
8.  $user = 'databseusername';
9.  $pass = 'databasepassword';
10.
11. //-------------------
12. $department = "music";
13. $first_name = "paul";
14.
15. //-------------------
16. $dbh = new PDO("mysql:host=localhost;dbname=$dbname", $user, $pass);
17. $stmt = $dbh->prepare
        ("SELECT * FROM staff where department = :dept
        and first_name = :forename");
18. $stmt->bindValue(":dept", $department, PDO::PARAM_STR);
19. $stmt->bindValue(":forename", $first_name, PDO::PARAM_STR);
20.
21. //-------------------
22. if ($stmt->execute()) {
23.    while ($row = $stmt->fetch()) {
24.       print_r($row);
25.    }
26. }
27. ?>
```

Code File: 12_database_access/php_pdo_objects_basic.php

The above example shows that Instead of using the question mark (?) to define the placeholder we use the named placeholder with a colon character (:)   We then reference the named placeholder in the bindValue. So in the above example we use department = :dept to reference dept in the SQL statement and then in the bindValue statement we use the placeholder name.

The basic syntax of the bind value is:

bindValue($parameter , $variable, $data_type, $length, $driver_options)

parameter
This is the placeholder name.

variable
This is the name of the PHP variable to bind to the SQL statement parameter.

data_type (optional)
The data type for the parameter.

PDO::PARAM_BOOL (for boolean)
PDO::PARAM_NULL (for SQL NULL)
PDO::PARAM_INT (for SQL INTEGER)
PDO::PARAM_STR (for string types)
PDO::PARAM_LOB (for Large OBject types)
PDO::PARAM_STMT (for a recordset type, currently not supported)
PDO::PARAM_INPUT_OUTPUT (for an INOUT parameter of a Stored Procedure)

Length (optional)
The length of the data type.

driver_options (optional)
These are optional driver values such as defining the character set.

Using bindParam and named placeholders

The other method is to use **bindParam()** is illustrated below.

```
1.  <?php
2.
3.  //----------------------
4.  //SQL fetch using bindParam
5.  error_reporting( E_ALL | E_STRICT | E_DEPRECIATED );
6.
7.  //----------------------
8.  $dbname = 'databasename';
9.  $user = 'databseusername';
10. $pass = 'databasepassword';
11.
12. //----------------------
13. $dbh = new PDO("mysql:host=localhost;dbname=$dbname", $user, $pass);

14. $stmt = $dbh->prepare
    ("SELECT * FROM staff where department = :dept
    and first_name = :forename");
15. $stmt->bindParam(":dept", $department, PDO::PARAM_STR);
16. $stmt->bindParam(":forename", $first_name, PDO::PARAM_STR);
17.
18. //----------------------
19. $department = "music";
20. $first_name = " paul";
21. if ($stmt->execute()) {
22.   while ($row = $stmt->fetch()) {
23.     print_r($row);
24.   }
25. }
26. ?>
```

Code File: 12_database_access/php_pdo_objects_basic.php

This is almost the same as using **bindValue()** except that **bindParam()** expects a variable (it doesn't matter if the variable is assigned something or not at this point).

In this example, the **$department** and **$first_name** variables can be placed after the **bindParam()** function unlike with **bindValue()** where you need to know the value of the parameters when you call **bindValue()**. The **bindParam()** is bound as a reference to the specified name while the **bindValue** binds a value.

So what is the advantage of one over the other? Using bindParam does give an advantage where you call the execute statement, then change the values and call the execute statement again. This is useful where you have to create multiple executes (say you are doing multiple insert rows) but you do not have to re-bind each time.

TASK 7 - SQL modify

The method in working with SQL Modify statements is really the same as with SQL fetch statements. In the example below the prepare statement is using an insert statement to create new rows.

```
1.  <?php
2.
3.  //--------------------
4.  //Example of SQL insert with PDO
5.  error_reporting( E_ALL | E_STRICT | E_DEPRECIATED );
6.
7.  //--------------------
8.  $dbname = 'databasename';
9.  $user = 'databseusername';
10. $pass = 'databasepassword';
11. $dbh = new PDO("mysql:host=localhost;dbname=$dbname", $user, $pass);

12. $stmt = $dbh->
    prepare("INSERT INTO staff (first_name, last_name) VALUES (?, ?)");
13. $stmt->bindParam(1, $first_name);
14. $stmt->bindParam(2, $last_name);
15.
16. //--------------------
17. // insert one row
18. $first_name = 'Fred';
19. $last_name = 'Bloggs';
20. $stmt->execute();
21.
22. //--------------------
23. // insert another row with different values
24. $first_name = 'Pete';
25. $last_name = 'Smith';
26. $stmt->execute();
27. ?>
```

Code File: 12_database_access/php_pdo_objects_basic.php

NOTE: *The question mark placeholder (?) is used in this example rather than named placeholder, and the **bindParm()** method then uses numbers to identify which parameter is being referenced. You can use named placeholders if you find them more convenient.*

Using other types of modify statements is very similar to the INSERT statement. An example of a simple UPDATE prepare statement on the staff table is as follows:

```
1.  $stmt=$dbh-
    >prepare("UPDATE staff SET email = ? WHERE loginid = ?");
```

It is advisable to use try / catch statements around PDO and print out friendly error messages or otherwise it is possible that an error will display internal details that you do not want users to see. The following Tasks illustrate the use of try / catch in different types of situations.

TASK 8 - SQL insert with try / catch and PDO

```php
1.  <?php
2.
3.  //---------------------
4.  //Example of SQL insert with try / catch and PDO
5.  error_reporting( E_ALL | E_STRICT | E_DEPRECIATED );
6.
7.  //---------------------
8.  $dbname = 'databasename';
9.  $user = 'databseusername';
10. $pass = 'databasepassword';
11.
12. //---------------------
13. try {
14. $dbh = new PDO("mysql:host=localhost;dbname=$dbname", $user, $pass);
15. $stmt = $dbh->prepare
    ("INSERT INTO staff (first_name, last_name) VALUES (?, ?)");
16.
17. //---------------------
18. //Using positional numbers for the parameters
19. $stmt->bindParam(1, $first_name);
20. $stmt->bindParam(2, $last_name);
21.
22. //---------------------
23. // insert one row
24. $first_name = 'Fred';
25. $last_name = 'Bloggs';
26. $stmt->execute();
27.
28. //---------------------
29. // insert another row with different values
30. $first_name = 'Pete';
31. $last_name = 'Smith';
32. $stmt->execute();
33. $dbh = null;
34. } catch (PDOException $e) {
35.     print "Error!: " . $e->getMessage() . "<br/>";
36.     die();
37. }
38. ?>
```

Code File: 12_database_access/php_pdo_objects_basic.php

TASK 9 – An example of SQL Fetch with try / catch

```php
1.  <?php
2.  //-----------------------
3.  //Example of fetching data with try / catch and PDO
4.  error_reporting( E_ALL | E_STRICT | E_DEPRECIATED );
5.  //-----------------------
6.  $dbname = 'databasename';
7.  $user = 'databseusername';
8.  $pass = 'databasepassword';
9.  //-----------------------
10. try {
11.     $dbh=new PDO("mysql:host=localhost;dbname=$dbname", $user, $pass);
12.     foreach($dbh->query('SELECT * from staff') as $row) {
13.         print_r($row);
14.     }
15.     $dbh = null;
16. } catch (PDOException $e) {
17.     print "Error!: " . $e->getMessage() . "<br/>";
18.     die();
19. }
20. ?>
```

Code File: 12_database_access/php_pdo_objects_basic.php

TASK 10 - SQL fetch and PDO reading into a $table array

```php
1.  <?php
2.      //------------------
3.      // Example of fetching data from a database using PDO
4.      // using the shortcut
5.               ->query() method here as there no variables
6.      // in the select statement.
7.  error_reporting( E_ALL | E_STRICT | E_DEPRECIATED );
8.  try {
9.          $dbhost = "localhost";
10.         $dbname = 'databasename';
11.         $user = 'databaseusername';
12.         $pass = 'databasepassword';
13.
14.      //------------------
15.      //Connect to the database
16.      $dbh = new PDO("mysql:host=" . $dbhost . ";dbname=" .
                        $dbname, $user, $pass);
17.      //------------------
18.      // the sql query
19.      $sql = "SELECT * FROM staff";
20.
21.      //------------------
22.      // statement handle
```

```
23.        $sth = $dbh->query($sql);
24.
25.        //------------------
26.        // set the fetch mode
27.        $sth->setFetchMode(PDO::FETCH_ASSOC);
28.        echo("---------------------------------------------<br/>");
29.        echo("An example of a while loop<br/>");
30.        while($row = $sth->fetch()) {
31.            echo( $row["first_name"] . "<br/>" );
32.            $table[] = $row;
33.        }
34.    $dbh = null;
35. }  catch (PDOException $e) {
36.     print "Error!: " . $e->getMessage() . "<br/>";
37.     die();
38. }
39.
40. //------------------
41. echo("<br/><br/>");
42. echo("---------------------------------------<br/>");
43. echo("An example of looping around an array<br/>");
44.
45. //------------------
46. if ($table) {    //Check if there are any rows to be displayed
47.    //Retrieve each element of the array
48.    foreach($table as $d_row) {
49.      echo($d_row["first_name"] . " " . $d_row["last_name"] . "<br/>" );
50.    }
51. }
52.
53. //------------------
54. echo("---------------------------------------<br/>");
55. echo("An example of printing one element from the array<br/>");
56. echo($table[0]["first_name"]);
57. ?>
```

Code File: 12_database_access/php_pdo_objects.php

The above example illustrates the use of **setFetchMode** to determine how the rows will be returned. We often use **FETCH_ASSOC** as it returns the rows as an array indexed by column name. There are a number of other options that can be found in the fetch method described in the PHP manual.

This is the list of fetch options available in PDO:

PDO::FETCH_LAZY
PDO::FETCH_ASSOC
PDO::FETCH_NAMED
PDO::FETCH_NUM
PDO::FETCH_BOTH

PDO::FETCH_OBJ
PDO::FETCH_BOUND
PDO::FETCH_COLUMN
PDO::FETCH_CLASS
PDO::FETCH_INTO
PDO::FETCH_FUNC
PDO::FETCH_GROUP
PDO::FETCH_UNIQUE
PDO::FETCH_KEY_PAIR
PDO::FETCH_CLASSTYPE
PDO::FETCH_SERIALIZE
PDO::FETCH_PROPS_LATE

As mentioned previously, the most common is probably **FETCH_ASSOC** and is one of the easiest to use.

TASK 11 - SQL fetch using named values

```php
1.  <?php
2.
3.    //------------
4.    //Example of fetching data from a database using PDO
5.    //This uses a prepared statement using named values and try / catc
      h
6.  error_reporting( E_ALL | E_STRICT | E_DEPRECIATED );
7.  try {
8.        $dbhost = "localhost";
9.        $dbname = 'databasename';
10.       $user = 'databaseusername';
11.       $pass = 'databasepassword';
12.
13.       //------------
14.       $first_name = "%paul%";
15.
16.       //------------
17.       //Connect to the database
18.       $dbh = new PDO("mysql:host=" . $dbhost . ";dbname=" .
                    $dbname, $user, $pass);
19.
20.       //------------
21.       //the sql query using a named placeholder
22.       $sql = "SELECT * FROM staff WHERE first_name LIKE :first_name ";
23.
24.       //------------
25.       //statement handle
26.       $sth = $dbh->prepare($sql);
27.       $sth->execute(array(":first_name" => $first_name));
28.       $sth->setFetchMode(PDO::FETCH_ASSOC);
29.       echo("<br/><br/>");
30.       echo("---------------------------------------<br/>");
31.       echo("An example of printing values from a select statement
                with parameters<br/>");
32.
33.       //------------
34.       while($row = $sth->fetch()) {
35.          echo( $row["first_name"] . "<br/>" );
36.          $table[] = $row;
37.       }
38.     $dbh = null;
39. } catch (PDOException $e) {
40.     print "Error!: " . $e->getMessage() . "<br/>";
41.     die();
42. }
43. ?>
```

Code File: 12_database_access/php_pdo_objects.php

Summary

At last, we have reached a Chapter where we show how to use PHP to connect to a database and then display and update the data. It has taken a while to get here because we have to understand many basic concepts of programming. However, I hope that you can see the programming is relatively straightforward.

The next few Chapters will take this further, where we look at using forms to interact with the database.

Topics for Review

[1] What are the advantages in using PDO over mysqli functions when you connect to a database?

[2] Why can't you use mysql functions instead of mysqli functions?

[3] What is the difference between bindParam and **bindValue**? What is the advantage of bindParam over **bindValue**?

[4] What is the difference between **mysqli_fetch_array()** and **mysqli_fetch_assoc()**

13 - Using PHP and MySQL

What is in this Chapter?

* Writing a simple database driven feedback form.
* Using an include file to hold the connection script.

In this Chapter, we will use PHP to connect a simple feedback form to a MySQL database. The form will have data input fields and the information will be stored in a MySQL database table.

There are a number of security issues that you must be aware of when creating a PHP script that interacts with a MySQL database:

* Validate all user input on the server side. That is to say, use PHP to validate the data input rather than relying on JavaScript on the client side. In particular, watch out for SQL injection.
* Set the permissions of the database user to the minimum required for the application. So for example, if you are creating an application that only reads from a database, make sure that the user has read only permissions - that is SQL SELECT permissions.

The MySQL Database and Table

You will need to have access to a MySQL database that you normally connect to using **phpMyAdmin**. You should create a database called **tutorials** if you have not already done so.

TASK 1 - Creating the table

We first need to create the "feedback" table.

(1) Login into your MySQL administration **phpMyAdmin** and select the **tutorials** database where you will create the table.

(2) Click on the SQL button and copy in the text below into the form and then click **Go**. Your feedback table will be created for you.

```
1.   CREATE TABLE feedback (
2.   user_id MEDIUMINT UNSIGNED NOT NULL AUTO_INCREMENT,
3.   first_name VARCHAR(15) NOT NULL,
4.   last_name VARCHAR(30) NOT NULL,
5.   email VARCHAR(40) NOT NULL,
6.   comments VARCHAR(1000) NOT NULL,
7.   feedback_date DATETIME NOT NULL,
8.   age INT NULL,
9.   PRIMARY KEY (user_id)
10.  );
```

Code File: 13_using_php_and_mysql/create_feedback_sql_script.txt

Building the connection script and form

TASK 2 - Creating the database connection script

We need to make the connection to the database and we will be using an include file to contain the details so that we can use this file in other pages.

The connection requires the database username /password, the database name and host name

(1) Create a page in your text editor. If you are using a text editor such as Dreamweaver, delete all HTML leaving a blank page. Save the page in your **includes** folder in the current tutorials folder with the file name **connect.php**.

(2) Copy the code below onto the new page.

```
1.  <?php
2.  //---------------
3.  //Database connection details to MySQL
4.  // Use constants for database settings
5.  DEFINE ('DBUSER', 'Your database user');
6.  DEFINE ('DBPASSWORD', 'Your password');
7.  DEFINE ('DBHOST', 'localhost');
8.  DEFINE ('DBNAME', 'Your database name');
9.  //Make a connection to the database
10. $link = mysqli_connect(DBHOST, DBUSER, DBPASSWORD, DBNAME);
11.
12. //---------------
13. //Check the connection
14. if (!$link) {
15.     printf("Connection failed: %s\n", mysqli_connect_error());
16.     exit();
17. }
18. ?>
```

Code File: 13_using_php_and_mysql/script01/includes/connect.php

(3) For 'Your database user', 'Your password', 'Your database name' substitute your details. Note that the database name may have a prefix depending on how your web hosting is set up (e.g. 12345_tutorials may be your database name).   The DBHOST is often **localhost** but this depends on your hosting provider.

For example:

```
1.  DEFINE ('DBUSER', '45169');
2.  DEFINE ('DBPASSWORD', 'password');
3.  DEFINE ('DBHOST', 'localhost');
4.  DEFINE ('DBNAME', '4169_tutorials');
```

(4) Save the file and upload it to your **includes** folder on your web server.

TASK 3 - Creating the Feedback Page

This task is where we create the feedback PHP page to store the feedback data in the MySQL database table as created above. We will use form fields for the user to enter data and a SQL INSERT statement to store the data in the database.

Your feedback page will look something like the following figure:

Please enter your feedback

First Name:

Last Name:

Email Address:

Comments:

Submit

(1) Create a new web page called **feedback.php**.   If you have created it using Dreamweaver, remove any HTML code in the page.

(2) Copy the code below onto **feedback.php**.

```php
1. <?php
2.
3. //This script allows a user to enter in details
4. //into a form and then post it to the database.
5. //The script could be used for any situation
6. //that requires data request from user.
7.
8. // connect to the database.
9. require_once('includes/connect.php');
10.
11. //Check if the form has been posted,
12. //if not then display the form
13. if (isset($_POST['submit'])) {
14.
15.   // Check if the first name has been entered.
16.   if (emptyempty($_POST['first_name'])) {
17.       $message = 'Please enter your first name';
18.       displayform($message); //Display error message
19.       exit();
20.   } else {
21.       $first_name = $_POST['first_name'];
22.   }
23.
24.   // Check if the last name has been entered
25.   if (emptyempty($_POST['last_name'])) {
26.       $message = 'Enter your last name';
27.       displayform($message); //Display error message
28.       exit();
29.   } else {
30.       $last_name = $_POST['last_name'];
31.   }
32.
```

```
33.  // Check if the email address has been entered
34.  if (emptyempty($_POST['email'])) {
35.      $message = 'Enter your email address';
36.      displayform($message); //Display error message
37.      exit();
38.  } else {
39.      $email = $_POST['email'];
40.  }
41.
42.    // Check if any comments have been entered
43.    if (emptyempty($_POST['comments'])) {
44.        $message = 'Enter your comments';
45.        displayform($message); //Display error message
46.        exit();
47.    } else {
48.        $comments = $_POST['comments'];
49.    }
50.
51.    //Check if all entries have been entered
52.    //We may also want to do more data validation on the inputs
53.    if ($first_name && $last_name && $email && $comments) {
54.
55.     // Create the SQL
56.     $query = "INSERT INTO feedback (first_name, last_name,
                email, comments,
57.      feedback_date) VALUES ('$first_name', '$last_name', '$email',
58.        '$comments', NOW() )";
59.
60.      $result = mysqli_query( $link, $query );
61.
62.      //Check the result, do other processing e.g. sending an email
63.      if ($result) {
64.          $message = 'Thank you for your feedback';
65.          displayform($message);
66.          exit();
67.
68.      } else { //If there is a problem, then display an error message
69.          $message = 'Please try again - ' . mysqli_error() . '';
70.          displayform($message);
71.          exit();
72.      }
73.
74.    } else {
75.        $message .= 'You have not filled in all the required fields';
76.        displayform($message);
77.        exit();
78.    }
79.
80. }
81. else
82. {
83.    displayform(" ");  //Display the form without a message
84. }
85.
86. mysqli_close($link);
```

```
87.
88. //---------------------------------------------
89. //This is the form
90. function displayform($message) {
91.
92.    // Display the message if there is one.
93.    if (isset($message)) {
94.       echo '<font color="red"><p>'. $message . '</p></font>';
95.    }
96.
97. ?>
98.
99. <form action="<?php echo $_SERVER['PHP_SELF']; ?>" method="post">
100.
101. <table>
102.
103. <tr>
104. <td colspan="2"><h2>Please enter your feedback</h2></td>
105. </tr>
106.
107. <tr>
108. <td><p><strong>First Name:</strong></p></td>
109. <td><input type="text" name="first_name" size="30" maxlength="30"
       value="<?php if (isset($_POST['first_name']))
       echo $_POST['first_name']; ?>" /></td>
110. </tr>
111.
112. <tr>
113. <td><p><strong>Last Name:</strong></p></td>
114. <td><input type="text" name="last_name" size="30" maxlength="30"
       value="<?php if (isset($_POST['last_name']))
       echo $_POST['last_name']; ?>" /></td>
115. </tr>
116.
117. <tr>
118. <td><p><strong>Email Address:</strong></p></td>
119. <td><input type="text" name="email" size="40" maxlength="40"
       value="<?php if (isset($_POST['email']))
       echo $_POST['email']; ?>" /></td>
120. </tr>
121.
122. <tr>
123. <td><p><strong>Comments:</strong></p></td>
124. <td><textarea name="comments" rows="7" cols="48" value=
    "<?php if (isset($_POST['comments'])) echo $_POST['comments'];?>" />
    </textarea>
    </td>
125. </tr>
126.
127. <tr>
128. <td></td>
129. <td><input type="submit" name="submit" value="Submit" /></td>
130. </tr>
131.
132. </table>
```

```
133.
134. </form>
135. <?php
136. }
137. //---------------------------------------
138. ?>
```

Code File: 13_using_php_and_mysql/script01/feedback.php

(3) Save the file and publish it to your Web server. Open the page and test it in your Web browsers. Fill in some data and submit the form. In **phpMyAdmin**, open the database and select the **feedback** table. You should see that the table now contains one record. Click on the **Browse** icon to read the record entry.

The **PHP** script first checks if the submit button was pressed using **isset($_POST['submit'])**. If not, the form is displayed. Note that the values of the form fields will be prefilled if the form was already used. Also note the use of the **displayform($message)** function that is used to display an appropriate message.

Each form entry is tested and if there is no entry in the field, the form is displayed allowing you to re-enter more data.

After all the entries are tested, the SQL INSERT query is created and then executed.

If everything works, the form is displayed; otherwise, an error message is displayed.

TASK 4 - Improving the feedback form

The feedback page works but there are issues to do with handling double quote marks in the data entry. We look at this a later Chapter where we show how to use the **PDO** method of connecting to databases.

In addition, there is a requirement to validate the data before it is stored in the database. This is to ensure that no one is entering data or malicious scripts to try to cause problems. We look at data validation in later Chapters.

TASK 5 - Further exercises

Now that you have the application working, modify it to request the age of the person. The database table already contains the age column but there is no code in the HTML form or in the PHP script.

Modify the HTML part of the page to add in the age field and then modify the PHP script to insert this field into the database.

As age is an integer, you should also add in PHP code to test if the value entered is a numeric value or not.

Summary

This Chapter describes in detail how to connect from PHP to a MySQL table and database.   It then shows a feedback form and the code that inserts data into a table. This is a basic form but it does require improvements before we use it in a live system to ensure that it validates the data when it saves to the database.

Topics for Review

[1] What advantages are there in placing the database connection string in an include file?

[2] How do you test a data input as being a numeric value?

14 - Further PHP and MySQL

What is in this Chapter?

* A database connection string.
* Viewing data from a database.
* Looping around an array to display the table data.
* Improving security in the code.

This Chapter will look at the connection string in more detail to make the connection to the MySQL database.

TASK 1 - Connection string include file

To connect to a MySQL database we need to make a connection using the required details of username / password, database name and database host. You create these for each of your MySQL databases often using the control panel provided by your hosting company.

We normally place our connection details into an include file so that we can define the connection string once and then use the same include file over and over again. This makes maintenance of the site much easier if you have to change to a different database.

The file below is called **connect.php,** and is a typical include file for this technique.

```php
1.  <?php
2.  //Database connection details to MySQL
3.  // Use constants for database settings
4.  DEFINE ('DBUSER', 'Your database user');
5.  DEFINE ('DBPASSWORD', 'Your password');
6.  DEFINE ('DBHOST', 'localhost');
7.  DEFINE ('DBNAME', 'Your database name');
8.  //Make a connection to the database
9.  $link = mysqli_connect(DBHOST, DBUSER, DBPASSWORD, DBNAME);
10. //Check the connection
11. if (!$link) {
```

```
12.     printf("Could not connect to database: %s\n",
            mysqli_connect_error());
13.     exit();
14. }
15. ?>
```

Code File: 14_further_php_and_mysql/script01/includes/connect.php

The above connection to the database uses the **mysqli_connect()** function:

```
1.  $link = mysqli_connect($host, $user, $password, $database_name);
```

This function opens a new connection to the database and returns a link reference.

$username, and **$password** are database user privileges that you should have set within the MySQL database system. Quite often the **$host** is localhost but this may not always be the case if the database is on a different server. **$database_name** is the name of the database that you have created.

The **$link** connection is checked and if it is false then an error message is displayed.

Notice that we have used constants (DEFINE) to set the database host, username, password and database name, although this is not a requirement and any variable can be used.

Retrieving data from a database table

In this part, we will use SQL **SELECT** query and **PHP** to return results for a database table.

Once we have successfully connected to the database, we now use the **mysqli_query** function with an SQL statement to query the database as one parameter and the $link reference as the other parameter as follows:

```
1.  $query = " SELECT * FROM staff ";
2.  $result = mysqli_query( $link, $query );
```

We then test that there are no errors:

```
1.  if (!$result) {
2.      printf("Error in connection: %s\n", mysqli_error($link));
3.      exit();
4.  }
```

If **$result** returns a false value, then there was an error to deal with, in this example by printing the error message and then ending the script as there is no point in continuing.

To retrieve data from a MySQL table we use the **SELECT** SQL query and the PHP function **mysqli_fetch_assoc()** to retrieve the data into an associative array.

The basic construction for reading records is:

```
1.   while ($row = mysqli_fetch_assoc ($result)) {
2.   // Do something with $row.
3.   }
```

This is usually used in a way similar to the following:

```
1.   //Fetch the result into an associative array
2.   while ( $row = mysqli_fetch_assoc( $result) ) {
3.     $table[] = $row; //add each row into the $table array
4.   }
5.   //This gives us an associative array in $table to access in the
6.   //same way as any associative array
7.   if ($table) {    //Check if there are any rows to be displayed
8.       //Retrieve each element of the array
9.       foreach($table as $d_row) {
10.      // Output the row details
11.      echo($d_row["first_name"] . " " . $d_row["last_name"] . "<br/>");
12.      }
13.      echo("Number of rows : " . count($table) );
14. }
15. else
16. {
17. echo("there are no records in the table");
18. }
```

We can also use **mysqli_fetch_array()** instead of the **mysqli_fetch_assoc()** function.

The **mysqli_fetch_array()** function takes an optional parameter specifying what type of array is returned which can be MYSQLI_ASSOC for associative array, MYSQLI_NUM for indexed array , or MYSQLI_BOTH for both. An associative array allows you to refer to column values by name, while an indexed array requires you to use numbers (starting at 0 for the first column returned).

Referring to a column by number (for example **$row[3]**) will be slightly faster than referring to a column by name (for example **$row['column_name']**) but the latter is easier to work with and is the preferred way.

So these are the three possible options:

mysqli_fetch_array() Constants

Constant	Example
MYSQLI_ASSOC	$row['column']
MYSQLI_NUM	$row[0]
MYSQLI_BOTH	$row[0] or $row['column']

The default setting of the function is MYSQLI_BOTH so normally we do not use the constants at all.

TASK 2 - Viewing the feedback data

In this task, we will create a page that will display the feedback table details.

Note that the script uses include files that we created in previous Chapters.

(1) Create a new web page called **view_feeedback.php**. If you are using Dreamweaver, remove the entire HTML from the page that Dreamweaver has created.

(2) Copy the following code into the page:

```
1.  <?php
2.  //This script displays all the comments
3.  //from the feedback table
4.  $pagetitle = "Feedback display";
5.  include ('includes/header.php'); //the header
6.  ?>
7.      <h1>User feedback</h1>
8.  <?php
9.  require_once ('includes/connect.php'); // Connect to the db.
10. //Create the SQL query
11. $query = "SELECT user_id, first_name, last_name, email,
12. comments FROM feedback ORDER BY feedback_date ASC";
13. $result = mysqli_query( $link, $query );
14. //-------------
15. if (!$result) {
16.     printf("Error in connection: %s\n", mysqli_error($link));
17.     exit();
18. }
19. //-------------
20. //Fetch the result into an associative array
21. while ( $row = mysqli_fetch_assoc( $result ) ) {
22.     $table[] = $row;  //add each row into the table array
23. }
24. //-------------
```

```
25. ?>
26. <table>
27. <tr>
28.     <td><strong>First Name</strong></td>
29.     <td width="10"> </td>
30.     <td><strong>Last Name</strong></td>
31.     <td width="10"> </td>
32.     <td><strong>Email</strong></td>
33.     <td width="10"> </td>
34.     <td><strong>Comments</strong></td>
35. </tr>
36. <?php
37. //-------------
38. if ($table) { //Check if there are any rows to be displayed
39.     //Retrieve each element of the array
40.     foreach($table as $d_row) {
41.       ?>
42.       <tr>
43.         <td><?php echo($d_row["first_name"]); ?></td>
44.         <td width="10"> </td>
45.         <td><?php echo($d_row["last_name"]); ?></td>
46.         <td width="10"> </td>
47.         <td><?php echo($d_row["email"]); ?></td>
48.         <td width="10"> </td>
49.         <td><?php echo($d_row["comments"]); ?></td>
50.       </tr>
51.       <?php
52.     }
53. }
54. ?>
55. </table>
56. <p>Number of records : <?php echo(mysqli_num_rows($result)); ?></p>
57. <?php
58. mysqli_close($link);
59. ?>
60. <br/><br/><br/><br/>
61. <?php
62. include ('includes/footer.php'); // the footer
63. ?>
```

Code File: 14_further_php_and_mysql/script01/view_feedback.php

The following files are also needed but you should have these from a previous exercise and should all be located in the **includes** folder: **connect.php, header.php, footer.php,** and **layout.css**

(3) The include file **connect.php** should be located in the **includes** folder:

```php
1.  <?php
2.  //Database connection details to MySQL
3.  //----------------------
4.  // Use constants for database settings
5.  DEFINE ('DBUSER', 'Your database user');
6.  DEFINE ('DBPASSWORD', 'Your password');
7.  DEFINE ('DBHOST', 'localhost');
8.  DEFINE ('DBNAME', 'Your database name');
9.  //----------------------
10. //Make a connection to the database
11. $link = mysqli_connect(DBHOST, DBUSER, DBPASSWORD, DBNAME);
12. //----------------------
13. //Check the connection
14. if (!$link) {
15.    printf("Could not connect to database: %s\n",
           mysqli_connect_error());
16.    exit();
17. }
18. ?>
```

Code File: 14_further_php_and_mysql/script01/includes/connect.php

(4) The **header.php** file also located in the **includes** folder:

```php
1.  <!DOCTYPE html>
2.  <html>
3.  <head>
4.  <meta charset="UTF-8" />
5.  <title><?php echo($pagetitle); ?></title>
6.  <link rel="stylesheet" href="includes/layout.css" type="text/css"
           media="screen" />
7.  </head>
8.  <body class="oneCol">
9.  <div id="container">
10.    <div id="mainContent">
11. <!-- START OF MAIN CONTENT BELOW HERE -->
```

Code File: 14_further_php_and_mysql/script01/includes/header.php

(5) The **footer.php** file also located in the **includes** folder:

```
1.  <!-- MAIN CONTENT ENDS HERE -->
2.  </div>
3.     Copyright © <?php echo (date("Y")); ?>    <strong>|</strong>  Page
    updated <?php echo( date ("F Y", getlastmod())); ?>
4.  <!-- end #container --></div>
5.  </body>
6.  </html>
```

Code File: 14_further_php_and_mysql/script01/includes/footer.php

(6) The **layout.css** file should be located in the **includes** folder:

```
1.  body {
2.          font: 100% Verdana, Arial, Helvetica, sans-serif;
3.          background:#E6E6E6;
4.          margin: 0;
5.          padding: 0;
6.          text-align: center;
7.          color: #000000;
8.  }
9.  .oneCol #container {
10.         width: 46em;
11.         background: #FFFFFF;
12.         margin: 0 auto;
13.         border: 1px solid #000000;
14.         text-align: left;
15. }
16. .oneCol #mainContent {
17.         padding: 0 20px;
18. }
```

Code File: 14_further_php_and_mysql/script01/includes/layout.css

(7) Upload the files to the web server and test it.

Exercise 14.1

Now that you have the above page working, modify the code to include the registration date and the person's age in the results.

To do this you will need to modify the SQL statement and modify the table display to include the new fields.

As the registration date is a date field, format the display to make the format as:

day month year

Improving security in the code

Whenever we connect to a database, we have to make sure that the user is not trying to damage the database by injecting scripts or trying to run SQL.

(1) Try to set the permissions of the database user to the minimum required, so for example, if you are only reading data, then the user should only have SELECT permissions. It is normally not necessary to allow a user to have ALTER permissions.

(2) Validate all data to check the date type (number, string etc.). Data validation should be performed on data from all text boxes in forms and on query strings.

(3) Use regular expressions to make sure submitted data matches what you would expect it to be. So for example, a name would consist of a to z characters the – character and the ' character. This should be done in **PHP** rather than using JavaScript client side code.

(4) Convert data into HTML using **htmlspecialchars** before you save it into a database. You would use this when you are saving large text blocks into a database. It converts characters such as < and > that are used in html, into their html equivalent character set. This means that if someone enters the word **<javascript** into the database, it will be changed into **<javascript** and will not be executed on a web page.

(5) Use the **mysqli_real_escape_string()** . function. This function cleans data by escaping certain characters.

```
1.  $data = mysqli_real_escape_string ($link, $data);
```

This function acts like **addlashes()** and should be used with any text fields in your forms.

TASK 3 - Using mysqli_real_escape_string();

To overcome problems with certain characters in SQL statements like quote marks, we will use the **mysqli_real_escape_string()** function. You need this when you attempt to save strings that have quote marks in them. So for example, the word **don't** will cause a SQL INSERT statement to fail because of the quote mark. The **mysqli_real_escape_string()** function will make this **don\'t**. The function is also able to take into account the character set of the connection and it will escape characters based on that.

The technique is also useful to help prevent SQL injection where someone attempts to damage your system by inserting scripts into your database.

```php
1.  <?php
2.  function mysqli_escape($data, $link) {
3.      $data = htmlspecialchars($data, ENT_NOQUOTES);
4.      return mysqli_real_escape_string($link, $data);
5.  }
6.  ?>
```

All the techniques have been combined into one user defined function shown above.

We can put this into an include file and use it for each input similar to the following:

For example:

```php
1.  $last_name = mysqli_escape($_POST["last_name"], $dbc);
```

NOTE: *The function htmlspecialchars to convert certain characters into html format. In this case, the option ENT_NOQUOTES is included so that single quotes and double quotes are not converted into html because we are already escaping those characters.*

In another Chapter, we look at using PDO as a means to connect to a database instead of **mysqli**. PDO is probably a better method to use when working with databases, as you do not have to worry about quote marks and it can connect to a wide range of database types whereas **mysqli** is for MySQL databases.

TASK 4 - Adding in the function

In this task, we will add in the above function to the **feedback.php** script that we created in the previous Chapter.

(1) Create a new file called **misc.php** and save it into the **includes** folder. If you are using Dreamweaver, remove all the HTML code from the file.

(2) Copy the above function **mysqli_escape** into the **misc.php** file.

```php
1.  <?php
2.  //escape data inputs
3.  function mysqli_escape($data, $link) {
4.      $data = htmlspecialchars($data, ENT_NOQUOTES);
5.      return mysqli_real_escape_string($link, $data);
6.  }
7.  ?>
```

14_further_php_and_mysql/script01/includes/misc.php

(3) Open **feedback.php**

(4) For each of the inputs add in the **mysqli_escape** code.

(5) For example, the $first_name is:

```
1.  $first_name = mysqli_escape($_POST['first_name'], $dbc);
```

(6) In **feedback.php,** you need to add in a reference to the **misc.php** as an include file as follows:

```
1.  require_once("includes/misc.php");
```

(7) Upload the files to the web server, not forgetting the **misc.php** file and then test the code.

Complete script for feedback.php

The complete script for the new **feedback.php** is. The listing is quite long but the file is available in the code download for the book.

```
1. <?php
2. //This script allows a user to enter in details
3. //into a form and then post it to the database.
4. //The script could be used for any situation
5. //that requires data request from a user.
6.
7. //This version includes the escape data function in an include file
8. //and a check to see if the email address has already been entered.
9. //----------------
10. // connect to the database.
11. require_once('includes/connect.php');
12. require_once('includes/misc.php');   // escape data function added
13.
14. //Check if the form has been posted,
15. //if not then display the form
16. if (isset($_POST['submit'])) {
17.
18.     // Check if the first name has been entered.
19.     if (emptyempty($_POST['first_name'])) {
20.         $message = 'Please enter your first name';
21.         displayform($message); //Display error message
22.         exit();
23.     } else {
24.         $first_name = mysqli_escape($_POST['first_name'], $link);
25.     }
26.
27.     // Check if the last name has been entered
28.     if (emptyempty($_POST['last_name'])) {
```

```
29.            $message = 'Enter your last name';
30.            displayform($message); //Display error message
31.            exit();
32.        } else {
33.            $last_name = mysqli_escape($_POST['last_name'], $link);
34.        }
35.
36.        // Check if the email address has been entered
37.        if (emptyempty($_POST['email'])) {
38.            $message = 'Enter your email address';
39.            displayform($message); //Display error message
40.            exit();
41.        } else {
42.            $email = mysqli_escape($_POST['email'], $link);
43.        }
44.
45.        // Check if any comments have been entered
46.        if (emptyempty($_POST['comments'])) {
47.            $message = 'Enter your comments';
48.            displayform($message); //Display error message
49.            exit();
50.        } else {
51.            $comments = mysqli_escape($_POST['comments'], $link);
52.        }
53.
54.    //Check for previous comments by this email address
55.    $query = "SELECT user_id FROM feedback WHERE email = '$email'";

56.    $result = mysqli_query( $link, $query );
57.    if (!$result) {
58.        printf("Error in connection: %s\n", mysqli_error($link));
59.        exit();
60.    }
61.    if (mysqli_num_rows($result) > 0) {
62.        $message = 'You have already entered a comment';
63.        displayform($message);
64.        exit();
65.    }
66.
67.    //Check if all entries have been entered
68.    //We may also want to do more data validation on the inputs
69.    if ($first_name && $last_name && $email && $comments) {
70.
71.        // Create the SQL
72.        $query = "INSERT INTO feedback (first_name, last_name, email,
              comments, feedback_date) VALUES ('$first_name', '$last_name',
              '$email', '$comments', NOW() )";
73.
74.        $result = mysqli_query( $link, $query );
75.
76.        //Check the result, do other processing e.g.sending an email
77.        if ($result) {
78.            $message = 'Thank you for your feedback';
79.            displayform($message);
80.            exit();
```

```
81.
82.      } else {// If there is a problem, then display an error message
83.           $message='Please try again - ' . mysqli_error($link) . '';
84.           displayform($message);
85.           exit();
86.      }
87.
88.    } else {
89.        $message .= 'You have not filled in all the required fields';
90.        displayform($message);
91.        exit();
92.    }
93.
94. }
95. else
96. {
97.     displayform(" ");   //Display the form without a message
98. }
99.
100. mysqli_close($link);
101.
102. //-----------------------------------------------------
103. //This is the form
104. function displayform($message) {
105.
106.   // Display the message if there is one.
107.   if (isset($message)) {
108.     echo '<font color="red"><p>'. $message . '</p></font>';
109.   }
110.
111. ?>
112.
113. <form action="<?php echo $_SERVER['PHP_SELF']; ?>"
                    method="post">
114.
115. <table>
116.
117. <tr>
118. <td colspan="2"><h2>Please enter your feedback</h2></td>
119. </tr>
120.
121. <tr>
122. <td><p><strong>First Name:</strong></p></td>
123. <td><input type="text" name="first_name" size="30"
                    maxlength="30"
                    value="<?php if (isset($_POST['first_name']))
                    echo $_POST['first_name']; ?>" /></td>
124. </tr>
125.
126. <tr>
127. <td><p><strong>Last Name:</strong></p></td>
128. <td><input type="text" name="last_name" size="30"
                    maxlength="30"
                    value="<?php if (isset($_POST['last_name']))
                    echo $_POST['last_name']; ?>" /></td>
```

```
129. </tr>
130.
131. <tr>
132. <td><p><strong>Email Address:</strong></p></td>
133. <td><input type="text" name="email" size="40"
                 maxlength="40"
                 value="<?php if (isset($_POST['email']))
                 echo $_POST['email']; ?>" /></td>
134. </tr>
135.
136. <tr>
137. <td><p><strong>Comments:</strong></p></td>
138. <td><textarea name="comments" rows="7" cols="48"
                 value="<?php if (isset($_POST['comments']))
                 echo $_POST['comments']; ?>" /></textarea></td>
139. </tr>
140.
141. <tr>
142. <td></td>
143. <td><input type="submit" name="submit" value="Submit" /></td>
144. </tr>
145.
146. </table>
147.
148. </form>
149. <?php
150. }
151. //-------------------------------------------------
152. ?>
```

Code File: 14_further_php_and_mysql/script01/feedback_2.php

Counting records and mysqli_num_rows

In this section we will use the **mysqli_num_rows()** to count the number of rows retrieved.

We can use this to add further functionality such as displaying the number of comments or to check if someone has already entered comments by checking if the number of rows is equal to 1. If the person has already entered comments, we can stop them adding comments again.

Exercise 14.2

In **view_feedback.php**, enter in some code to display the number of comments that have been entered.

Add **mysqli_num_rows()** to the **view_feedback.php** page as follows:

```
1.   <p>Number of records: <?php echo(mysqli_num_rows($resource)); ?></p>
```

Exercise 14.3

In **feedback.php**, enter some code to check if the user has already entered a comment. To do this we create a SQL SELECT statement that looks for the email address. The number of rows is counted and if the number of rows is more than 0, then the email address already exists.

The following code will provide the above functionality:

```
1.  //Check for previous comments by this email address
2.  $query = "SELECT user_id FROM feedback WHERE email = '$email'";

3.  $result = mysqli_query( $link, $query );
4.  if (!$result) {
5.      printf("Error in connection: %s\n", mysqli_error($link));
6.      exit();
7.  }
8.  if (mysqli_num_rows($result) > 0) {
9.      $message = 'You have already entered a comment';
10.     displayform($message);
11.     exit();
12. }
```

Summary

This Chapter continues with the feedback form and improves it by adding in an include file to store the connection string. The Chapter also illustrates how to display data from a database using an associative array and a **foreach** loop combining PHP and HTML. This technique is very important when working with data from a database and you need to understand it as we use it in later Chapters.

Topics for Review

[1] Review how to fetch data using mysqli_fetch_assoc and a while loop.

[2] Review how to loop through an array of rows using a foreach loop to display data.

[3] What advantage is there in using the DEFINE for database settings?

[4] Consider the issues that may arise if the permissions of the database user is set to high.

15 - Error Handling and Debugging

What is in this Chapter?

* Error handling for security.
* Error types and reporting errors.
* Debugging methods.
* Good programming practice.

It is common to have errors when writing code. To be able to fix them we need an understanding of error types. We can expect syntax errors - which are those caused by incorrectly writing PHP code, logical errors - where the code works but does not do what was expected, and there are run time errors - where a problem happens during the running of the code.

Error types

Syntax errors

These types of errors are ones where the page fails completely with an error message that will help to identify its located.   These will be fatal errors and the page cannot recover. The error message will usually give the line number for you to look at.

The type of errors might be:

* Leaving off the semi-colon (;) at the end of a line.
* Not closing a loop with a bracket or using the wrong bracket type.
* Calling a function that does not exist.
* Not closing a string with quote marks or using the wrong quote marks.
* Not putting $ in front of a variable name.
* Missing an include file.

Exercise 15.1

See if you can come up with some more examples of syntax errors that you have seen.

Logical errors

Logical errors are those where the code works, (that is there are no error messages), but the code does not do what it is supposed to do. One method to find the issue is to use **echo()** statements to display information and then an **exit()** statement to stop the script. Using this method, you can work your way through the code until you find the problem area.

Types of logical errors to look out for:

* Doing a calculation with the wrong formula.
* Incorrect SQL statements when working with databases.
* A database connection string is not correct.
* Data does not pass from one web page to another when you are using forms. This is sometimes caused by an error in the **$_POST or $_GET** statements, or possibly by incorrect HTML code.
* A page takes a long time to load which indicates a database error or possibly an error in a loop.

Exercise 15.2

See if you can come up with some more examples of logical errors that you have seen.

Run time errors

Another form of error is a run-time error where the page runs but displays a **warning** or a **notice** message or some other message such as indicating that a function is depreciated in that version of **PHP**.

A **notice** message is an advisory message meaning, "You probably shouldn't be doing what you're doing, but you can do it anyway." A typical notice message may occur when you have an uninitialized variable.

A **warning** is a message saying, "You are doing something wrong and it is very likely to cause errors, so you should fix it." A typical warning message is where you are using a function but have called it with the wrong number of arguments.

Notices and warnings will not stop your script but you need to look at them and attempt to have no notices or warnings in your application.

Handling error messages in PHP

So we can see from the previous section that messages could be output to the HTML page which can mean:

* Security issues - It is possible that file paths or other system information could be displayed in a browser.
* Page formatting issues - When an error occurs and the error message is output into the HTML, the HTML may become broken and so the layout of the page becomes broken.

However, we can control the messages that are displayed if an error occurs in our script.

Choosing what errors to report in PHP

We can set our **PHP** scripts to report or ignore different levels of errors.

Error Reporting Levels

We can control the reporting level using the **error_reporting()** function that takes a number as an argument to define the required error reporting. The following is a list of the more common error numbers:

Number	Constant	Report On
1	E_ERROR	Fatal run-time errors.
2	E_WARNING	Non-fatal run time errors.
4	E_PARSE	Parse errors.
8	E_NOTICE	Notices.
2048	E_STRICT	Code recommendations.
8192	E_DEPRECIATED	Functions that will be depreciated.
32767	E_ALL	All errors and warnings except strict and depreciated.

These error levels can generally be divided into three types:

* **Notices** - Do not stop the execution of the script and may not be a problem. This would include messages about undefined variables or variables that have not been set.
* **Warnings** - Indicate a potential problem but do not stop the script.
* **Errors** - Stop a script from continuing and will be such things as incorrect PHP syntax, missing semicolons, etc.

Normally we want **ALL** errors, warnings and notices to be displayed during development or otherwise we may miss an error that can turn into something significant.

Once the scripts are complete, we then change the error reporting to the minimum level so that the user does not see any messages that may compromise security.

To control the error reporting we can use the **error_reporting()** function within an include file. This function takes a number or constant as listed in the table above.

```
1.  error_reporting(0); // Show no errors.
```

A setting of 0, turns error reporting off completely. Errors will still occur, but they are not displayed on the page.

Alternatively:

```
1.  error_reporting(E_ALL); //Show all errors except strict and
    depreciated
```

Or:

```
1.  error_reporting( E_ALL | E_STRICT | E_DEPRECATED );//Show all errors
```

Use the above line when developing an application so that you see **ALL** possible errors, notices, warnings, and any strict or depreciated function problems that may show a serious potential issue.

Notice that the numbers can be added to customise the level of error reporting, so we can use the bitwise operators - **| (or), ~ (not), & (and)** – with the constants.

In the following example, we are showing all errors except notice errors:

```
1.  error_reporting(E_ALL & ~E_NOTICE & ~E_STRICT); // Show any non-
    notice errors.
```

Use the above when the application is finished and has been distributed. This will display warnings but not notices or any strict messages.

We want to adjust the error reporting for all of our scripts so that we can easily switch depending on whether the site is live or being developed. To do this we will create a configuration include file in the next task.

TASK 1 - Controlling error reporting in a web application

(1) Create a new **PHP** script in your text editor. If we are using a text editor such as Dreamweaver, delete all HTML leaving a blank page. Save the script into the **includes** folder with the file name **error.php**.

(2) Add the script below to set the error reporting to the highest level.

```
1.  error_reporting( E_ALL | E_STRICT | E_DEPRECIATED );//Set the level
    of error reporting
```

For development purposes, we will want **PHP** to notify us of all errors and warnings.

Once development is complete, change this to:

```
1.  error_reporting( E_ALL & ~E_NOTICE & ~E_STRICT );
```

You may want to add this line into your include file but comment it out.

(3) Save the script and upload it to the Web server.

We can give the file any extension but .php is more secure as the code is not readable through the Web browser.

(4) In order to use this file include it into top of every script.

```
1.  include( 'includes/error.php' );
```

Exercise 15.3

Open the **register.php** file (or any other file that you know is working) and add in the error reporting include file.

Enter in:

```
1.  include( 'includes/error.php' );
```

Debugging PHP

Use the print() or echo() and exit() functions

The most common method of working through a script is to use the **echo()** and **exit()** functions at different locations within the script.

This can be used to track variables through the script.

The **exit()** function will make the script stop at a particular point making it easier to see what the value of a variable is at that point.

So, if we were retrieving data from a database we could create a set of echo statements as follows to check the returned values:

```
1.  echo(“firstname: $row[“firstname”] . “<br/>”);
2.  echo(“lastname: $row[“lastname”] . “<br/>”);
3.  echo(“age: $row[“age”] . “<br/>”);
4.  exit();
```

Once we have looked at those variable, we can then just comment out the complete block by using the /* and */ comment tags leaving the code in place in case we want to do further testing.

The **echo()** statement is particularly useful when debugging SQL statements as you can display the complete statement and then try it in **phpMyAdmin** to get further error details.

Use the print_r() function

A handy test function to use is **print_r()** that will automatically display all the contents of an array.

So the array:

```
1.  $county = array(“1” => “Cornwall”, “2” => “Devon”, “3” => “Somerset”
    , “4” => Wiltshire”, “5” => “Avon”);
```

can be displayed with:

```
1.  print_r($county);
```

and will give something like:

```
Array  ( [1] => [Cornwall], [2] => [Devon], [3] => [Somerset],
[4]=>[Wiltshire], [5]> [Avon] )
```

Reducing the code down to its minimum

Some **PHP** scripts are very complex and one debugging method is to comment out most of the code to take it to a bare minimum, and then slowly build it back up. If you have coded in functions or classes, this should be straightforward.

try / catch PHP 5

Version **PHP** 5 onwards includes the try / catch exception handling.

Exception handling

A try / catch block is meant to catch exceptions. An exception would be something like divide by zero that causes a program exception, and which we can catch.

An error on the other hand is not usually recoverable. An example of an error would be forgetting to place a comma (;) at the end of a line or not enclosing a string with quote (") marks.

In the case of divide by zero, if you use a try / catch block, program execution will continue because you have caught the exception.

Each try must have at least one corresponding catch block. You can have multiple catch blocks to catch different classes of exceptions.

When an exception is thrown, the code following the statement will not be executed and **PHP** will then attempt to find the first matching catch block.

The general form of a try / catch block is:

```
1.  try
2.  {
3.      $a = 1;
4.      $b = 0;
5.      $c = $a / $b;
6.  }
7.  catch (Exception $e)
8.  {
9.      echo($e->getMessage());
10. }
```

Other functions of the exception class are:

```
getMessage();       // message of exception
getCode();          // code of exception
getFile();          // source filename
getLine();          // source line
getTrace();         // an array of the backtrace()
getPrevious();      // previous exception
getTraceAsString(); // formatted string of trace
```

TASK 2 - Exercise in try / catch errors

Exercise 15.4

Write a simple **PHP** try / catch script to cover the problem of divide by zero.

Debugging and testing SQL

The techniques used to debug SQL queries in **PHP** is really the same as with debugging **PHP** scripts.

(1) We can print out any applicable SQL queries in our **PHP** script using the **echo()** function.

(2) We can run the query in the MySQL client or other tool. Once we have the SQL query we can run it in **phpMyAdmin**, or similar.

(3) We can rewrite the query in its most basic form, and then keep adding elements and columns back until we discover which clause is causing the problem.

To debug and test **PHP** that interacts with databases, you will find it a great benefit to have test data in your SQL tables. One way to do this is to create a script with INSERT statements. This will save time if you have to re-create your database.

Other methods of debugging

The issue with PHP is that it is not a compiled language and so is more difficult to debug than other languages like Java or Visual Basic.

However, there are a number of third-party applications that help debugging. The Dreamweaver editor, and programs similar to Dreamweaver like Brackets have syntax checking and highlighting to help prevent errors as you code the program. They also include facilities for search / replace and other management functions for connecting to a remote web server.

Coding Best Practices

This is a summary of some PHP coding practices which you may find useful:

Familiarise yourself with the PHP Manual

The PHP Manual is a very extensive resource covering not just the syntax and functions that make up the language but includes practical tips and usage.

A useful feature is the user contributor notes showing example code with explanations of particular issues.

https://www.php.net/manual/en/index.php

Make sure that you use error_reporting

The error_reporting function allows you to display warnings and other messages depending on the level that you set. This is important during development to see possible problems.

During development, use something like this:

```
1.  error_reporting( E_ALL | E_STRICT | E_DEPRECIATED );
```

In your production version, use the following:

```
1.  error_reporting( E_ALL & ~E_NOTICE & ~E_STRICT );
```

Do your programming in an IDE (Integrated Development Environment)

IDE's are programming environments that include such features as syntax highlighting, code completion and even debugging. These include Brackets, Sublime, and commercial products like Dreamweaver. Nearly all of them are better than using a simple text editor such as NotePad.

Don't Repeat Yourself

DRY programming (**D**on't **R**epeat **Y**ourself) is where you use common functions and classes rather than copying code from one place to another. If you discover an error or an improvement in a function or class that you have written once, changing that one function is easy.

Use <?php ?>

Do not use <? ?> to define your PHP scripts even though it may work in some **PHP** installations it may not work in all.

Code to a consistent standard and format your code

Working to a coding standard is important to keep your code neat and easy to read. If you use sensible names for variables and functions, it will make your code much easier to read a few months after writing it.

Unfortunately, coding standards for **PHP** are different between frameworks such as Cake, Symphony and the WordPress frameworks.

The PSR standards produced by the PHP-FIG (PHP Framework Interop Group) is a standard for use in all PHP frameworks.

The PSR-1 Basic Coding Standards can be viewed at:
https://www.php-fig.org/psr/psr-1/

The overview of this standard says:

* Files MUST use only <?php and <?= tags.
* Files MUST use only UTF-8 without BOM for PHP code.
* Files SHOULD either declare symbols (classes, functions, constants, etc.) or cause side-effects (e.g. generate output, change .ini settings, etc.) but SHOULD NOT do both.
* Namespaces and classes MUST follow an "autoloading" PSR: [PSR-0, PSR-4].
* Class names MUST be declared in StudlyCaps, for example: **LargeParcel**
* Class constants MUST be declared in all uppercase with underscore separators, for example: **const ENCODING_8BIT = '8bit';**
* Method names MUST be declared in camelCase, for example: **isHTML()**

The important thing is that you should always try to be consistent in the way that you define your names.

PSR-1 is just one of the standards that you can view on the PSR web site.

Use comments in your code

Make sure that you fully comment your code, functions and classes. You should comment each class object and every function. For functions, it is conventional to describe its purpose and then list its inputs and outputs parameter with their data types similar to the following:

```
1.  //------------------------------------------------------------
2.  /**
3.  * Purpose    :    Given the recid, returns if a physical item or not
4.  * Outputs    :    Returns 1 (physical item) or 0 (digital item)
5.  * @return integer
6.  */
7.  function getisphysicalrecid( $recid ) {
8.        .   .   .   .   .   .   .
```

```
 9.          .    .    .    .    .    .    .
10.          .    .    .    .    .    .    .
11.          .    .    .    .    .    .    .
12.      return   $value;
13. }
```

Install a development environment on your local computer such as UniformServer

WAMP (**W**indows, **A**pache, **M**ySQL, **P**HP) or LAMP (**M**ac, **A**pache, **M**ySQL and **P**HP) are available and relatively easy to install on your own personal computer. In the Appendix of this book, I describe UniformServer which has the advantage that it will work even on a USB stick.

You can use this as your development server enabling you to easily set up and test web pages.

Validate and sanitise all user input

Never trust any data inputs into your application.

Validation is the process of ensuring that input data falls within the expected extent of valid program values.   So for example, if you were asking for someone's age, you would expect it to be an integer value in the range from 1 to 100.

Sanitization on the other hand is to do with the elimination of unwanted characters from the input by means of removing, replacing, encoding, or escaping certain characters.

These are required to prevent you application crashing or even causing damage to your database.

Use PDO

Use PDO and parameterised queries when you connect to databases as this gives good protection against SQL injection and PDO allows connections to a range of database systems. Another method is to use **mysqli_** functions with parameterised queries however; **mysqli_** functions only work with MySQL databases.

Code with objects

OOP (**O**bject **O**riented **P**rogramming) uses objects to represent parts of the application. It helps to reduce duplicate code, breaking the problem into sections that are more manageable and easier to maintain.

Minimise database interaction

Always aim to minimise your database interaction to improve performance. In particular, do not put database queries in side loops.

Use try / catch

The try / catch programming were shown in a previous section of this Chapter and are particularly useful where you may get a problem with communicating with an external element. For example database connections, http request and so on.

Learn git

git is a version control system that is used to track changes in source code during software development. It is particularly useful for coordinating work between multiple programmers. **GitHub** is a web based service for service control and is a location for **git** repositories.

Learn Bootstrap or similar framework

You can make your web pages look good by using a framework such as Bootstrap. You can easily create pages that look good and work well in different devices, tables, phones and desktop.   The latest version of Bootstrap is version 4 available from https://getbootstrap.com/

Summary

Finding bugs in PHP is not always straightforward, so it is important to write code in functions. Once you have developed a function that you know works, you can use it many times without adding in new bugs. PHP 5 introduces the try catch method to help catch exceptions such as not connecting to a server, or divide by zero errors.

Topics for Review

[1] What are the main error reporting levels that we would work with in a PHP script?

[2] How do you show all error messages?

[3] Explain what the print_r() function does.

[4] How would you debug SQL?

16 - Cookies and Sessions

What is in this Chapter?

* Using cookies and sessions.
* Creating, deleting and accessing cookies.
* Using session variables.
* A shopping cart using sessions.
* Creating a login system.

The HTTP protocol used by browsers to communicate with the web server is stateless. This means that each request from the web browser is independent of every other request you make and hence the server is unable to tell that the requests came from the same person.

The server has no in-built method to store user's data between requests.

There are a number of ways of overcoming this issue, such as using hidden form variables, but the techniques we look at in this section is using cookies and sessions that has proved to be a successful technique.

Why do we want to maintain state?

* We may want to hold information that a user has entered into a form before you submit it to a database.
* We want to display specific adverts to certain users based on previous browsing.
* We want to track a user through a web site to see which pages they have viewed.
* We want to improve the user experience so that they see different pages depending on their previous browsing.
* We want a user to login to an area and we want to allow access to certain pages depending on their login.
* We want to hold shopping cart information for a user.
* ... and many more reasons to maintain state ....

Cookies and Sessions

Sessions allow you to store data temporarily on the web server. You can think of sessions as being global variables that are available to any of your PHP scripts, while the browser (the session) is open. Closing the browser will close the session and delete the data on the web server. The process that this uses is to create a temporary cookie on your computer to identify the session number; the PHP script is then able to identify the data on the web server using this session number.

A cookie (sometimes called an HTTP cookie, web cookie, or browser cookie) is a small text file on your computer that you read using a PHP script located on the domain that created the cookie in the first place. So a cookie created by a PHP script on https://www.withinweb.com/index.php can only be read by a PHP script that is somewhere on the web site https://www.withinweb.com

A cookie can be either **permanent** or **temporary**. If it is permanent, it will stay on the computer after the browser is closed, and will remain on the computer until you delete it or until it expires. A temporary cookie is one that expires when the browser is closed.

Cookies

The following diagram illustrates the process where your PC requests a page and the server sends back a cookie that is then stored on your computer.

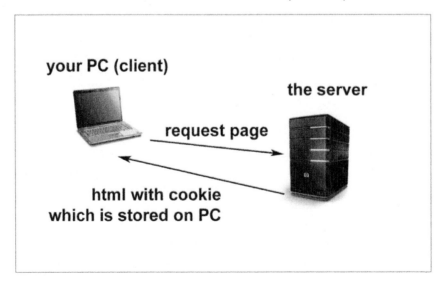

Showing Cookies in Chrome

You can view and delete the cookies that are being used on Chrome by:

* On your computer, open Chrome.

* At the top right, click the three vertical dots menu and select "**Settings**".

* This will display the settings menu where you then select "**Advanced**".

* Click "**Privacy and security**" and you should see "**Site settings**".

* Click on "**Cookies**" and then "**See all cookies and site data**".

If you remove cookies, you will be signed out of websites and your saved preferences could be deleted.

Setting Cookies

Cookies are set in PHP via the **setcookie()** function as a name / value pair:

```
1.  setcookie (name, value);
2.  setcookie ('first_name', 'Paul');
```

The second line of code will send a cookie to the browser with a name of first_name and a value of Paul.

You can use either double quote marks or single quote marks.

NOTE: *The cookie name must not have spaces in it.*

When programming with cookies we have to send the cookie to the client before any other information.   So we have to make sure that no HTML - not even white space - is sent before a cookie is sent, otherwise an error will occur.

So for example:

```
1.  <?php
2.  echo("this is a cookie");
3.  setcookie ('first_name', 'Paul');
4.  ?>
```

will generate a PHP error because the echo statement is before the setting of the cookie.

Accessing Cookies

To retrieve a value from a cookie, you use **$_COOKIE** which is a superglobal variable meaning it is available throughout the script.   **$_COOKIE** is an associative array, so we use the cookie name as the key.

To retrieve the value of the cookie called first_name we would use:

```
1.  $thecookievalue = $_COOKIE['first_name'];
```

Cookie Parameters

In addition to the cookie name value pair, **setcookie()** has up to four other optional arguments of **expiration, path, domain** and **secure**.

```
1.  setcookie ('name', 'value', expiration, 'path', 'domain', secure);
```

The four optional arguments are **expiration, path, domain** and **secure**.

Expiration:

This defines the time in seconds for the cookie to exist on your computer. The time is specified in seconds from the epoch (the epoch is midnight on January 1st 1970). If it is not set, the cookie will be deleted from your computer when the user closes the web browser. Quite often we set the expiration time by adding a particular number of minutes or hours to the current time, calculated using the **time()** function.

As an example of this, the following line sets the expiration time of the cookie to be 1 hour (3600 seconds) from the current time:

```
1.  setcookie ('name', 'value', time()+3600);
```

NOTE: *The expiration value is an integer and so you do not put quote marks around it.*

NOTE: *The time is based on the server time, so if the server time is incorrect, the cookie that is put down on the computer will have the incorrect expire time.*

Path and domain:

The path and domain arguments are used to limit a cookie to a specific folder within a web site (the path) or to a specific domain. For example, you could restrict a cookie to exist only when a user is within a particular folder or subfolders of a domain.

The following example means the cookie is only available for pages in the admin folder.

```
1.  setcookie ('name', 'value', time()+3600, '/admin/');
```

If we use:

```
1.  setcookie ('name', 'value', time()+3600, '/', '.withinweb.com');
```

The / indicates that the same cookie can be used in all folders of the domain and the .withinweb.com means that the same cookie can be used in subdomains of withinweb.com, which would be for example: http://study.withinweb.com as well as the main site: http://www.withinweb.com

Secure:

The last optional parameter is the secure flag that defines that the cookie should only be sent over a secure HTTP connection (https). A **1** indicates that a secure connection must be used, and **0** to use a normal connection.

```
1.  setcookie ('name', 'value', time()+3600, '/admin/', ' ', 1);
```

The parameters must be entered in the function in the correct order and any parameter that is not required should be set to NULL.   Note that the expiration value parameter and the secure value parameter are both integers and do not have to have quote marks around them.

Delete a Cookie

We can delete cookies using the **setcookie()** function.

If we create a cookie as:

```
1.  setcookie("first_name", "Paul");
```

To delete the cookie we just use:

```
1.  setcookie("first_name");
```

We can also set an expiration date to a time in the past if we wish:

```
1.  setcookie("first_name", "", time()-300);
2.
```

Exercise 16.1

(1) Using Dreamweaver or other text editor, create a new PHP page.

(2) If you are using Dreamweaver, you can delete all the HTML code and save the page as **cookie_write.php**

(3) Create a cookie with name of **myname** as follows:

```
1.  <?php
2.  setcookie("myname", "Paul");
3.  ?>
```

Code File: 16_cookies_sessions_logins/cookie_write.php

Upload this file to the web server.

(4) Now create another php page called **cookie_read.php**

(5) In this page, enter the code to display the cookie:

```
1.  $myname = $_COOKIE["myname"];
2.  echo($myname);
```

Code File: 16_cookies_sessions_logins/cookie_read.php

Upload the page to the web server.

(6) Now run the first page **cookies_write.php** in your browser. This will display a blank page, then without closing your browser run the second page **cookies_read.php**. This should display the value of the cookie that you created.

This created a temporary cookie that is deleted when you close the browser. So, if you now close the browser, and then start the browser again and then display the page **cookies_read.php,** it will create an error message showing it could not find the cookie.

To overcome the error message, change the **cookie_read.php** to:

```
1.  if (isset($_COOKIE['myname'])) {
2.      $myname = $_COOKIE['myname'];
3.      echo($myname);
4.  }
5.  else
6.  {
7.      echo("The cookie is not set");
8.  }
```

Code File: 16_cookies_sessions_logins/cookie_read2.php

Now, if the cookie does not exist, it will display a message.

Exercise 16.2

Modify **cookies_write.php** so that it uses a cookie that expires in the future.

(1) To do this, change the **setcookie** to the following:

```
1.  setcookie( "myname", "Paul", time()+(60*60*24) );
```

This will mean the cookie will stay on the machine for 24 hours.

Code File: 16_cookies_sessions_logins/cookie_write2.php

(2) Upload the file to the web server, run the file in the browser and then run the **cookie_read.php** file to see that the cookie is displayed. Close the browser and open the browser again, and then run the **cookie_read.php** file to see if the cookie is still present.

NOTE: *The time is taken from the server, so there may be issues if the server is in a different time zone then the local PC. Some programmers say the minimum expiration time should be 25 hours to overcome any issues with time zones.*

Exercise 16.3

This exercise illustrates creating an array of products that you might want to use if you are working with a shopping cart. The cookie name is called products.

(1) Using Dreamweaver or other editor create a new **PHP** file. If you are using Dreamweaver, delete the HTML from the page and save the file as **cookies_write3.php**

(2) Copy the following code into the PHP page.

```php
1.  <?php
2.  $products = array ("shirtlarge", "shirtsmall", "computermouse");
3.      foreach($products as $item)
4.      {
5.         setcookie("cookieproducts[$item]", $item, time() + (60*60*24));
6.      }
7.  ?>
```

Code File: 16_cookies_sessions_logins/cookie_write3.php

This creates an array of cookies called **cookieproducts**. The products would be shirtlarge, shirtsmall, coatdark, coatlight and should be stored in a non-expiring cookie.   Note that the products have to have no spaces because they will be the names of the cookie.

(3) Now create a web page called **cookies_read3.php** to read and display the items as follows:

```
1.  <?php
2.      if (isset($_COOKIE[cookieproducts])) {
3.          foreach ($_COOKIE[cookieproducts] as $name => $value) {
4.              $name = htmlspecialchars($name);
5.              $value = htmlspecialchars($value);
6.              echo "$name : $value <br />\n";
7.          }
8.      }
9.  ?>
```

Code File: 16_cookies_sessions_logins/cookie_read3.php

(4) Test the page to make sure that it works. Notice that we are using a foreach to loop around the cookies.

Show all cookies

When you run a PHP script in a browser that creates a cookie on your computer, that cookie is only available to PHP scripts that run on that same domain that created them. So a cookie created with the script http://www.yourserver.com/create.php can only be read from a PHP script run from http://www.yourserver.com

However, you can display all cookies that have been created on your computer from a particular domain using the following script:

```
1.  <?php
2.  //Displaying all cookies that have been set from this domain
3.  foreach($_COOKIE as $key => $value)
4.  {
5.    echo $key . " => " . $value;
6.  }
7.  ?>
```

Sessions

Sessions are another way of retaining data and making them available from one page to another, but sessions are temporary and only exist while the browser is kept open. Session data is stored on the web server in special files. The server creates a unique ID and this is used to identify the session data itself. The session UID is stored on your web browser using a cookie.

If the user has disallowed cookies in their web browser, PHP is clever enough to detect this and the session UID is then transferred from page to page using the GET parameter in the page URL.   This process is automatic and we can still use sessions in our code even when the browser disallows cookies.

We could use cookies all the time rather than sessions but there are some advantages to sessions. Sessions are more secure in that all the information is stored on the server.   Also, some users turn off cookies in their browsers but sessions can still work even if cookies are turned off.

Setting Session Variables

To use sessions, we have to place **session_start()** at the top of every web page that makes use of sessions. When the PHP page is run, the function **session_start()** tries to send a cookie with a name of **PHPSESSID** and a numerical value that identifies the session.

The reason that **session_start()** has to be called before any other data is sent to the browser is that it is sending a cookie.

Once the session has been started, session values can be defined and accessed using the **$_SESSION** function as a name / value pair as follows:

```php
1.  <?php
2.  $_SESSION['key'] = 'value';
3.  ?>
```

So examples of sessions would be:

```php
1.  <?php
2.  $_SESSION['recordid'] = '27';
3.  $_SESSION['usertype'] = 'admin';
4.  ?>
```

Deleting session variables

A session is deleted when the browser is closed. Otherwise, we can delete an individual session by using the **unset** function as follows for the session name of 'username':

```php
1.  <?php
2.  unset($_SESSION['username']);
3.  ?>
```

To delete every session variable, we can do the following **$_SESSION**.

```
1.  <?php
2.  $_SESSION = array();
3.  ?>
```

To remove all the session data from the server, use **session_destroy()**:

```
1.  <?php
2.  session_destroy();
3.  ?>
```

TASK 1 - A session test program

As an example, the following is a simple script that shows if sessions are working correctly on your web server. This script is handy if you are having issues with sessions and you want to make sure that the server is correctly set up.

Upload the script to your web server and load the page in a web browser. The first time the page loads, it will display a message saying that the session has started. You then click on the link and it will reload the page where it should display the welcome back message saying that sessions are working correctly.   If the welcome back message does not display, then it indicates that the session has not been created.

```
1.  <?php //session_test.php
2.  // This is a tiny standalone diagnostic script to test that sessions
3.  // are working correctly on a given server.
4.  //
5.  // Just run it from a browser.    The first time you run it will
6.  // set a new variable, and after that it will try to find it again.
7.  // The random number is just to prevent browser caching.
8.  //---------------
9.  session_start();
10. if (!isset($_SESSION["test"])) {    // First time you call it.
11.     echo "<P>No session found - starting a session now.";
12.     $_SESSION["test"] = "welcome back!";
13. //---------------
14. } else {                            // Subsequent times you call it
15.     echo "<P>Session found - ".$_SESSION["test"];
16.     echo "<P>Sessions are working correctly</P>";
17. }
18. //---------------
19. echo "<P><A HREF=\"session_test.php?random=".rand(1,10000)."\">Reloa
    d this page</A></P>";
20. ?>
```

Code File: 16_cookies_sessions_logins/session_test.php

TASK 2 - A session array script

The following code illustrates how you might handle more information in a session. This creates an array called 'cart' to store the quantities of particular items.

```php
1.  <?php session_start();
2.  //---------------
3.  //Initialise an array:
4.  $_SESSION['cart'] = array();
5.  //---------------
6.  //Add items with their quantities:
7.  $_SESSION['cart']['Boxers'] = 4;
8.  $_SESSION['cart']['T-shirts'] = 2;
9.  $_SESSION['cart']['Socks'] = 5;
10. //---------------
11. //We can print out the complete structure using:
12. print_r($_SESSION['cart']);
13. //---------------
14. //Array
15. //(
16. //    [Boxers] => 4
17. //    [T-shirts] => 2
18. //    [Socks] => 5
19. //)
20. //---------------
21. //To update the quantities.
22. $_SESSION['cart']['Socks'] = $new_quantity;
23. $_SESSION['cart']['Socks'] += $quantity;
24. ?>
```

Exercise 16.4

(1) Create a new web page called **sessions_write.php**. If you have used Dreamweaver to create the page, delete the html code and enter in the opening and closing tags:

```php
1.  <?php
2.  ?>
```

(2) At the top of the page just after **<?php** enter **session_start();**

(3) We want to use a session variable to store a username so we can use:

```php
1.  $_SESSION["username"] = "My username";
```

(4) Upload the file to your web server and run the web page in your web browser to make sure that there are no errors.

(5) We now want to read the session variable that we have created, so at the bottom of the page we can use:

```
1.  echo($_SESSION["username"]);
```

(6) Upload the file to the web server and run the web page in your browser to make sure that there are no errors. It should display the value that you set in the session variable.

Exercise 16.5

We want to create a simple shopping cart in a web page called **cart.php**.

We will use an array to create the product information as follows:

```
1.  <?php
2.  $products = {"product A", "product B", "product C"};
3.  $amounts = {"19.99", "10.99", "2.99"};
4.  ?>
```

We can assume that this array will be available to all pages that we create. In this exercise, we will use this array although we could hold the product information in a database.

First we want to display the product information using a **for loop**. Each row will need an "Add to Cart" link as well.

To store the product information we can use a session array:

```
1.  <?php
2.  $_SESSION["cart"][$rec] = $rec;
3.  ?>
```

Where **$rec** is the product array number.

The cart itself can be accessed using a **foreach** loop using:

```
1.  <?php
2.  foreach ( $_SESSION["cart"] as $value ) {
3.      echo($value);
4.  }
5.  ?>
```

We need to have a way to add and remove the products from the array and we can do this by using a href link like **<a href="cart.php?add=...."></a>** You can then program the page so that when the post name 'add' is received, it adds that item to the cart.

A shopping cart using sessions

This section illustrates a relatively simple shopping cart using PHP sessions to store the cart details, quantities and total cart amount. The cart has an 'add to cart', 'remove from cart' and displays the total value of the cart.

The following listing is the complete cart. The code is rather long but it is available in the download for the book.

```php
1. <?php session_start();
2. #cart.php - A simple shopping cart with add, and remove links
3. //Define the products and cost
4. $products = array("product A", "product B", "product C");
5. $amounts = array("19.99", "10.99", "2.99");
6. //---------------------------
7. //initialise sessions
8. if ( !isset($_SESSION["total"]) ) {
9.      $_SESSION["total"] = 0;
10.     for ($i=0; $i< count($products); $i++) {
11.            $_SESSION["qty"][$i] = 0;
12.            $_SESSION["amounts"][$i] = 0;
13.      }
14. }
15. //---------------------------
16. //Reset
17. if ( isset($_GET['reset']) )
18. {
19.     if ($_GET["reset"] == 'true')
20.     {
21.         unset($_SESSION["qty"]);      //The quantity for each product
22.         unset($_SESSION["amounts"]); //The amount from each product
23.         unset($_SESSION["total"]);   //The total cost
24.         unset($_SESSION["cart"]);    //Which item has been chosen
25.     }
26. }
27. //---------------------------
28. //Add
29. if ( isset($_GET["add"]) )
30. {
31.     $i = $_GET["add"];
32.     $qty = $_SESSION["qty"][$i] + 1;
33.     $_SESSION["amounts"][$i] = $amounts[$i] * $qty;
34.     $_SESSION["cart"][$i] = $i;
35.     $_SESSION["qty"][$i] = $qty;
36. }
37. //---------------------------
38. //Delete
39. if ( isset($_GET["delete"]) )
40. {
41.     $i = $_GET["delete"];
42.     $qty = $_SESSION["qty"][$i];
43.     $qty--;
44.     $_SESSION["qty"][$i] = $qty;
```

```
45.     //remove item if quantity is zero
46.     if ($qty == 0) {
47.         $_SESSION["amounts"][$i] = 0;
48.         unset($_SESSION["cart"][$i]);
49.     }
50.     else
51.     {
52.         $_SESSION["amounts"][$i] = $amounts[$i] * $qty;
53.     }
54. }
55. ?>
56. <h2>List of All Products</h2>
57. <table>
58. <tr>
59.     <th>Product</th>
60.     <th width="10px"> </th>
61.     <th>Amount</th>
62.     <th width="10px"> </th>
63.     <th>Action</th>
64. </tr>
65. <?php
66.    for ($i=0; $i< count($products); $i++) {
67.        ?>
68.        <tr>
69.            <td><?php echo($products[$i]); ?></td>
70.            <td width="10px"> </td>
71.            <td><?php echo($amounts[$i]); ?></td>
72.            <td width="10px"> </td>
73.            <td><a href="?add=<?php echo($i); ?>">Add to cart</a></td>
74.        </tr>
75.        <?php
76.    }
77. ?>
78. <tr>
79.     <td colspan="5"></td>
80. </tr>
81. <tr>
82.     <td colspan="5"><a href="?reset=true">Reset Cart</a></td>
83. </tr>
84. </table>
85. <?php
86. if ( isset($_SESSION["cart"]) ) {
87. ?>
88. <br/><br/><br/>
89. <h2>Cart</h2>
90. <table>
91.     <tr>
92.     <th>Product</th>
93.     <th width="10px"> </th>
94.     <th>Qty</th>
95.     <th width="10px"> </th>
96.     <th>Amount</th>
97.     <th width="10px"> </th>
98.     <th>Action</th>
99. </tr>
```

```
100. <?php
101. $total = 0;
102. foreach ( $_SESSION["cart"] as $i ) {
103.    ?>
104.    <tr>
105.       <td><?php echo( $products[$_SESSION["cart"][$i]] ); ?></td>
106.       <td width="10px"> </td>
107.       <td><?php echo( $_SESSION["qty"][$i] ); ?></td>
108.       <td width="10px"> </td>
109.       <td><?php echo( $_SESSION["amounts"][$i] ); ?></td>
110.       <td width="10px"> </td>
111.    <td><a href="?delete=<?php echo($i); ?>">Delete from cart</a></td>
112.    </tr>
113.    <?php
114.    $total = $total + $_SESSION["amounts"][$i];
115. }
116. $_SESSION["total"] = $total;
117. ?>
118. <tr>
119.    <td colspan="7">Total : <?php echo($total); ?></td>
120. </tr>
121. </table>
122. <?php
123. }
124. ?>
```

Code File: 16_cookies_sessions_logins/cart.php

The cart example uses the following sessions to maintain the state of the cart:

$_SESSION["qty"][i]   Stores the quantity for each product

$_SESSION["amounts"][i]   Stores the price from each product

$_SESSION["cart"][i]   Identifies which items have been added to the cart

$_SESSION["total"]   Stores the total cost

The sessions are actually arrays so in the case of:

$_SESSION["qty"][i]

is the quantity for the element with number i.

Description of the shopping cart code

We start by defining the PHP to use sessions by:

session_start();

This has to be at the very top of the PHP page.

Next, we set up our products and populate our sessions. In this example, we are using a fixed array of product descriptions and amounts. You may want to do this in your application or you could read in the data into the $product and $amounts array from a database.

```
3.   //Define the products and cost
4.   $products = array("product A", "product B", "product C");
5.   $amounts = array("19.99", "10.99", "2.99");
6.   //---------------------------
7.   //initialise sessions
8.   if ( !isset($_SESSION["total"]) ) {
9.       $_SESSION["total"] = 0;
10.      for ($i=0; $i< count($products); $i++) {
11.          $_SESSION["qty"][$i] = 0;
12.          $_SESSION["amounts"][$i] = 0;
13.      }
14. }
```

We use the $_SESSION["total"] to test if the session exists. If it has not been set, then we set up our sessions arrays.

The following code resets all the data in the sessions when a link is clicked by un-setting the session:

```
15. //---------------------------
16. //Reset
17. if ( isset($_GET['reset']) )
18. {
19.     if ($_GET["reset"] == 'true')
20.     {
21.        unset($_SESSION["qty"]); //The quantity for each product
22.        unset($_SESSION["amounts"]);//The amount from each product
23.        unset($_SESSION["total"]);   //The total cost
24.        unset($_SESSION["cart"]);    //Which item has been chosen
25.     }
26. }
```

The following code adds an item to the sessions when the 'Add to Cart' link is clicked:

```
27. //-----------------------------
28. //Add
29. if ( isset($_GET["add"]) )
30. {
31.     $i = $_GET["add"];
32.     $qty = $_SESSION["qty"][$i] + 1;
33.     $_SESSION["amounts"][$i] = $amounts[$i] * $qty;
34.     $_SESSION["cart"][$i] = $i;
35.     $_SESSION["qty"][$i] = $qty;
36. }
```

and the following deletes an item from the cart when the 'Delete from Cart' link is clicked:

```
37. //-----------------------------
38. //Delete
39. if ( isset($_GET["delete"]) )
40. {
41.     $i = $_GET["delete"];
42.     $qty = $_SESSION["qty"][$i];
43.     $qty--;
44.     $_SESSION["qty"][$i] = $qty;
45.     //----------
46.     //remove item if quantity is zero
47.     if ($qty == 0) {
48.         $_SESSION["amounts"][$i] = 0;
49.         unset($_SESSION["cart"][$i]);
50.     }
51.     else
52.     {
53.         $_SESSION["amounts"][$i] = $amounts[$i] * $qty;
54.     }
55. }
```

The rest of the code is the visual display using a table and various loops to show the product lists and the cart details together with the links.

The web cart page display

The following illustrates the web page that you will see when you run the **cart.php** file on a web server and then add items to the cart.

```
List of All Products

Product   Amount    Action
product A  19.99     Add to cart
product B  10.99     Add to cart
product C  2.99      Add to cart

Reset Cart




Cart

Product   Qty  Amount         Action
product B  1    10.99    Delete from cart
product C  1    2.99     Delete from cart
Total : 13.98
```

Using sessions to create a login admin system

One of the areas where sessions are used is in securing web pages so that you have to login to get to a particular page.

This is done by:

(1) Display a web page with a form to request a username / password

(2) The user enters their username / password and then the script checks that these are correct. The user details may be stored in a database and read from the database.

(3) If the person is valid, a session is created that may look something like:

```
1.  $_SESSION["access"] = "yes";
```

You may also set other session variables if you want different levels of user access. So, you might set something like:

```
1.  $_SESSION["access"] = "yes";
2.  $_SESSION["username"] = "gibbpv";
3.  $_SESSION["usertype"] = "superuser";
```

(4) Once the person has been validated and the sessions have been created we can then redirect the user to the first page, or if the user is not valid, we can display the login form with some sort of error message.

(5) We then have to create an include file that is included in every PHP page and checks whether the session has been set. If someone goes to one of the PHP pages without logging in, it will find that the session is not set and display an appropriate message.

We will create a number of pages with a couple of include files to illustrate this.

The structure that we will be creating will look like this:

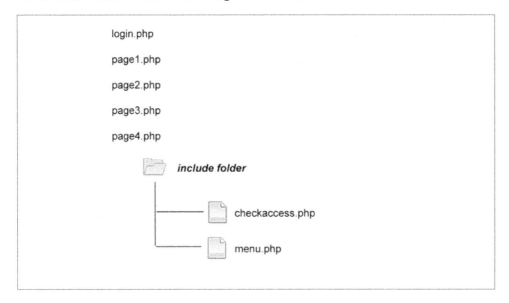

login.php

page1.php

page2.php

page3.php

page4.php

include folder

checkaccess.php

menu.php

TASK 3 - Create a login form

```php
1.  <?php
2.  session_start();
3.
4.  //-------------------------------------------------
5.  if ( isset($_POST["Submit"]) ) {
6.          $username = $_POST["username"];
7.          $password = $_POST["password"];
8.          if ( authenticate($username, $password) ) {
9.              $_SESSION["access"] = "yes";
10.             include("includes/menu.php");
11.         }
12.         else
13.         {
14.             loginform();
15.         }
16. }
17. else
18. {
19.         loginform();
20. }
```

```
21.
22. //-----------------------------------------------------
23. function authenticate($username, $password) {
24.        if ( $username == "username" && $password == "password" ) {
25.                return true;
26.         }
27.         else
28.         {
29.                return false;
30.         }
31. }
32.
33. //-----------------------------------------------------
34. function loginform() {
35. ?>
36. <form name="login" action="" method="post">
37.      <input type="text" name="username" /><br/>
38.      <input type="password" name="password" /><br/>
39.      <input type="submit" name="Submit" value="Submit" /><br/>
40. </form>
41. <?php
42. }
43. ?>
```

Code File: 16_cookies_sessions_logins/script01/login.php

(1) Create a file called **login.php** and copy the above text into it.

(2) Upload the file to your tutorial web server.

TASK 4 - Create an authentication include file

```
1.   <?php
2.   session_start();
3.
4.   //------------
5.   if ( isset ( $_SESSION['access'] ) ) {
6.           if ($_SESSION['access'] != "yes") {
7.                   errormessage();
8.                   exit;
9.           }
10. }
11. else
12. {
13.         errormessage();
14.         exit;
15. }
16.
17. //-----------------------------------------------------
18. function errormessage() {
```

```
19. ?>
20.  <h2>You do not have access to this page.</h2>
21.  <h2>Click <a href="login.php">here</a> to return to login page</h2>
22. <?php
23. }
24. ?>
```

Code File: 16_cookies_sessions_logins/script01/includes/checkaccess.php

(1) Create a file called **checkaccess.php** and copy the above text into it.

(2) Upload this file to the **includes** folder on your web server.

TASK 5 - Create dummy php pages

```
1.  <?php
2.      include("includes/checkaccess.php");
3.      include("includes/menu.php");
4.  ?>
5.  <h1>Page 1</h1>
```

(1) Create a set of **PHP** pages to test the login system.

(2) We want to create **page1.php, page2.php, page3.php, page4.php** and **page5.php** similar to the example above.

(3) These are essentially identical except that each has a different <h1> text.

(4) Save all the files to your tutorials web site.

TASK 6 - Create a menu page

```
1.  <a href="page1.php">Menu link 1</a><br/>
2.  <a href="page2.php">Menu link 2</a><br/>
3.  <a href="page3.php">Menu link 3</a><br/>
4.  <a href="page4.php">Menu link 4</a><br/>
5.  <a href="page5.php">Menu link 5</a><br/>
```

(1) Create a new web page called **menu.php** and copy the above text into the file.

Code File: 16_cookies_sessions_logins/script01/includes/menu.php

(2) Upload the file to the web server in the **include** folder.

TASK 7 - Testing the login system

The login has the username of '**username**', and password of '**password**' and is hard coded into the login page. A better solution is to read the username and passwords from a database table.

(1) Display the **login.php** form in the web browser and enter an invalid username / password to test that it does not login.

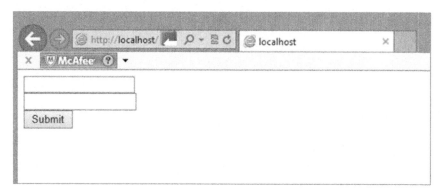

(2) Now enter the valid username / password into the login form. This should display the menu and you should be able to click through on each page.

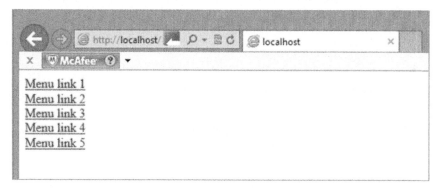

(3) Exit the web browser to close all the session and start the browser up again. This time display one of the dummy pages in the web browser. This should say you are not logged in.

Summary

In this Chapter, we looked at maintaining state using the two methods of cookies and sessions. We looked at why we need to maintain state and the difference between the two methods. With cookies, we showed how to create and delete a cookie and with sessions, we showed how to create a PHP shopping cart script and a script to protect pages using sessions.

Topics for Review

[1] Explain the differences between cookies and sessions.

[2] Why do we sometimes want to maintain state in a web page?

[3] How do you define secure cookies?

[4] Run the sessions test script on your server.

17 - Modifying Records

What is in this Chapter?

* How to create an edit form.
* How to create a delete form.

In this Chapter, we look at how to edit an existing record and how to delete an existing record using PHP and SQL.

To do this we use the SQL **UPDATE** statement and the SQL **DELETE** statement on the desired records.

We also need to be able to pass data between **PHP** web pages so that we know what record we are working with.

The techniques forms the basis of more complex administration sites where you can create, edit and delete entries as used in a content management system or any site that has a requirement for someone to modify existing data.

Passing values between pages

We will look at **GET** and **POST** which are two methods to transfer data from one web page to another.

The first method is to make use of HTML's hidden input type.

```
1.   <input type = "hidden" name = "coursetype" value = "parttime" />
```

As long as the code is between the form tags, the variable **$_POST['coursetype']** will have a value of 'parttime' when posted to a handling **PHP** script (assuming the form uses the **POST** method)

The second method is to append a value to the scripts URL like this:

```
http://www.mywebsite.com/page.php?coursetype=parttime
```

This technique emulates the **GET** method of an HTML form. With this example **page.php** receives a variable called **$_GET['coursetype']** with a value of 'parttime'.

We can use either of these methods to pass data between web pages.

In order to demonstrate the **GET** method, we will create a new version of **view_feedback.php**. This will provide links to edit or delete an existing user. The links will pass the user's ID to the handling pages.

TASK 1 - Adding in edit and delete links

The usual method of updating records is to have an href link in the list of results from the table. When the user clicks on the link, it takes them to another page using a record id in the href link. The record id is used to collect information from the database that is then displayed to the user so that it can be edited.

First, we need to make two small changes to the **view_feedback.php** script.

(1) Open the **view_feedback.php** script in Dreamweaver or in another editor and find the HTML code:

```
1.  <td><strong>First Name</strong></td>
2.  <td width="10"> </td>
3.  <td><strong>Last Name</strong></td>
4.  <td width="10"> </td>
5.  <td><strong>Email</strong></td>
6.  <td width="10"> </td>
7.  <td><strong>Comments</strong></td>
```

add in the following underneath the last </td> to extend the table:

```
1.  <td width="10"> </td>
2.  <td><strong>Edit</strong></td>
3.  <td width="10"> </td>
4.  <td><strong>Delete</strong></td>
```

(2) Find the following code:

```
1.  <td><?php echo($d_row["first_name"]); ?></td>
2.  <td width="10"> </td>
3.  <td><?php echo($d_row["last_name"]); ?></td>
4.  <td width="10"> </td>
5.  <td><?php echo($d_row["email"]); ?></td>
6.  <td width="10"> </td>
7.  <td><?php echo($d_row["comments"]); ?></td>
```

add in the following underneath the last </td> to extend the table:

```
1.  <td width="10"> </td>
2.  <td><?php echo("<a href='edit_feedback.php?user_id=" .
        $d_row["user_id"] . "'>Edit</a>"); ?> </td>
3.  <td width="10"> </td>
4.  <td> <?php echo("<a href='delete_feedback.php?user_id=" .
        $d_row["user_id"] . "'>Delete</a>"); ?></td>
```

Code File: 17_modifying_records/script01/view_feedback.php

(3) Upload the file to the web server and make sure that it runs in the browser.

We have added in two links that will transfer the primary key of the record to the new page edit_feedback.php and delete_feedback.php.

TASK 2 - Creating the edit_feedback.php page

The **edit_feedback.php** page is actually quite similar to the **feedback.php** page that inserts new records into the feedback table.

(1) Create a new web page called **edit_feedback.php**. If you are using Dreamweaver, delete all HTML code and then copy the following text into the page. The code is quite long but you can find it in the download code for the book.

```php
1. <?php
2.
3. //Version with escape data function added
4.
5. require_once('includes/connect.php'); // Connect to the database.
6. require_once('includes/misc.php'); //has the mysqli escape function
7. //---------------
8. //collect the user_id either from a get
9. //statement or from a post statement
10. if ( isset($_GET["user_id"]) || isset($_POST["user_id"]) ) {
11.
12.     if ( isset($_GET["user_id"]) ) {
13.         $user_id = $_GET["user_id"];
14.     }
15.     else {
16.         $user_id = $_POST["user_id"];
17.     }
18.
19.     if (!is_numeric($user_id)) {
20.         exit;
21.     }
22.
23. }
24. else
25. {
26.     exit;
27. }
```

```
28.
29. //Check if the form has been posted,
30. //if not then display the form
31. if (isset($_POST['submit'])) {
32.
33.   // Check if the first name has been entered.
34.   if (emptyempty($_POST['first_name'])) {
35.     $message = 'Please enter your first name';
36.     displayform($message, $user_id, $link); //Display error message
37.       exit();
38.   } else {
39.       $first_name = mysqli_escape($_POST['first_name'], $link);
40.   }
41.
42.   // Check if the last name has been entered
43.   if (emptyempty($_POST['last_name'])) {
44.     $message = 'Enter your last name';
45.     displayform($message, $user_id, $link); //Display error message
46.     exit();
47.   } else {
48.     $last_name = mysqli_escape($_POST['last_name'], $link);
49.   }
50.
51.   // Check if the email address has been entered
52.   if (emptyempty($_POST['email'])) {
53.     $message = 'Enter your email address';
54.     displayform($message, $user_id, $link);//Display error message
55.     exit();
56.   } else {
57.     $email = mysqli_escape($_POST['email'], $link);
58.   }
59.
60.   // Check if any comments have been entered
61.   if (emptyempty($_POST['comments'])) {
62.     $message = 'Enter your comments';
63.     displayform($message, $user_id, $link);//Display error message
64.     exit();
65.   } else {
66.     $comments = mysqli_escape($_POST['comments'], $link);
67.   }
68.
69.   //Check the entries have been entered.
70.   //We could also enter in other validation here
71.   if ($first_name && $last_name && $email && $comments) { //If every
   thing is OK.
72.
73.   // Make the query.
74.   $query = "UPDATE feedback SET first_name = '$first_name',
75.     last_name = '$last_name',
76.     email = '$email', comments = '$comments', feedback_date = NOW()
       WHERE user_id = $user_id";
77.
78.   $result = mysqli_query( $link, $query );
79.
80.   //Check the result, do other processing such as sending an email
```

```
81.     if ($result) {
82.         $message = '<p>Feedback updated</p>';
83.         displayform($message, $user_id, $link);
84.         exit();
85.
86.     } else { //If there is a problem, then display an error message
87.         $message = '<p>Error in updating feedback table.</p><p>' .
            mysqli_error($link) . '</p>';
88.          displayform($message, $user_id, $link);
89.          exit();
90.     }
91.
92.   } else {
93.   $message.='<p>You have not filled in all the required fields</p>';
94.     displayform($message, $user_id, $link);
95.     exit();
96.   }
97.
98. } // End of the main Submit conditional.
99. else
100. {
101.   displayform(" ", $user_id, $link);
102. }
103.
104. mysqli_close($link);
105.
106. //-------------------------------------------------------------
107. //This is the form
108. function displayform($message, $user_id, $link) {
109.
110. $pagetitle = 'Edit a feedback entry';
111. include ('includes/header.php');   //the header
112.
113. ?>
114.     <h1>User feedback</h1>
115. <?php
116.
117.   // Print the message if there is one.
118.   if (isset($message)) {
119.       echo '<font color="red"><p>'. $message . '</p></font>';
120.   }
121.
122. //collect the data for this given $user_id
123. $query = " SELECT user_id, first_name, last_name, email,
124. comments FROM feedback WHERE user_id = $user_id ";
125.
126. $result = mysqli_query( $link, $query );
127.
128. if (!$result) {
129.     printf("Error in connection: %s\n", mysqli_error($link));
130.     exit();
131. }
132.
133. //Fetch the result into an associative array
134. while ( $row = mysqli_fetch_assoc( $result ) ) {
```

```
135.     $table[] = $row;    //add each row into the table array
136. }
137.
138. if ( count($table) != 1 ) {
139.     exit;
140. }
141. else
142. {
143.     //Collect the values from the database
144.     $first_name = $table[0]["first_name"];
145.     $last_name = $table[0]["last_name"];
146.     $email = $table[0]["email"];
147.     $comments = $table[0]["comments"];
148. }
149.
150. ?>
151.
152. <form action="<?php echo $_SERVER['PHP_SELF']; ?>"
                     method="post">
153.
154. <input type="hidden" name="user_id"
                 value="<?php echo($user_id); ?>" />
155.
156. <table>
157.
158. <tr>
159. <td colspan="2"><h2>Update the entry</h2></td>
160. </tr>
161.
162. <tr>
163. <td><p><strong>First Name:</strong></p></td>
164. <td><input type="text" name="first_name" size="30"
         maxlength="30" value="<?php echo($first_name); ?>" /></td>
165. </tr>
166.
167. <tr>
168. <td><p><strong>Last Name:</strong></p></td>
169. <td><input type="text" name="last_name" size="30"
         maxlength="30" value="<?php echo($last_name); ?>" /></td>
170. </tr>
171.
172. <tr>
173. <td><p><strong>Email Address:</strong></p></td>
174. <td><input type="text" name="email" size="40"
         maxlength="40" value="<?php echo($email); ?>" /></td>
175. </tr>
176.
177. <tr>
178. <td><p><strong>Comments:</strong></p></td>
179. <td><textarea name="comments" rows="7" cols="48"
         value="<?php echo($comments); ?>" /><?php echo($comments); ?>
         </textarea></td>
180. </tr>
181.
182. <tr>
```

```
183. <td></td>
184. <td><input type="submit" name="submit" value="Submit" /></td>
185. </tr>
186.
187. </table>
188.
189. </form>
190. <?php
191. include ('includes/footer.php'); // the footer
192. }
193. //-------------------------------------------
194. ?>
```

Code File: 17_modifying_records/script01/edit_feedback.php

(2) Upload the file to the web server.

(3) Run the **view_feedback.php** page in your web browser and when you click on one of the edit links, it should display the values for that user_id on the page.

(4) Modify some of the text and submit the changes.

(5) Look at the database in **phpMyAdmin** and check that the data has been entered.

The technique used in the script is as follows:

* Read the **user_id** either from the **$_GET** statement or from the **$_POST** statement.
* Check if the form has been posted using the submit button.
* If the form has not been submitted, display the form, collecting the data for this **user_**id from the database**.**
* If the form has been submitted, update the database with the defined data.

Breaking down the above code, first read the **user_id** using either GET or POST statement:

```
1.  <?php
2.  //---------
3.  //collect the user_id either from a get statement or from a
        post statement
4.  if ( isset($_GET["user_id"] || isset($_POST["user_id"]) ) {
5.      if ( isset($_GET["user_id"] ) {
6.          $user_id = $_GET["user_id"];
7.      }
8.      else {
9.          $user_id = $_POST["user_id"];
```

```
10.     }
11.
12.     if (!is_numeric($user_id)) {
13.         exit;
14.     }
15. }
16. else
17. {
18.     exit;
19. }
20. ?>
```

The SQL query is now an UPDATE statement:

```
1.  $query = "UPDATE feedback SET first_name = '$first_name', last_name
    = '$last_name', email = '$email', comments = '$comments',
    feedback_date = NOW() WHERE user_id = $user_id";
```

We use another SQL query to get the user details for this user_id:

```
1.  <?php
2.  //----------
3.  //collect the data for this given $user_id
4.  $query = " SELECT user_id, first_name, last_name, email,
5.  comments FROM feedback WHERE user_id = $user_id ";
6.  //----------
7.  $result = mysqli_query( $link, $query );
8.  if (!$result) {
9.     printf("Error in connection: %s\n", mysqli_error($link));
10.    exit();
11. }
12. //----------
13. //Fetch the result into an associative array
14. while ( $row = mysqli_fetch_assoc( $result ) ) {
15.     $table[] = $row;     //add each row into the table array
16. }
17. if ( count($table) != 1 ) {
18.     exit;
19. }
20. else
21. {
22.     //Collect the values from the database
23.     $first_name = $table[0]["first_name"];
24.     $last_name = $table[0]["last_name"];
25.     $email = $table[0]["email"];
26.     $comments = $table[0]["comments"];
27. }
28. ?>
```

In the form field, we add in a hidden field to be used when the data is posted back from the form:

```
1.  <input type="hidden" name="user_id" value="<?php echo($user_id); ?>"
    />
```

Each of the form fields has their value entered similar to the following:

```
1.  <input type="text" style="background:#cccccc" name="first_name" size
    ="30" maxlength="30" value="<?php echo($first_name); ?>" />
```

Exercise 17.1

The database feedback table contains an extra field of age that is an integer data type.

Modify the above **edit_feedback.php** page to include the age field in the UPDATE query and in the displays.

Exercise 17.2

Modify the **edit_feedback.php** script to include the header.php and footer.php files to give the same layout.

TASK 3 - Creating the delete_feedback.php page

Deleting a record requires the SQL **DELETE** query. However, deleting the record is more complicated in that we need to ask the user if they actually want to delete the record.

The process is:

* The page first checks that it has received a numeric user ID.
* A message asks if this user should be deleted.
* The user ID is stored in a hidden form input.
* The user is then deleted upon submission of the form.

(1) Create a new **PHP** file and save it as **delete_feedback.php**. If you are creating it in Dreamweaver, delete all the HTML code.

(2) Copy the following into the file.

```
1.  <?php
2.  //Delete a record
3.  //-----------
4.  //Connect to the database.
5.  require_once('includes/connect.php');
6.  //-----------
```

```
7.  //collect the user_id either from a get statement or
        from a post statement
8.  if ( isset($_GET["user_id"]) || isset($_POST["user_id"]) ) {
9.
10.     if ( isset($_GET["user_id"]) ) {
11.         $user_id = $_GET["user_id"];
12.     }
13.     else {
14.         $user_id = $_POST["user_id"];
15.     }
16.
17.     if (!is_numeric($user_id)) {
18.         exit;
19.     }
20. }
21. else
22. {
23.     exit;
24. }
25. if ( isset($_POST["action"]) ) {
26.
27.   if ( $_POST["action"] == "Yes" ) {
28.
29.       $query = " DELETE FROM feedback WHERE user_id = $user_id ";
30.       $result = mysqli_query( $link, $query );
31.
32.     if ($result) { //If it worked show a message or send an email
33.         $message = 'Record deleted';
34.         displayform($message, $user_id);
35.         exit();
36.     } else { //If there is a problem, then display an error message
37.         $message = 'Error in feedback table - ' .
                mysqli_error($link) . '';
38.         displayform($message, $user_id);
39.         exit();
40.     }
41.
42.   }
43.   else
44.   {
45.       displayform("Action cancelled", $user_id);
46.   }
47.
48. }
49. else
50. {
51.   displayform("Are you sure you want to delete this record?",
        $user_id);
52. }
53. //----------------------------------------------------------
54. function displayform($message, $user_id) {
55.
56. $pagetitle = 'Delete a feedback entry';
57. include ('includes/header.php');  //the header
58. ?>
```

```
59.    <h1>User feedback</h1>
60. <?php
61.
62. // Print the message if there is one.
63. if (isset($message)) {
64.    echo '<font color="red"><p>'. $message . '</p></font>';
65. }
66. ?>
67. <h2>Delete this record -  Select Yes or Cancel</h2>
68. <form action="<?php echo $_SERVER['PHP_SELF']; ?>" method="post">
69. <input type="hidden" name="user_id" value="<?php echo($user_id); ?>"
    />
70. <p><strong>Delete :</strong><input type="submit" name="action" value
    ="Yes" /></p>
71. <p><strong>Cancel :</strong><input type="submit" name="action" value
    ="Cancel" /></p>
72. </form>
73. <?php
74. include ('includes/footer.php'); // the footer
75. }
76. //----------------------------------------------------------
77. ?>
```

Code File: 17_modifying_records/script01/delete_feedback.php

(3) Upload the file to the web server and run the **view_feedback.php** page. Test it by clicking on the delete link and seeing that the record was deleted.

Exercise 17.3

Modify the **delete_feedback.php** script to include **the header.php** and **footer.php** files to give the same layout.

Summary

This Chapter shows the next step in working with form data to modify existing data. We created a set of files that we can use to edit and delete values in our table. You should now see how you could create a complete set of files that enables you to administer the table data.

Topics for Review

[1] Show how to pass a value using the GET method.

[2] Explain the advantages and disadvantages between the POST and GET methods.

18 - Classes

What is in this Chapter?

* Some concepts of Object Oriented Programming.
* Terminology.
* Inheritance.
* Constructors and Destructors.

Object oriented programming (OOP) is the "in thing" in programming. Some languages like Java are based entirely around objects and you cannot do anything in Java without them.

However, OOP techniques were bolted on to PHP such that early versions did not have full support for the concepts. Many PHP programs are actually hybrids of procedural and object programming.

PHP has come a long way since its early days in its support for OOP, but you still do not have to write all your code in objects. PHP 7 in particular has much more clearer support.

In this Chapter, we will look at objects and classes that will allow you to understand why they are so important in modern programming.

Basic principles

Object Oriented Programming uses techniques to take 'real world' concepts and make them into programs. This technique allows you to develop **'DRY'** programming or 'Don't Repeat Yourself' programming making code maintenance much easier.

To start with, many developers get confused with the terms objects and classes, and some appear to use the terms interchangeable. However, they are not the same.

A class is the definition or classification of the concept that we are trying to represent, and it groups together variables and methods into reusable code blocks. So, we could have a class called **'vehicle'** that says it has an engine and wheels, and it has methods of 'increase speed' and 'breaking'. We could then have objects of this class that are specific instances.

So we might have an instance of **vehicle** which is an object called **'familycar'** having four wheels, an engine and a certain acceleration and breaking. We could have another instance of **vehicle** which is an object called **'motorbike'** having two wheels and an engine, and the speed and breaking would be much quicker than the **familycar**.

Both **familycar** and **motorbike** are of type **vehicle** and have the same basic structure.

Classes form the structure of data and actions, and use that information to build objects. More than one object can be built from the same class at the same time, each one independent of the others.

An object is an attempt to program the real world. So we could have an object defined as **vehicle** which we can understand as a physical thing.

However, we do not have to create objects that represent physical things. We could create an object that sends emails for example.

The procedural approach

Say that we wish to write a program to create, update and delete person details, such as name, address, job title and so on. If we program in a procedural way, we may find somewhere in the code, a function that creates an array for the persons details. We may also find a function that reads and writes the data from the database into the array. Quite often, the only way that we can see a connection between the two functions is the name of the functions themselves, if the programmer considered the issue. Or the functions have been placed in to one common file.

With the object-oriented approach, we group together all the pieces of code for the person details into one conceptual unit. Placing the code together into units is the basic idea of object oriented programming. All OOP languages have some way in which to group together code and data, but they also have one or more of the following concepts: inheritance, polymorphism and encapsulation.

Object Oriented Terminology

There are three principles of Object Oriented Programming.

- Inheritance
- Encapsulation
- Polymorphism

Inheritance

If we write code to define something like a motor **vehicle**, we may want to have a slightly different version of a vehicle. For example, we might want to code a **goods vehicle** that can carry materials rather than people. To do this we use inheritance, that allows us to define a class (a **goods vehicle**), based on another class (a **motor vehicle**) and then add or change the implementation of some functions. The original class (the **motor vehicle**) is the parent where the child class (the **goods vehicle**) inherits the function and data definitions unless you specify otherwise.

Encapsulation

Encapsulation is where data variables and function code in the class are not accessible directly from outside the class. We can define which variables and functions are **private**, that is the scope of the variable or function is within the class, or **public** where the scope allows them to be accessed outside the class. The purpose of this is to hide the inner workings of the class so that the programmer only has access to easy interfaces.

Polymorphism

Polymorphism is where the developer writes a base class that defines the object and writes subclasses to build the different behaviours the object may have. We can call the same method in different objects and the object-oriented system is able to pick up the correct behaviour for the particular object that we have created.

Creating an Object

When working with classes and objects we use the following terminology:

Methods - these are functions defined in the class.

Properties or data members - these are data variables in the class.

Instance - this is an implementation of the class to create an object.

TASK 1 - An implementation of a class

Example of a class as used in PHP:

```
1.  <?php
2.
3.  class Box {
4.
5.      private $_length;
6.      private $_width;
7.      private $_height;
8.
9.      public function __construct($length, $width, $height) {
10.         $this->_length = $length;
11.         $this->_width = $width;
12.         $this->_height = $height;
13.     }
14.
15.     public function volume() {
16.         return $this->_length * $this->_width * $this->_height;
17.     }
18.
19. }
20. ?>
```

Code File: 18_classes/box_class_01.php

Explanation of each line:

```
3.  class Box
```

The above line defines the class. Note that the word 'class' is all lowercase and normally by convention we define the class name with the first letter being uppercase.

```
5.  private $_length;
6.  private $_width;
7.  private $_height;
```

These are **properties** or **data members** of the class and are not normally accessible directly. Their values are accessed through functions of the class. In this class, I have used the convention where data properties start with an underscore character.

```
9.  public function __construct($length, $width, $height) {
10.     $this->_length = $length;
11.     $this->_width = $width;
12.     $this->_height = $height;
13. }
```

The above is the **constructor** that loads the properties with their values at initialisation. Note the constructor function is **__construct**. Also note the use of the keyword $this which is the way you reference values of this class.

In older versions of PHP, you may see the following used as the constructor:

```
9.  public function Box($length, $width, $height) {
10.        $this->_length = $length;
11.        $this->_width = $width;
12.        $this->_height = $height;
13. }
```

In this case, the constructor name is the same as the name as the class, which in this example is Box. In PHP 7, this technique is no longer valid and you will receive an error message.

```
15. public function volume() {
16.       return $this->_length * $this->_width * $this->_height;
17. }
```

The above is a **method** that calculates the volume using the properties.

Now that we have defined the Box class, we can create instances of the class in the following way:

```
1.  <?php
2.
3.  $myBox = new Box(20,10, 5);
4.  $myVolume = $myBox->volume();
5.  echo("Volume = " . $myVolume . "<br/>");
6.
7.  ?>
```

Code File: 18_classes/box_class_02.php

Explanation of each line:

```
3.  $myBox = new Box(20,10, 5);
```

The above defines the object that we have called $myBox

```
4.  $myVolume = $myBox->volume();
```

The above calculates and returns the answer. Note the syntax that we use to reference the method of volume(). We use the -> operator to access or change property values.

We can then display the answer in the normal way:

```
5.  echo("Volume = " . $myVolume . "<br/>");
```

The definitions of each class modifier types

Functions and properties use **public, protected** or **private** to modify the level of access. The following explains these:

public. Public members can be accessed from outside an object by using
$object->publicMember
and by accessing it from inside a method via the $this variable
$this->publicMember
This is also true if another class **inherits** a public member in which case it can be accessed from outside the derived class's objects and from inside its methods.

protected. Protected members can be accessed only from within an object's method - for example,
$this->protectedMember.
The same rule applies if another class **inherits** a protected member in which case it can be accessed from within the derived object's methods via the $this variable.

private. Private members are similar to protected members because they can be accessed only from within an object's method. However, they cannot be accessed from a derived object's methods. Note that in a class that relates to another class, you can define private members with the same name and they will be completely unrelated.

TASK 2 - Inheritance

The following extends the Box class to a Parcel class. Note the use of
parent::__construct to enable the **$length, $width, $height** to be passed into the parent class:

```
1.  <?php
2.
3.  class Parcel extends Box {
4.
5.      private $_deliveryAddress;
6.      private $_weight;
7.
8.      //Constructor
9.      public function __construct($length, $width, $height,
                $deliveryAddress, $weight)
10.     {
```

```
11.
12.         parent::__construct($length, $width, $height);
13.
14.         $this->_deliveryAddress = $deliveryAddress;
15.         $this->_weight = $weight;
16.
17.     }
18.
19.     //Public method
20.     public function cost() {
21.
22.             $volume = $this->volume();
23.
24.             if ($volume <= 200)
25.             {
26.                 return 5;
27.             }
28.             else
29.             {
30.                 return 10;
31.             }
32.
33.     }
34.
35. }
36.
37. ?>
```

Code File: 18_classes/parcel_class_01.php

The complete code for the new inherited class is as follows:

```
1.  <?php
2.
3.  class Box {
4.
5.      protected  $_length;
6.      protected  $_width;
7.      protected  $_height;
8.
9.      public function __construct($length, $width, $height) {
10.          $this->_length = $length;
11.          $this->_width = $width;
12.          $this->_height = $height;
13.      }
14.
15.      public function volume() {
16.          return $this->_length * $this->_width * $this->_height;
17.      }
18.
19. }
20.
21. $myBox = new Box(20,10, 5);
22. $myVolume = $myBox->volume();
```

```
23. echo("Volume = " . $myVolume . "<br/>");
24.
25. class Parcel extends Box {
26.
27.   private $_deliveryAddress;
28.   private $_weight;
29.
30.   public function __construct($length, $width, $height,
            $deliveryAddress, $weight) {
31.
32.       parent::__construct($length, $width, $height);
33.
34.       $this->_deliveryAddress = $deliveryAddress;
35.       $this->_weight = $weight;
36.
37.   }
38.
39.   public function cost() {
40.
41.       $volume = $this->volume();
42.
43.       if ($volume <= 200)
44.       {
45.         return 5;
46.       }
47.         else
48.       {
49.         return 10;
50.       }
51.
52.   }
53.
54. }
55.
56. $myParcel = new Parcel(20,10, 5, '10 Bristol Road', '210');
57. $myCost = $myParcel->cost();
58. $myVolume = $myParcel ->volume();
59. echo("Volume = " . $myVolume . " Cost = " . $myCost . "<br/>");
60.
61. ?>
```

Code File: 18_classes/parcel_class_02.php

This is how we create an instance of the Parcel class:

```
1.   $myParcel = new Parcel(20,10, 5, '10 Bristol Road', '210');
2.   $myCost = $myParcel->cost();
3.   $myVolume = $myParcel->volume();
4.   echo("Volume = " . $myVolume . " Cost = " . $myCost . "<br/>");
```

Notice that when we define the object Parcel we pass in all the variables required for the base class and the extended class. The parent::__construct passes the required variables to the base class.

Also, notice that we have changed the property type of the Box class to **protected**.

Constructors and Destructors

Constructor methods are called when the object is created and so are used to initialise variables and perform other tasks before it is used.

The destructor method concept is similar to that of other object-oriented languages. The destructor method is called when there are no other references to a particular object.

We use __**construct()** to represent the constructor and __**destruct()** to represent the destructor.

In previous versions of PHP, you could use a constructor method with the same name as the class. That is no longer allowed, and you have to use the __**construct()** keyword.

Another example

To reinforce the concepts of OOP we will continue by creating a 'Person' class with various properties and methods. We will then extend the person class to an 'Employee' class that will have some special properties. We will also see that we can create an array of objects and then output the details of all objects in the array.

This is our person class:

```php
1.  <?php
2.
3.  class Person {
4.
5.      //-------------------------------
6.      // private properites
7.      protected $_name;
8.      protected $_dateofbirth;
9.      protected $_weight;
10.
11.     //-------------------------------
12.     // constructor
13.     public function __construct( $name, $dateofbirth, $weight )
14.     {
15.         $this->_name = $name;
16.         $this->_dateofbirth = $dateofbirth;
17.         $this->_weight = $weight;
18.     }
19.
20.     //-------------------------------
21.     // methods that return information about the person
```

```
22.     public function get_name()
23.     {
24.         return $this->_name;
25.     }
26.
27.     public function get_dateofbirth()
28.     {
29.         return $this->_dateofbirth;
30.     }
31.
32.     public function get_age()
33.     {
34.         $today = new DateTime();
35.         $diff = $today->diff(new DateTime($this->_dateofbirth));
36.             return $diff->y;
37.     }
38.
39.     public function get_weight()
40.     {
41.         return $this->_weight;
42.     }
43.
44.     //-----------------------------
45.     // methods that change values of properties
46.     public function change_name($name)
47.     {
48.         $this->_name = $name;
49.     }
50.
51.     public function add_weight($weight)
52.     {
53.         $this->_weight = $this->_weight + $weight;
54.     }
55.
56.     public function lose_weight($weight)
57.     {
58.         $this->_weight = $this->_weight - $weight;
59.     }
60.
61.     //-----------------------------
62.     // print the person details
63.     public function printall()
64.     {
65.       echo("<br/>-----------------------------------<br/>");
66.       echo("NAME: " . $this->_name . " DATEOFBIRTH: " .
              $this->_dateofbirth . " WEIGHT: " .
              $this->_weight . "<br/>");
67.       echo("-----------------------------------<br/><br/>");
68.     }
69.
70. }
71. ?>
```

File Code: 18_classes/person_class_01.php

In this class we start with the protected properties of **$_name, $_dateofbirth** and **$_weight** and we populate them using the constructor. We use the protected keyword rather than private keyword because we intend to extend the class and this will allow us to access the properties from the child class.

We then have a set of public methods that either return information or change values.

Note that we have a method **get_age()** that uses the date of birth to calculate the age of the person.

We can now use our class person by initialising a couple of users.

```
1.  <?php
2.  $paul = new Person('Paul Gibbs', '1957-04-03', 160);
3.  $john = new Person('John Smith', '1970-04-05', 210);
4.  ?>
```

We can now do various things to the person object such as losing weight.

```
1.  <?php
2.
3.  $paul = new Person('Paul Gibbs', '1957-04-03', 160);
4.  $john = new Person('John Smith', '1970-04-05', 210);
5.
6.  $paul->lose_weight(10);
7.
8.  echo("Paul's weight is now: " . $paul->get_weight(10) . "<br/>");
9.  echo("Paul's age is: " . $paul->get_age() . "<br/>");
10. echo("-----------------------------<br/><br/>");
11.
12. $paul->printall(); // display all details
13.
14. ?>
```

We can also add our objects to an array and loop through the array to get particular details.

```
1.  <?php
2.
3.  $paul = new Person('Paul Gibbs', '1957-04-03', 160);
4.  $john = new Person('John Smith', '1970-04-05', 210);
5.
6.  $people[] = $paul;
7.  $people[] = $john;
8.
9.  foreach( $people as $person ) {
10.     echo "The name is " . $person->get_name() . "<br/>";
11.     echo "This person is ".$person->get_age()." years old.<br/>";
12. }
```

```
13.
14. ?>
```

We can now create a second class called **employee** that inherits from the base class. This class has the extra properties of salary and start date.

```php
1.  <?php
2.
3.  class Employee extends Person {
4.
5.      //------------------------------
6.      // private properties
7.      private $_salary;
8.      private $_startdate;
9.
10.     //------------------------------
11.     // constructor
12.     public function __construct($name, $dateofbirth, $weight,
                $salary, $startdate)
13.     {
14.         parent::__construct( $name, $dateofbirth, $weight );
15.
16.         $this->_salary = $salary;
17.         $this->_startdate = $startdate;
18.
19.     }
20.
21.     //------------------------------
22.     // methods that return information about the person
23.     public function get_salary()
24.     {
25.         return $this->_salary;
26.     }
27.
28.     public function get_startdate()
29.     {
30.         return $this->_startdate;
31.     }
32.
33.     //------------------------------
34.     // print the person details
35.     public function printall()
36.     {
37.        echo("NAME: " . parent::_name . "DATEOFBIRTH: " .
                parent::_dateofbirth . "WEIGHT: " . parent::_weight .
                "SALARY: " . $this->_salary . "STARTDATE: " .
                $this->_startdate .  "<br/>");
38.     }
39. ?>
```

Note the constructor class of Employee uses the **parent::_construct** to populate the properties of the base **Person** class.

We can now create instances of an employee using the **Employee** class:

```php
1.  <?php
2.
3.  $pete = new Employee('Pete Coles', '1990-06-07', '200', 20000,
        '2012-06-04');
4.  $pete->printall();
5.  $paul = new Person('Paul Gibbs', '1960-02-01', 160);
6.  $paul->printall();
7.
8.  ?>
```

File Code: 18_classes/employee_class_02.php

Notice how we use the method **printall**. In the last example, pete is an employee and hence when we use **$pete->printall();** we display all the employee data. On the other hand, paul is a person and when we print it out we just get the details of a person. We are using the same method name, but the objects are able to execute the correct **printall** method.

Using the OOP approach means that there is some extra work to set up the class, but after the class has been defined, creating and modifying people is easy.

For small projects, the difference may not seem much, but as your application grows, OOP will significantly reduce your workload.

NOTE: *Not everything needs to be object oriented. You could create a function that handles something small without turning it into a class. You have to make your own judgement when to work with the object-oriented methods or to work with the procedural methods.*

Class diagram for Person and Employee

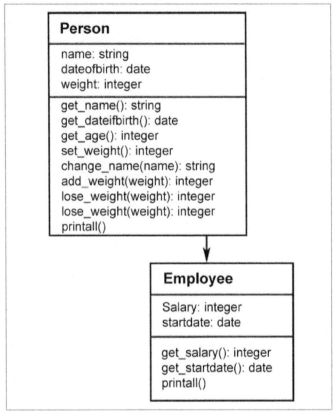

Exercise 18.1

Create a class called 'EmailOut' with private properties:

toAddress
fromAddress
subject
body

Create a public constructor that populates these variables and create a public method that sends out the email using the PHP **mail** function.

Code File: 18_classes/email_class.php

Summary

Object Oriented Programming is very extensive subject, but this Chapter covers much of the basic concepts that you will come across. We have seen how to define a class and then create the object from the class. We have also seen the concept of inheritance and constructors.

Topics for Review

[1] What is the syntax for a constructor?

[2] Explain the meaning of public, protected and private members.

[3] List the three principles of Object Oriented Programming.

19 - File Handling

What is in this Chapter?

* File permissions.
* Reading and writing text in files.
* Creating and deleting directories and file manipulation.
* Finding out what files there are in a particular directory.
* Uploading files or images to your webserver.

Text files are useful if you want to store small amounts of data rather than using a database. For example, you could hold a list of product item details that you are selling on your web site and read the data into an array for display.

File permissions on the server

If you have to write data to a text file on a web server, or you have to copy, rename, delete or do any kind of file manipulation, the file or folder will require the correct permissions.

To change file or folder permissions in Dreamweaver, open the site up in the remote view and right click on the file or folder. Select 'permissions' and then choose the kind of permissions that you want. This would be 666 if you want to write and manipulate files.   Most other ftp clients will have a similar technique where you can see and change the file permissions.

File permissions can be a little esoteric in Linux operating systems, however, as a web programmer, you do not need a deep understanding and you will probably only come across the issue when you are working with text files, or are uploading files to the server.

Short explanation of file permissions

If we look at a directory listing from a Linux server, it will look something like:

```
drwxr-xr-x   6 eva          users        1024 Jun  8 16:46 reports
-rw-------   1 eva          users        1564 Apr 28 14:35 splus
-rw-------   1 eva          users        1119 Apr 28 16:00 splus2
-rw-r--r--   1 eva          users        9753 Sep 27 11:14
ssh_known_hosts
-rw-r--r--   1 eva          users        4131 Sep 21 15:23
swoutput.php
-rw-r--r--   1 eva          users       94031 Sep  1 16:07 fishing.php
```

What does it all mean?

* The first column gives the type of the file (e.g., directory or ordinary file) and the file permissions.

* The second column is the number of links to the file.

* The third and fourth columns are the user who owns the file and the group of users to which the file belongs. You almost certainly do not need to worry about groups, as you probably only belong to the default group 'users'.

* The fifth column is the size of the file in bytes.

* The next three columns are the time at which the file was last changed (for a directory, this is the time at which a file in that directory was last created or deleted).

* The last column is the name of the file.

What we are interested in is the collection of letters on the left hand side. You may already know that these letters define permissions, but what do the 'r', 'w' and 'x' actually mean.

You can see that there are 10 slots in the listing. The first slot tells us what type it is and is often a dash (-) meaning it is a regular file. A 'd' is for directory, 'l' is for link, and a 'c' for character device.

The other 9 slots are our three permissions for our three entities. The first three are for the owner, then group, then other.

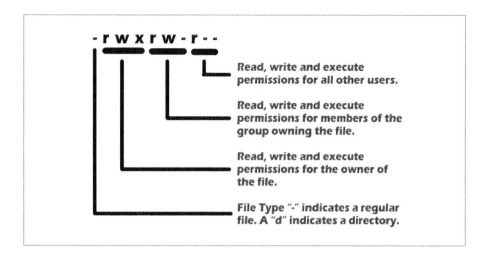

'**r**' 'read' permission. This allows you to read, view, or otherwise open the file depending on context.

'**w**' 'write' permission. This allows you to edit or delete the file.

'**x**' 'execute' permission. This allows you to run the file as a program.

These are collected together in threes representing the three entities of owner, group, and other.

Owner: Typically, the owner is the person who creates the file. The majority of system files are owned by root.

Group: Groups create a way to share files between users, for example, a team of designers who are working together on a project. Groups may also be used to allow access to certain devices, such as DVD drives or printers.

Other: As the name implies, this permission applies to everybody else. We need to pay particular attention to this permission because if it is set to read or write then anybody can view, edit, or delete the file.

So what does 775 and 664 mean?

Quite often, the three elements are displayed using a number that represents the binary value of each of the three elements.

So **rwx** is 7, while **rw-** is 6. Hence, 664 is rw-rw-r-- which means the owner can read and write, the group can read and write, but all other users are read only.

Once your web site is configured and stable, write-protect critical directories and files by changing directory permissions to 755, and file permissions to 644. They should never be 777; the ideal is 644 for files and 755 folders.

Your ftp client will have a way to modify the file permissions, either by ticking boxes for each permission, or by entering a numerical value such as 644.

Working with text files

The typical way in which you will work with a text file is something like:

* Open the file that you are going to work with by associating a file handle.
* Read or write to the file using the file handle.
* Close the file using the file handle.

TASK 1 - Opening a file

Code File: 19_file_handling/file.php

(1) In your text editor create a new PHP web page called **file.php**. If you are using Dreamweaver, remove all the html code from the page.

(2) Enter the following:

```
1.   <?php
2.
3.   //file.php
4.
5.           $filename = "data.txt";
6.
7.           if  (  !$fp = fopen($filename, "r") )
8.           {
9.               die ("cannot open file $filename");
10.          }
11.
12.          fclose($fp);
13.
14. ?>
```

The $fp is the file pointer that is used for reading and writing operations.

(3) Upload the file to your web space and run it in your web browser and see what happens.

(4) Create a text file called data.txt and upload it to the web space and run **file.php** in your browser again.

The fopen() function

fopen() () takes two arguments. The first argument is the file name. The file name can be relative to the location of this PHP file, or absolute with the full path name of the file in the form "/myfiles/www/data.txt" or it can be a url or an ftp path name to a different server.

The second argument is the mode, which can be:

r   Read only access

r+ Read and write access

w Write access only

w+ Read and write access, any existing data will be lost if the file does not exit and PHP will attempt to create the file

a Appending only. Write to the end of the file, if the file does not exist then **PHP** will attempt to create the file

a+ Open for reading and appending. Data is written to the end of the file, if the file does not exist, then PHP will attempt to create it.

TASK 2 - Writing to the file

Code File: 19_file_handling/file1.php

(1) In **file.php**, change the mode from r to w+

(2) Before the **fclose()** line enter the following:

fwrite($fp, "this is some text);

(3) Your file will now look like:

```
1.  <?php
2.
3.          //file1.php
4.
5.          $filename = "data.txt";
6.
7.          if (  !$fp = fopen($filename, "w+") )
8.          {
9.              die ("cannot open file $data.txt");
10.         }
11.
12.         fwrite($fp, "this is some text");
13.
14.         fclose($fp);
15.
16. ?>
```

(4) Upload the file to your web server, and run **file.php** in your web browser. When you examine the data.txt file you should see the extra text.

TASK 3 - Reading from the file

Code File: 19_file_handling/file2.php

There are a number of ways of reading the contents of a file. One method is to read a block of characters into an array until the end of the file is reached as follows:

```
1.  while (!feof($file_handle) ) {
2.          $line_of_text[] = fgets($file_handle);
3.  }
```

fgets($file_handle) means to read a line or until an end of line is found.

(1) Modify **file.php** with the above code added and an extra bit of code to display the text in the array.

The **file.php** code will now look like:

```php
1.  <?php
2.
3.          //file2.php
4.
5.          $filename = "data.txt";
6.
7.          if  (  !$fp = fopen("data.txt", "w+") )
8.          {
9.              die ("cannot open file $data.txt");
10.         }
11.
12.         fwrite($fp, "this is some text\r\n");
13.         fwrite($fp, "this is some more text\r\n");
14.         fwrite($fp, "this is even more text\r\n");
15.
16.         fclose($fp);
17.
18.         $file_handle = fopen("data.txt", "rb");
19.
20.         while (!feof($file_handle) ) {
21.             $line_of_text[] = fgets($file_handle);
22.         }
23.
24.         fclose($file_handle);
25.
26.         foreach ($line_of_text as $key => $value) {
27.             echo($value . "<br/>");
28.         }
29.
30. ?>
```

(2) Upload the file to the web server and run it in your web browser. It should display the text that was entered into the file.

File and folder manipulation

There are a number of PHP functions that can be used to work with files and folders.

Some of these functions may need permissions to be modified on the server for them to work.

copy()   copy a file

rename()   rename a file

file_exists()   shows if the file exists

basename()   returns the base part of a file name

Example file operations

The following example illustrates a way of displaying files that are within a folder. The base folder is defined using **getcwd()** and then all files are echoed to the web page except for the name of the current running script. This technique is something that could be used as the basis of a file explorer.

```php
1.  <?php
2.
3.  //Simple example to list files in a given folder
4.  //This will display all the content of $basefolder
5.  //but will not display the folder references . and ..
6.  //nor will it display current file name.
7.
8.  $basefolder = getcwd();
9.
10. if ($handle = opendir($basefolder)) {
11.     echo "<p>Directory entries for <strong>$basefolder</strong></p>";

12.
13.     /* This is the correct way to loop over the directory. */
14.     while (false !== ($entry = readdir($handle))) {
15.
16.         if ( ($entry != ".") && ($entry != "..") &&
17.             ($entry != basename($_SERVER['PHP_SELF'])) )
18.         {
19.             echo "$entry<br/>";
20.         }
21.     }
22.
23.     closedir($handle);
24.
25. }
26. ?>
```

Code File: 19_file_handling/filelist.php

Uploading files to a web server

A file upload is quite often a feature of web applications, and **PHP** has the functionality to do this.

The web page below (**upload.html**) includes a form showing the basic features:

```
1.  <html>
2.  <head>
3.  <title>Upload form</title>
4.  </head>
5.  <body>
6.
7.  <br/><br/><br/><br/><br/>
8.
9.  <form action="uploadfile.php" method="post"
        enctype="multipart/form-data">
10.   Your Photo: <input type="file" name="photo" size="25" /><br/><br/>
11.   <input type="submit" name="submit" value="Submit" />
12. </form>
13.
14. </body>
15. </html>
```

Code File: 19_file_handling/upload.html

The points to note are:

* The action of the <form> element is **uploadfile.php** which is the **PHP** file that will contain the script to handle the processing.

* The enctype describes how the form data will be encoded. In this case we are using multipart/form-data meaning that no characters are encoded. This value is required when you are using forms that have a file upload control.

* The method is post.

When you display this page in your browser, you will see a page similar to the following:

Your Photo: [   ] Browse...

Submit

Clicking on the **Browse** button will allow you to select a file from your local computer. Then click on **Submit** will post the data to the PHP file **uploadfile.php** that contains the required code.

In **uploadfile.php** we use the **$_FILES** superglobal variable to return an associative array of items uploaded to the script via the HTTP POST method.

So for the above form we would use **$_FILES['photo']['name']** to access the name of the file.

There are a number of other parameters available as follows:

```
1.  <?php
2.
3.  $_FILES['field_name']['name'];
4.  $_FILES['field_name']['size'];
5.  $_FILES['field_name']['type'];
6.  $_FILES['field_name']['tmp_name'];
7.  $_FILES['field_name']['error'];
8.
9.  ?>
```

When the file has been uploaded, it is uploaded to a temporary directory defined by $_FILES['field_name']['tmp_name']

The temporary directory is defined in the **php.ini** file as temp_dir and should exist in your **php.ini** file.

If you are having problems uploading, check that the temp_dir is correctly defined.

Once the file is in the temp_dir we can then move it using the php **move_uploaded_file** function. Note that this function requires the full path of the source file and the destination file.

An example of an upload script is shown below. The script first checks that a file has been selected and then checks that the file is less than 1 Mbytes. It then checks if the file has the correct file extension, which in this case has to be either png, jpg or gif files.

If it passes the tests, the file is moved out of the temp directory into the final directory. The destination folder for this example is the same location folder as the script itself. You can move the script to any folder providing the folder exists.

You may come across permission problems, as the destination folder will require write access in which case try setting folder permissions to 771 or 751.

```php
1.  <?php
2.
3.  $message = "";
4.
5.  //If a file was uploaded:
6.  if($_FILES['photo']['name'])
7.  {
8.
9.     //if no errors...
10.    if(!$_FILES['photo']['error'])
11.    {
12.       //Get the name of the temp file
13.       $temp_file_name = $_FILES['photo']['tmp_name'];
14.       //Defines max file size of 1 Mbytes
15.       if($_FILES['photo']['size'] > (1024000))
16.       {
17.           $message .= 'Your file is too large';
18.       }
19.       else
20.       {
21.
22.         if ( !preg_match('/\\.(png|jpg|gif)$/i',
                $_FILES['photo']['name']) )
23.         {
24.             $message .= "Wrong file type.";
25.         }
26.         else
27.         {
28.         //Move the file to the uploads folder
29.         //full path of destination folder is the current folder name
30.           $destination = getcwd() . "/";
31.           move_uploaded_file($_FILES['photo']['tmp_name'],
                $destination.$_FILES['photo']['name']);
32.             $message .= 'The file has been uploaded.';
33.         }
34.
35.       }
36.
37.    }
38.    //If there is an error
39.    else
40.    {
41.        //Define the returned message
42.       $message .= 'Your upload triggered the following error:  '.
              $_FILES['photo']['error'];
43.    }
44. }
45.
46. echo($message);
47.
48. echo("<br/>");
49. echo("<br/>");
50. echo("====================================<br/>");
51. echo("Debug information<br/>");
52. echo("Name of upload file: " . $_FILES['photo']['name'] . "<br/>");
```

```
53. echo("<br/>");
54. echo("Name of temp file " . $temp_file_name) . "<br/>";
55. echo("<br/>");
56. echo("Destination: " . $destination.$_FILES['photo']['name']) .
       "<br/>";
57. echo("=====================================<br/>");
58. echo("<br/>");
59. echo("<br/>");
60. //echo(phpinfo());
61.
62. ?>
```

Code File: 19_file_handling/uploadfile.php

NOTE: *That the maximum file upload will be restricted by the **php.ini** settings of upload_max_filesize and post_max_size.*

```
;------------------------------------------------
; Maximum allowed size for uploaded files.
upload_max_filesize = 8M

; Must be greater than or equal to upload_max_filesize
post_max_size = 8M
;------------------------------------------------
```

Summary

This Chapter has shown how to handle text files. We can open, read and write text files and perform various file operations. We have also seen how to upload files to the web server. Working with files is a straightforward process and has many uses in a web application.

Topics for Review

[1] Explain what r, w and x represent in file permissions.

[2] What is the enctype value in a <form> tag used for uploading files?

[3] Where is the setting for the maximum allowed size for uploaded files?

[4] How do you open a file using PHP?

20 - Regular Expressions and Data Validation

What is in this Chapter?

* Regular expression structure.
* Some examples of regular expressions.
* Data validation methods.

Regular expressions are patterns that match strings. You use them to create complex true or false tests on strings. So if you want to know if a string contains a particular arrangement of characters, then regular expressions can do that.

In addition, they can extract substrings and make complex substitutions.

Regular expressions are very important in web development as we use them to **validate** data inputs to prevent someone entering data in the database that may cause harm. It is possible to write a very complex validation filter with a regular expression in just one line of code. For example, you may want to restrict surnames to being 3 to 10 characters long, with the characters being in the range of a to z, hyphen and single quote, but no others.

The two functions that we are interested in are **preg_match** and **preg_split**

preg_match will return true or false depending on whether the pattern is matching in a string, whereas **preg_split** will split a string into an array depending on the pattern.

An example of a simple regular expression would be:

```
1.  <?php
2.  $keywords = preg_split("/\s+/", "php  regular expressions");
3.  print_r( $keywords );
4.  ?>
```

The above will split a string into an array based on spaces in the string.

The output will be something like:

```
Array ( [0] => php [1] => regular [2] => expressions )
```

This shows that the first element is 'php' the second element is 'regular' and the third element is 'expressions'

The **preg_split** function looks like this:

```
1.  <?php
2.  array preg_split ( string $pattern , string $subject, [ optional fla
    gs ] );
3.  ?>
```

preg_split, takes a pattern to search for together with an input string and returns an array.

Meta characters

Meta characters are characters have special meaning within the pattern:

Character		Meaning
\	Back slash	Escape character
^		Indicates the beginning of a string
$	Dollar	Indicates the end of a string
.	Dot	Indicates any single character except a new line
|		Or
[	Left square	Start of a class
]	Right square	End of a class
(	Round left	End of a sub pattern
)	Round right	End of a sub pattern
{	Curly left	Start of a quantifier
}	Curly right	End of a quantifier

A pattern can be made up of **literal** characters. A literal is a pattern that means exactly what is written. So a pattern of **ce** will find a match in the word **reception** and in the word **services**.

Meta characters are special characters that have a meaning beyond their literal value.

The dot character means any single character except a newline so **ce.** will match cep and ces in the words **reception** and **services**.

If we wanted the dot character to be a dot character rather than a meta character, we place a \ in front of it.

Quantifiers

Character	Character
?	0 or 1
*	0 or more
+	1 or more
{x}	Exactly x occurrences
{x,y}	Between x and y exclusive
{x,)	At least x occurrences

Quantifiers are characters that allow for multiple occurrences so a* will match zero or more a's that is a, aa, aaa and so on. a? will match zero or 1 a

Character Classes

Class	Shortcut	Meaning
[0-9]	\d	Any digit
[\f\r\t\n\v]	\s	Any white space
[A-Za-z0-9_]	\w	Any word character
[^0-9]	\D	Not a digit
[^\f\r\t\n\v]	\S	Not white space
[^A-Za-z0-9_]	\W	Not a word character

Character classes are really shortcuts to the more common types of patterns that are used so **\s** is any white space, **\d** represents all digits or **[0-9]** and so on.

Notice that we can use the curly brackets quantifiers with the character classes to represent a series of characters, for example **[0-9]{3,5}** means any 3 to 5 digits in length, or just **\d{3,5}** to represent the same thing.

Some match examples

Example - simple search

Let's search the string "Hello World!" for the letters "ll":

```
1.  <?php
2.  //-----------------------------------------------
3.  if (preg_match("/ll/", "Hello World!", $matches)) {
4.      echo "<br/>Match was found <br />";
5.      echo $matches[0];
6.  }
7.  //-----------------------------------------------
8.  ?>
```

The letters "ll" exist in "Hello", so **preg_match** returns 1 and the first element of the $matches variable is filled with the string that matched the pattern.

The above example will display something like:

> 11

preg_match() returns the number of times pattern matches. That will be either 0 times (no match) or 1 time because **preg_match()** will stop searching after the first match.

preg_match_all() will continue until it reaches the end of subject. **preg_match()** returns FALSE if an error occurred.

Example - search with following characters

The regular expression in the next example is looking for the letters "ll", but looking for them with the following characters:

```php
1.  <?php
2.  //--------------------------------------------------
3.  if (preg_match("/ll.*/", "The History of Halloween", $matches)) {
4.     echo "<br/>Match was found <br />";
5.     echo $matches[0];
6.  }
7.  //--------------------------------------------------
8.  ?>
```

The above example will display something like:

> lloween

Example - validate phone function

The following is an example of how you might use a regular expression in a function to validate numbers such as a phone number:

```
1.  <?php
2.  //-------------------------------------------------
3.  /**
4.  * Purpose : Check input for particular characters
5.  * Only allow 0-9 , and space
6.  * returns false if invalid characters were found
7.  * @return boolean
8.  */
9.  function validate_phone($words) {
10.
11.         // The ^ defines the start of the string so the string
12.         // from the start has to have 0-9 or a space
13.         if ( preg_match( "/[^0-9 ]/", $words, $array ) )
14.             return false;      //invalid characters
15.         else
16.             return true;       //valid characters
17. }
18. ?>
```

Example - validate input function

The following is another example of using a regular expression to check for certain characters and numbers:

```
1.  <?php
2.  //-------------------------------------------
3.  /**
4.  * Purpose : Check input for particular  characters
5.  * Only allow a - z, A - Z , 0-9 , and space
6.  * returns false if invalid characters were found
7.  * @return boolean
8.  */
9.  function is_valid_input($words) {
10.
11.         if ( preg_match( "/[^0-9a-zA-Z, ]/", $words, $array ) )
12.             return false;  //invalid characters
13.         else
14.             return true;  //valid characters
15.
16. }
17. ?>
```

Exercise 20.1

Write a regular expression that looks for the following words in a phrase and displays a message to say if any of the phrases exist in the string.

Cow
pig
horse

Exercise 20.2

Write a regular expression that counts the number of words in a phrase. You might want to use preg_split for this as it returns an array of results.

Exercise 20.3

Divide a sentence into words and display each word on a separate line.

Code File: 20_regular_expression_validation/regular_expression_exercises.php

Validation input for PHP 5.2.0 onwards

PHP 5.2.0 onwards includes the **filter_var()** function that filters an input with a defined filter.

http://php.net/manual/en/filter.examples.validation.php

with filter types as listed here:

http://www.php.net/manual/en/filter.filters.php

As an example, there is a filter that is used to validate email addresses, **FILTER_VALIDATE_EMAIL. ,**

The following example shows how to use this in the **filter_var** expression:

```
1.  <?php
2.  //Validate an email address in PHP 5.2.0 onwards
3.
4.  $email_address = "me@example.com";
5.  if (filter_var($email_address, FILTER_VALIDATE_EMAIL)) {
6.     // The email address is valid
7.  } else {
8.     // The email address is not valid
9.  }
10. ?>
```

There are a whole range of different filters and filter flags for validation and sanitizing your data inputs; these make common data validation and filtering a lot easier than using regular expressions.

The validation filters include:

FILTER_VALIDATE_BOOLEAN
FILTER_NULL_ON_FAILURE
FILTER_VALIDATE_EMAIL
FILTER_VALIDATE_FLOAT
FILTER_VALIDATE_INT
FILTER_VALIDATE_IP
FILTER_VALIDATE_REGEXP
FILTER_VALIDATE_URL

These are used to check if a value matches a particular type.

Sanitize filters are used to remove or encode certain groups of characters from an input to protect your application from characters that may be potentially harmful. Each sanitize filter contains a set of flags that define what the filter should do.

For example, **FILTER_SANITIZE_STRING** is used to strip tags, or to strip and to encode special characters from an input string.

```
1.  <?php
2.  $name = "<strong>Paul Gibbs</strong> <script</script>";
3.  echo ( filter_var($name, FILTER_SANITIZE_STRING) );
4.  ?>
```

The above example will display "Paul Gibbs" without any of the html codes – it strips out all HTML.

Validation for Email Forms

When we work with a form that sends emails, we need to do a number of tests on the user input to prevent spam.

An incorrectly written form can allow someone to inject code so that your web server sends emails to other recipients using your server as a relay.

At first glance, it is not clear how a form can send emails to another email address, but it is possible to enter in bcc and cc into text fields and hence cause the email to send to those addresses.

You should treat an email form in the same way as for any user input where you validate and filter the inputs.

Validate email address

You should test any field that requires an email address to make sure it matches the format of an email address.

This can be done using a function like this:

```
1.  //--------------------------------------------------------
2.  //validate email address
3.  function is_valid_email($emailaddress)
4.  {
5.      if (filter_var( $emailaddress, FILTER_VALIDATE_EMAIL )) {
6.          return true;
7.      } else {
8.          return false;
9.      }
10. }
```

This uses the **filter_var()** function with the **FILTER_VALIDATE_EMAIL** parameter.

Validate text entered in other text fields

We can use functions as shown below to validate and check other fields. These examples use regular expressions and you can make them fit whatever input you want. They are similar to other validation scripts that we have shown previously.

```
1.  //---------------------------------------------------
2.  //Validate name as 3 to 20 characters a-Z ' and - characters
3.  function is_valid_name($words)
4.  {
5.      if (filter_var( "/[^a-zA-Z -\']{3,20}/",
                FILTER_VALIDATE_REGEXP ))
6.          return false;
7.      else
8.          return true;
9.  }
10.
11. //---------------------------------------------------
12. //Validate name as 0 to 255 characters a-Z ' and - characters
13. function is_valid_comments($words)
14. {
15.     if (filter_var( "/[^a-zA-Z -\']{0,255}/",
                FILTER_VALIDATE_REGEXP ))
16.         return false;
17.     else
18.         return true;
19. }
```

Remove line feed characters

In order to send emails the user needs to be able to put a new line code into the script so we must look for and remove any new line codes using something like the following function:

```
1.  //------------------------------------------------
2.  // Remove characters that are not required
3.  function process_email_text($text)
4.  {
5.
6.      $find = array(
7.          "/\r/",
8.          "/\n/",
9.          "/\x0a/",
10.         "/\x0d/"
11.         );
12.
13.     $name = preg_replace($find, ' ', $text);
14.
15.     return $name;
16.
17. }
```

Code File: 20_regular_expression_validation/process_email_text.php

You would apply this function to each of your input fields.

Remove characters that are specific to email spamming

We should also look for specific email codes such as bcc: for sending blind copy emails, cc: for copy emails and so on.

This can be done with a function like this:

```
1.  //------------------------------------------------
2.  // Check email text for any spam values
3.  function process_spam($text)
4.  {
5.
6.      $find = array(
7.          "Content-Type:",
8.          "mime-version",
9.          "bcc:",
10.         "cc:",
11.         "to:"
12.         );
13.
14.     foreach ($find as $value) {
15.         if ( stripos($text, $value) > 0 )
```

```
16.               {
17.                   return true;
18.               }
19.     }
20.
21.     return false;
22.
23. }
```

Code File: 20_regular_expression_validation/process_spam.php

In this example, a list of words is checked. If it finds a word, it returns true and will not send an email.

This can be used in the following way:

```
1.  if (process_spam($emailText))
2.  {
3.        // Do not send email
4.  }
5.  else
6.  {
7.        // Do something else
8.  }
```

Captcha Example

Web pages are very prone to automatic attacks from remote programs because a web page is available for the entire world to see. Automatic programs scan websites for certain types of forms that may be vulnerable. They are able to create data that is posted to the form to cause issues with databases and emailing.

Captcha forms are a very common method of checking that a submission is from a human rather than an automated program. **Captcha** scripts use dynamically created images that display a random string. The user must enter the random numbers or text into a text field for checking by the PHP script. It is difficult for automatic programs to read images correctly, so this is a good method to protect web submission forms.

Captcha scripts are often seen in forms that send emails and we show a simple example here.

First, create a new file called **captcha.php** and copy in the following code:

```
1.  <?php
2.
3.  session_start();
4.
5.  $text = rand(10000,99999);
6.  $_SESSION["vercode"] = $text;
7.
8.  $height = 25;
9.  $width = 65;
10. $image_p = imagecreate($width, $height);
11. $black = imagecolorallocate($image_p, 0, 0, 0);
12. $white = imagecolorallocate($image_p, 255, 255, 255);
13. $font_size = 14;
14.
15. imagestring($image_p, $font_size, 5, 5, $text, $white);
16. imagejpeg($image_p, null, 80);
17.
18. ?>
```

Code File: 20_regular_expression_validation/captcha.php

This generates a random number from 10000 to 99999 and assigns it to a session variable. It then creates a 25 x 65 pixel image with black background and white text. A new random image is created when the page is refreshed.

Next, we create a web form. Create a new file called **captcha_form.php** as shown below with the following code:

```
1.  <form action="captcha_ver.php" method="post">
2.  <p>
3.  Comment:<br/><textarea name="comment"></textarea>
4.  </p>
5.  <p>
6.  Enter Code <img src="captcha.php"><br/>
7.  <input type="text" name="vercode" />
8.  </p>
9.  <p>
10. <input type="submit" name="Submit" value="Submit" />
11. </p>
12. </form>
```

Code File: 20_regular_expression_validation/captcha_form.php

This form has a comment text area but the form can include any fields that you require. It also has the randomly generated image, a box for the verification code and a submit button.

Now we create the code that runs when the form is submitted. Create a new file called **captcha_ver.php** and copy in the following code:

```
1.  <?php
2.
3.  session_start();
4.  if ($_POST["vercode"] != $_SESSION["vercode"] OR
        $_SESSION["vercode"]=='')  {
5.      echo  '<strong>Incorrect verification code.</strong>';
6.  } else {
7.      // add form data processing code here
8.      echo  '<strong>Verification successful.</strong>';
9.  }
10.
11. ?>
```

Code File: 20_regular_expression_validation/captcha_ver.php

This code checks if the verification code you entered matches the code that was randomly generated.

Summary

In this Chapter, we covered regular expressions that are an important part of web form development enabling you to validate data. **PHP** can use the **preg_match** function or in later versions of **PHP,** you use the **filter_var** function. The **filter_var** function provides a simpler way of coding data validation and filtering.

Getting to grips with regular expressions can be difficult but searching on the internet should return a number of websites that give good examples.

Topics for Review

[1] What is the main use of regular expressions in PHP scripts?

[2] Show how to validate an email address using the filter_var() function.

[3] Explain the purpose of a captcha script

21 - PHP Security

What is in this Chapter?

* Apache web server php.ini file.
* Scripting security.

This Chapter discusses some of the issues that you will need to consider for security of your scripts and web site. We look at server configuration that helps to improve security and issues on PHP code security.

Web Server Configuration parameters

The configuration of the Apache web server is in a **php.ini** file. There are many parameters in the **php.ini** file, but we are only interested in ones that can help to improve the security of our PHP scripts. If you make changes to the **php.ini** file, you should stop and start the web server to make them take effect. However, you may not have access to the **php.ini** file or you may only be able to change certain settings because you are on a shared hosting system with other users.

safe_mode

No longer relevant to PHP 7 but is worth mentioning as a historical aside.
Always set **safe_mode** = on and set **safe_mode_gid** = off

Safe mode was deprecated in **PHP 5.3** and removed in **PHP 5.4.** Some say it was an ill-conceived idea and never really worked. It was a method to try to solve the problem of shared security to stop users accessing other user's files on the same-shared server. However, it could easily be overcome and hence the decision to deprecate it.

expose_php

Set **expose_php** to off

This parameter defines if the PHP version number is sent back to the browser in the header. Normally set this to off to hide the PHP version.

register_globals

It is recommended that you always set **register_globals** to off. This is the default setting in the **php.ini** file.

register_globals is a setting that registers the $REQUEST array's elements as variables. What this means is that anything passed as GET, POST or COOKIE becomes accessible as a variable.

So, http://www.domain.com/vars.php?myvar=123

without any further coding will automatically make any variable called **$myvar** to the value of 123.

Therefore, it is possible to modify variables in the code if you know what you are doing.

Leaving **register_globals** set to on is a security issue that can be exploited, and hence the default setting is off.

display_errors

.Set **display_errors** = off in production systems.

The **display_errors** parameter defines if errors are reported back to the user. In a production system, it is better not to have errors output to the user because it may be possible for them to gather information about database tables, connections and so on, which a user may then be able to exploit.

log_errors

Set **log_errors** = on and set **error_log** to a particular directory to find any errors.

This would be used in conjunction with **display_errors** = on. In a production system, you would normally set the **log_errors** to off.

PHP Code scripting security

XSS

XSS (Cross Site Scripting) is a method where the user inputs data to a form where the input contains scripts such as JavaScript like this:

<script>some JavaScript ...</script>

The JavaScript can cause the web page to redirect to another page or perform some other action. It can be stopped by validating and filtering the data and by converting the input to HTML before it is stored in the database.

So if you have a 'comments' form where there is an input box for your name, you might enter in the form something like:

<script>window.location='http://www.google.com/'</script>

If this is saved into a database without change, when it is rendered on a web page the page will redirect to somewhere else.

It is relatively straightforward to prevent by filtering out **<** and **>** characters along with other characters that should not be stored in the database. Also converting to HTML with the **htmlspecialchars** function will make the script unusable.

For example:

```
1.  $input = "<script>window.location='http://www.google.com/'</script>"
2.  $inputConv = htmlspecialchars($input, ENT_QUOTES);
```

makes the input string into:

```
&lt;script&gt;window.location=&#039;http://www.google.com/&#039;&lt;/
script&gt;
```

The **htmlspecialchars** function:

   '&' (ampersand) becomes '&'
   '"' (double quote) becomes '"' when ENT_NOQUOTES is not set.
   ''' (single quote) becomes ''' (or ') only when ENT_QUOTES is set.
   '<' (less than) becomes '<'
   '>' (greater than) becomes '>'

SQL Injection

SQL Injection is where a user exploits badly written PHP code by pushing SQL into input fields. This can be overcome by using parameterized queries in PHP and escaping characters such as quote marks and converting the input to HTML before it is passed to the database.

The vulnerability that is exploited is where SQL statements are built up by adding strings together. Using parameterized queries (or in the case of PHP these are called PDO) does not use this technique and hence helps to prevent SQL Injection. PDO also can define data types for fields so the data values have to have the correct data types further improving security.

Ways to Counter SQL Injection

The following describes some of the methods to prevent SQL injections, some of which we have already looked at in the descriptions on general PHP coding.

Database Permissions

Set the permissions on the database username / password as tightly as possible. If you are displaying data, there is no need for the user to have INSERT or UPDATE permissions on the database. One solution is to have two users. One with SELECT permissions for displaying data. The other with SELECT, INSERT and UPDATE permissions for interacting with forms that store data in the database.

Test all data input

You should have code that tests all form data and all URL query strings. For example, if you are passing data using a query string, a record id is usually integer, so test that they are actually integer values with a function such as **is_numeric** in PHP.

For example, a store URL may have a URL where a product is referenced like this: /product.php?id=3827

In this case, the id should always be an integer that you can test like this:

```
1.  if (  !is_numeric( $_GET['id'] ) ) {
2.     exit();
3.  }
```

Use correct data types and data sizes in the database

This means that if you have a column that stores names for example, the data size for the column only needs to be, say, 40 characters. There is no need to have a data size any larger than required and the data types should match the data you are storing.

Convert text to html

Before storing text in a database, convert it to HTML. This will change inputs such as the JavaScript <script> to its HTML equivalent that cannot be executed on a web page. Otherwise, a script such as:

<script src=http://website.com/xss.js></script>

if saved into a database, would then run the js file on a web page. Converting this to HTML will prevent this.

Filter out any characters that may cause issues, and are not required

Use regular expressions to test for the correct characters for any input.

Use parameterized queries

If you use parameterized queries for connection to the database, you eliminate string concatenation. You should always use parameterized queries rather than constructing the SQL. Ideally, use PDO as the method to connect to the database.

Check characters particularly with username / password

For example, if an entry is a username, it normally does not require any other characters other than a to z and 0 to 9 and it only needs to be say, 8 characters long.

Use the mysqli_real_escape_string

There are certain characters in SQL statements that can have special meaning and will cause a SQL statement to fail. The quote mark for instance. One way to overcome this is to use the **mysqli_real_escape_string** function that will escape characters depending on the character set used.

So, for example, SQL = " SELECT * FROM staff WHERE name = 'O'Reilly' " will fail because of the O'.

Using mysqli_real_escape_string will sort this out.

However, you can avoid all character escaping issues if you use prepared statements and binding as an alternative. This is a much better method and works because bound parameter values are NOT passed via the SQL statement syntax.

Code Injection

Code Injection is where the user enters the code into a PHP script using a form or appending data to a URL and is a more general term than XSS. This is overcome using validation and filtering on the data inputs. Therefore, use **filter_var** or regular expressions to make sure that users do not attempt to input characters that they should not be using.

The type of things a user can do with Code Injection is as described in the section above on XSS where a user might enter some JavaScript into a database. Code injection can happen through web forms or via URLs where the PHP script does not properly validate the data. In an extreme case it is possible for an attacker to execute server code by appending commands onto a URL or by posting server side code into a web form.

Data validation will depend on the particular input that you are testing, so for example, a telephone number should only contain numbers and should not be more than 15 numbers long, or someone's last name should only contain characters of letters a to Z, space, single quotation marks and dashes (-) character and should not be more that 20 characters long.

Here are a couple of examples of functions:

```
1.  //Name is 3 to 20 characters long consisting of a to Z, space, '
        mark and -.
2.  function is_valid_name($input) {
3.
4.      if ( preg_match( "/[^a-zA-Z '-]{3, 20}/", $input, $array ) )
5.          return false;        //invalid characters
6.      else
7.          return true;         //valid characters
8.
9.  }
```

```
1.  //Telephone number is 3 to 15 numbers consisting of 0 - 9
        characters and a space
2.  function is_valid_name($input) {
3.
4.      if ( preg_match( "/[^0-9 ]{3, 15}/", $input, $array ) )
5.          return false;        //invalid characters
6.      else
7.          return true;         //valid characters
8.
9.  }
```

Email Injection

Email injection is where users can inject email headers by entering in **Bcc** or other email parameters into a 'from' address and use that to relay emails through a web form. The built in PHP mail function is not particularly robust and there are other email systems such as **ZendMail**, that you might want to look at if you are going to do a lot of emailing from your website.

When you are using the PHP mail function in the following way:

```
1.  <?php
2.
3.  $to = "to@somewhere.com";
4.  $subject = "PHP Course";
5.  $body = "This is a test email\n\nfrom my website";
6.  $headers = "From: from@somewhereelse.com\r\n";
7.
8.  mail($to, $subject, $body, $headers);
9.
10. ?>
```

The potential vulnerability here is the **$headers** variable.

You might have a text box where you enter an email address and that is processed something like:

```
1.  $headers = "From: $fromAddress\r\n";
```

where **$fromAddress** is read in to the form from the text box.

If the user knows the vulnerability, the user can enter in the text box something like:

```
myadddress@domain.com%0ACc:recipien1t@domain.com,%0ABcc:recipient2@do
main.com
```

where each email address is separated by a line feed '**0x0A**' and we can use **CC** and **BCC** to send to multiple addresses.

Hence, we can use the form to act as a relay to send out multiple emails from someone's website.

This can be prevented by validating the user input for unusual characters using regular expressions or with the **filter_var** function.

Filters

Filters is a method that enables us to validate data that the user inputs. Filters are available in PHP 5.2 onwards and provide an easier way of doing data validation with PHP rather than using regular expressions. .

The Chapter on regular expressions explain filters, an example of which is:

```
1.  if (filter_var($emailaddress, FILTER_VALIDATE_EMAIL)) {
2.      echo 'VALID';
3.  } else {
4.      echo 'NOT VALID';
5.  }
```

This above filter is specifically for validating an email address but other filters provide for filtering of strings or numbers.

Summary

This Chapter covered web server configuration in the php.ini file and various issues to do with PHP code scripting such as cross-site scripting, SQL injection, and email injection. You need to be aware of all of these concepts, as some individuals will deliberately set out to cause you problems. Remember, your web page will be visible to the entire world and some programmers will spend endless amount of time just to break your application for no apparent reason other than the fun of it.

Topics for Review

[1] Explain what is XSS and how it can be countered.

[2] Explain what SQL Injection is and how it can be countered.

[3] What are parameterized queries and why they are so important?

22 - jQuery, Ajax and Bootstrap

What is in this Chapter?

* Using jQuery on web pages.
* Page elements.
* Examples of jQuery.
* AJAX and JSON.
* AJAX and PHP.
* Bootstrap framework.

jQuery is a JavaScript library for client side programming that runs in the web browser. In the past, working with JavaScript caused problems as different browsers implement browser standards differently. Code had to be written for the different browsers so was complicated to maintain and difficult to test.

jQuery is a JavaScript framework that uses a set of pre-defined functions compatible with modern browsers. When you use jQuery, you can be confident that it will work on the majority of browsers that are in use today, and as they release new versions of browsers, updates to jQuery will ensure it works with those as well.

Uses of jQuery

* Creating forms to do calculations on the client PC.
* Validating data before you submit data to a database.
* Creating displays that give a better user experience, for example, displaying error messages in data validation.
* Using the user interface plug ins such as accordion, date picker, progress bar and so on as shown in https://jQueryui.com/
* Using the many plug-ins that have been developed by other developers.
* Developing AJAX applications and working with JSON and PHP.

jQuery on your web page

There are two ways to incorporate jQuery into a web page, the first method is to download the JavaScript file from the jQuery web site, and the second method is to use a hosted JavaScript file.

Download the latest jQuery file

Go to https://www.jquery.com web site, go to the download page and download the latest version of the jQuery file. This will be in the form of a .js file that will be either uncompressed or compressed. The file will be called something like jquery-3.4.1.min.js depending on the jQuery version.

Move the file to a suitable location on your PC so that it will be part of your local web site. Place the **jquery.js** file into a folder called **js.**

For these examples I have renamed the file to just **jquery.js**, but you can leave it with its original filename if you wish.

Create a new web page called **jquery_01.html** and reference the JavaScript file as shown below. As it is located in the js folder, the reference will be **js/jquery.js**

```
1.   <!DOCTYPE html>
2.   <html>
3.   <head>
4.     <meta charset="UTF-8">
5.     <title>jQuery demo</title>
6.     <script src="js/jquery.js" type="text/javascript"></script>
7.   </head>
8.   <body>
9.
10.    Body of web page
11.
12.  </body>
13.  </html>
```

Code File: 22_jquery/jquery_01.html

Displaying this page in your web browser will just display the words "Body of web page" and as such, does not do anything else except to illustrate how the JavaScript is incorporated into the page.

Use a hosted js file such as from Google libraries

The other method is to use a hosted js file. Google places a copy of the jQuery library on their web site to allow you to refer to it. The only disadvantage is that you may want to work from a local computer not connected to the internet. Other than that, there is no real disadvantage.

All the code libraries are all listed at:

https://developers.google.com/speed/libraries/devguide

Look for the jQuery JavaScript snippet and copy it into your own web page. Create a new web page called **jquery_02.html** as follows:

```
1.  <!DOCTYPE html>
2.  <html>
3.  <head>
4.    <meta charset="UTF-8">
5.    <title>jQuery demo</title>
6.    <script src="https://ajax.googleapis.com/ajax/libs/jquery/3.4.1/j
    query.min.js"></script>
7.  </head>
8.  <body>
9.
10.   Body of web page
11.
12.  </body>
13.  </html>
```

Code File: 22_jquery/jquery_02.html

Displaying this page in your web browser will just display the words "Body of web page" and as such doesn't do anything else except to illustrate how the JavaScript is incorporated into the page.

Using jQuery

In this example, we will display a simple alert box to illustrate how to use jQuery.

jQuery requires the complete web page to be loaded before any JavaScript is run because it needs to have access to all elements of the document object model (DOM).

In jQuery, the preferred method is to use the ready method as follows:

```
1.  $(document).ready(function() {
2.  //runs any code here when ready
3.  });
```

A simplified version of this is:

```
1.  $(function() {
2.          //runs any code here when ready
3.  });
```

(1) Create a new html web page called **jquery_03.html**

(2) Remove all HTML code from the web page and then copy the following into it:

```
1.  <!DOCTYPE html>
2.  <html>
3.  <head>
4.      <meta charset="UTF-8">
5.      <title>jQuery demo</title>
6.      <script src="js/jquery.js" type="text/javascript"></script>
7.  </head>
8.  <body>
9.
10.         <script text="text/javascript">
11.         $(document).ready(function() {
12.           alert('web page is ready');
13.             });
14.         </script>
15.
16. </body>
17. </html>
```

Code File: 22_jquery/jquery_03.html

(3) Load the web page on to the web server and test it in a browser. It should display the popup box with 'web page is ready'.

The code $(name) is how jQuery identifies elements in the web browser. In this case, the 'name' is **document** that refers to the entire page. The ready() function is then applied to this. The argument of the ready() function is a function, in this case we are using a function definition without a name called an anonymous function.

So the anonymous function is called when the complete web page is available and ready.

Be careful of the syntax for this, in particular the last two brackets are curly bracket followed by ordinary bracket followed by semicolon. This technique uses **callback functions**, which is a function passed as a parameter to another function and you will see this method used a great deal in jQuery and AJAX calls.

Selecting Page Elements

We have seen that we use $(document) to select the web document itself. To select other page elements we use CSS selectors in place of document. This can be used to show and hide elements on a page or to perform other functions on the elements.

#name selects the element with an id of 'name'

.name selects every element with a class of 'name'

name selects every element of 'name' type, e.g. 'p' selects paragraphs, or 'a' selects links

So to select every link we use $('a') and to select the element with an id of caption we use $('#caption') Note that the element is enclosed in quote marks.

So, if you have an input box called miles:

<input type="text" name="miles" size="5" maxlength="10" **id="miles"** />

To select the value of what was entered in the miles box:

```
1.  if ($('#miles').val() > 0) {
2.      miles = $('#miles').val();
3.  }
```

Event Handling

Event handling is the process where we can monitor when the user takes some sort of action such as clicking a submit button, rolling the mouse over an image, or changing the value in a text box.

Event handlers use **selection.eventType(function);**

The selection would be $('.name') or $('a') or $('#name') while the eventType would depend on the element so it would be click, submit, mouseover and so on.

The following example illustrates two events, one that is a mouseover event on an image with a class (myPicture) and the other is a button click event with an id (loadfile).

```
1.  <!DOCTYPE html>
2.  <html>
3.  <head>
4.  <meta charset="UTF-8" />
```

```
5.   <title>Example event</title>
6.   <script
7.   src="https://ajax.googleapis.com/ajax/libs/jquery/3.4.1/jquery.min.j
     s"></script>
8.   </head>
9.
10.  <body>
11.
12.  <script type="text/javascript">
13.      $(document).ready(function(){
14.
15.          //alert("ready");
16.
17.          $(".myPicture").mouseover(function() {
18.              alert("Mouse over function called");
19.          });
20.
21.          $("#loadfile").click(function(){
22.              alert("Button clicked");
23.          });
24.
25.      });
26.  </script>
27.
28.  <img src="image.jpg" width="100px" height="100px"
         class="myPicture"/>
29.
30.  <br/>
31.
32.  <input type="button" id="loadfile" name="loadfile"
         value="Load File" />
33.
34.  </body>
35.  </html>
```

Code File: 22_jquery/event01.html

As in the previous example, we wait until the document has been loaded using the ready function before we define the events. When you click on the button, you should see an alert box and when you roll the mouse over the image, you should see another alert box.

Other mouse events that you may want to use are:

.click()   Click Event
.dblclick   Double Click
.focusout()   Focus out
.hover   Enters and leaves the element
.mousedown()   Mouse Down
.mouseenter()   Mouse enters an element
.mouseleaver() Mouse leaves an element

.mousemove()	Mouse move
.mouseout()	Mouse out
.mouseover()	Mouse over
.mouseup()	Mouse up
.toggle()	Alternate clicks.

A simple calculator

We can use jQuery to create a **car fuel calculator** to illustrate some of these points.

(1) Create a new web page called **jquery_04.html**

(2) Remove any HTML from the page and copy the following text:

```
1.   <!DOCTYPE html>
2.   <html>
3.   <head>
4.      <meta charset="UTF-8">
5.      <title>jQuery demo</title>
6.      <script src="js/jquery.js" type="text/javascript"></script>
7.   </head>
8.   <body>
9.
10.     <script text="text/javascript">
11.     $(document).ready(function() {
12.
13.         $('#fuelcost').submit(function() {
14.
15.         var miles, mpg, cost, validate, costpergallon,
                costpermile, total, message;
16.
17.             validate = true;
18.             message = '';
19.
20.             if ($('#miles').val() > 0) {
21.                 miles = $('#miles').val();
22.             }
23.             else
24.             {
25.                 message = 'Enter miles\r\n';
26.                 validate = false;
27.             }
28.
29.             if ($('#mpg').val() > 0) {
30.                 mpg = $('#mpg').val();
31.             }
32.             else
33.             {
34.                 message += 'Enter mpg';
35.                 validate = false;
36.             }
```

```
37.
38.             if ($('#cost').val() > 0) {
39.                 cost = $('#cost').val();
40.             }
41.             else
42.             {
43.                 cost = '140.9';
44.             }
45.
46.             if (validate == true)
47.             {
48.                 costpergallon = (cost * 4.5460951) / 100;
49.                 costpermile = costpergallon / mpg;
50.                 total = (miles * costpermile);
51.
52.                 alert(total);
53.                 return false;
54.             }
55.             else
56.             {
57.                 alert(message);
58.                 return false;
59.             }
60.         });
61.     });
62. </script>
63.
64. <form action="calculator.php" method="post" id="fuelcost">
65. <p>Miles: <input type="text" name="miles" size="5"
            maxlength="10" id="miles" /></p>
66. <p>MPG: <input type="text" name="mpg" size="5"
            maxlength="10" id="mpg" /></p>
67. <p>Pence / Litre - Optional (140.9p): <input type="text"
            name="cost" size="5" maxlength="10" id="cost" /></p>
68. <p><input type="submit" name="submit" value="Calculate!" /></p>
69. </form>
70.
71. </body>
72. </html>
```

Code File: 22_jquery/jquery_04.html

(3) Upload the page to your web server and test in your web browser.

This example uses an event handler to monitor for the submit button being pressed.

The form will post to the non-existent **calculator.php** file but we have set return false so that it does not ever post to that file.

A Calculator for Print Runs

Another example in the code available for download is a printer calculator

Code File: 22_jquery/printercalculator/

This is a little more extensive than the calculator example shown above as it introduces selections from the drop down boxes.

DOM Manipulation

One of the uses of jQuery is DOM (document object model) manipulation. What this means is that we can control attributes of the DOM using JavaScript, so for example we can hide or show table elements or divs depending on certain conditions, or we can change the colour of elements depending on selections.

The following example illustrates using a drop down list to show and hide divs and to show and hide tr elements of a table

(1) Create a new web page called **jquery_05.html**

(2) Remove any HTML from the page and copy the following text:

```
1.   <!DOCTYPE html>
2.   <html>
3.   <head>
4.   <meta charset="UTF-8" />
5.     <script src="js/jquery.js"></script>
6.   </head>
7.   <body>
8.
9.   <script language="javascript" type="text/javascript">
10.  $(document).ready(function () {
11.    $("#options").change(function () {
12.       $("#options option:selected").each(function ()
13.          {
14.
15.             if($(this).attr("id") == "TEXTAREA")
16.                {
17.                   $("#divtextarea").show();
18.                      $("#divtextbox").hide();
19.                      $("#divcheckbox").hide();
20.                      $("#divdropdown").hide();
21.                      $('.member').show();
22.                }
23.
24.             if($(this).attr("id") == "TEXTBOX")
25.                {
26.                      $("#divtextbox").show();
27.                      $("#divtextarea").hide();
```

```
28.                         $("#divcheckbox").hide();
29.                         $("#divdropdown").hide();
30.                         $('.member').show();
31.                 }
32.
33.             if($(this).attr("id") == "CHECKBOX")
34.                 {
35.                         $("#divtextbox").hide();
36.                         $("#divtextarea").hide();
37.                         $("#divcheckbox").show();
38.                         $("#divdropdown").hide();
39.                         $('.member').hide();
40.                 }
41.
42.             if($(this).attr("id") == "DROPDOWN")
43.                 {
44.                         $("#divtextbox").hide();
45.                         $("#divtextarea").hide();
46.                         $("#divcheckbox").hide();
47.                         $("#divdropdown").show();
48.                         $('.member').hide();
49.                 }
50.
51.             if($(this).attr("id") == "SELECT")
52.                 {
53.                         $("#divtextarea").hide();
54.                         $("#divtextbox").hide();
55.                         $("#divcheckbox").hide();
56.                         $("#divdropdown").hide();
57.                         $('.member').hide();
58.                 }
59.
60.         });
61.     }).change();
62. });
63. </script>
64.
65. <select name="options" id="options" class="OptionsStyle">
66.     <option value="SELECT" id="SELECT">SELECT</option>
67.     <option value="TEXTBOX" id="TEXTBOX">TEXTBOX</option>
68.     <option value="TEXTAREA" id="TEXTAREA">TEXTAREA</option>
69.     <option value="CHECKBOX" id="CHECKBOX">CHECKBOX</option>
70.     <option value="DROPDOWN" id="DROPDOWN">DROPDOWN</option>
71. </select>
72.
73. <div id="divtextarea">textarea</div>
74. <div id="divtextbox">textbox</div>
75. <div id="divcheckbox">checkbox</div>
76. <div id="divdropdown">dropdown</div>
77.
78. <table>
79. <tr class="member">
80.     <td>line 1 table row</td>
81. </tr>
82. <tr class="member">
```

```
83.       <td>line 2 table row</td>
84. </tr>
85. </table>
86.
87. </body>
88. </html>
```

Code File: 22_jquery/jquery_05.html

(3) Upload the page to your web server and test in your web browser.

Other examples

The site:

https://jqueryui.com/

includes a number of common User Interfaces you can incorporate into your own website with minimum effort and very little programming. In fact, you do not actually need to understand jQuery to be able to use these interfaces.

UI Accordion interface

As an example, we will use the Accordion interface illustrated below. Just copy and save as an html page. This example comes from **https://jqueryui.com/accordion/** that lists all the various options available.

Click headers to expand/collapse content that is broken into logical sections, much like tabs. Optionally, toggle sections open/closed on mouse over.

The underlying HTML mark-up is a series of headers (H3 tags) and content divs so the content is usable even without JavaScript enabled on the browser.

Create a new web page called **jquery_06.html** as follows:

```
1.  <!DOCTYPE html>
2.  <html>
3.  <head>
4.      <meta charset="UTF-8" />
5.      <title>jQuery UI Accordion - Default functionality</title>
6.      <link rel="stylesheet"
7.        href="http://code.jquery.com/ui/1.9.2/themes/base/jquery-
    ui.css" />
8.      <script src="http://code.jquery.com/jquery-1.8.3.js"></script>
9.      <script src="http://code.jquery.com/ui/1.9.2/jquery-
    ui.js"></script>
10.     <script>
11.     $(function() {
12.         $( "#accordion" ).accordion();
```

```
13.      });
14.      </script>
15.  </head>
16.  <body>
17.
18.  <div id="accordion">
19.      <h3>Section 1</h3>
20.      <div>
21.          <p>
22.          Mauris mauris ante, blandit et, ultrices a, suscipit eget
23.          ut neque. Vivamus nisi metus, molestie vel, gravida in, sit
24.          amet, nunc. Nam a nibh. Donec suscipit eros. Nam mi. Proin
25.          odio. Curabitur malesuada. Vestibulum a velit eu ante
26.          vulputate.</p>
27.      </div>
28.      <h3>Section 2</h3>
29.      <div>
30.          <p>
31.          Sed non urna. Donec et ante. Phasellus eu ligula. Vestibulum
32.          purus. Vivamus hendrerit, dolor at aliquet laoreet, mauris
33.          velit, faucibus interdum tellus libero ac justo. Vivamus
34.          suscipit faucibus urna.</p>
35.      </div>
36.      <h3>Section 3</h3>
37.      <div>
38.          <p>
39.          Nam enim risus, molestie et, porta ac, aliquam ac, risus.
40.          Phasellus pellentesque purus in massa. Aenean in pede.
41.          ac tellus pellentesque semper. Sed ac felis. Sed commodo,
42.          lacinia ornare, quam ante aliquam nisi, eu iaculis leo
43.          venenatis dui.</p>
44.              <ul>
45.                  <li>List item one</li>
46.                  <li>List item two</li>
47.                  <li>List item three</li>
48.              </ul>
49.      </div>
50.      <h3>Section 4</h3>
51.      <div>
52.      <p>Cras dictum. Pellentesque habitant morbi tristique senectus
53.      malesuada fames ac turpis egestas. Vestibulum ante ipsum primis
54.      orci luctus et ultrices posuere cubilia Curae; Aenean lacin
55.      vel est.</p>
56.      <p>Suspendisse eu nisl. Nullam ut libero. Integer dignissim.
57.      Class aptent taciti sociosqu ad litora torquent per conubia
58.      inceptos himenaeos.</p>
59.      </div>
60.  </div>
61.
62.  </body>
63.  </html>
```

Code File: 22_jquery/jquery_06.html

Menu Interface

jqueryui includes a menu system as described at **https://api.jqueryui.com/menu/**

Create a new web page called **jquery_07.html** as follows:

```
1.  <!DOCTYPE html>
2.  <html>
3.  <head>
4.  <meta charset="UTF-8">
5.  <title>menu demo</title>
6.  <link rel="stylesheet" href="http://code.jquery.com/ui/1.10.2/themes
    /smoothness/jquery-ui.css">
7.  <style>
8.  .ui-menu {
9.  width: 200px;
10. }
11. </style>
12. <script src="http://code.jquery.com/jquery-1.9.1.js"></script>
13. <script src="http://code.jquery.com/ui/1.10.2/jquery-
    ui.js"></script>
14. </head>
15. <body>
16. <ul id="menu">
17. <li><a href="#">Item 1</a></li>
18. <li><a href="#">Item 2</a></li>
19. <li><a href="#">Item 3</a>
20. <ul>
21. <li><a href="#">Item 3-1</a></li>
22. <li><a href="#">Item 3-2</a></li>
23. <li><a href="#">Item 3-3</a></li>
24. <li><a href="#">Item 3-4</a></li>
25. <li><a href="#">Item 3-5</a></li>
26. </ul>
27. </li>
28. <li><a href="#">Item 4</a></li>
29. <li><a href="#">Item 5</a></li>
30. </ul>
31. <script>
32. $( "#menu" ).menu();
33. </script>
34. </body>
35. </html>
```

Code File: 22_jquery/jquery_07.html

Date Picker

On the web site **http://jqueryui.com/datepicker/** there is an example on creating a date picker. Create a web page and create the date picker, then modify the script to add in the dateFormat to give a UK format rather than the default US format.

You will need to look up the API documentation at
http://api.jqueryui.com/datepicker/ and look at the dateFormat method to see
how to do it.

Code File: 22_jquery/datepicker.html

Image Galleries, Sliders and Carousels

https://galleria.io/ is a free and open source gallery

https://wowslider.com/

Illustrates what can be done with jQuery.

Bootstrap

http://getbootstrap.com

Bootstrap is a framework for creating web page layouts more easily than writing css
code yourself.

AJAX and jQuery

We use **AJAX** to load the part of a web page in the background without the whole
page having to reload. jQuery includes code that allows the jQuery AJAX functions
to work correctly over different browsers. In the next section, we look at look at
AJAX, and how to use it with PHP.

AJAX

AJAX stands for "**A**synchronous JavaScript and **X**ML" and is a set of web technologies where a client request can update part of a web page without having to reload the whole web page. The method is noticeable in modern web email systems such as Google, Yahoo and Microsoft email clients where parts of the page changes without the whole page being reloaded in the browser.

Asynchronous means that the processing happens in the background and does not interrupt the normal display of other parts of the web page.

Many **AJAX** applications do not actually use XML, despite the X in **AJAX** – they tend to use data in the form of plain text or html, or in **JSON** (JavaScript **O**bject **N**otation) which we will look at later in this Chapter. The underlying call is **XMLHttpRequest** from the browser originally developed by Microsoft and then taken up by all other browser developers and is now a standard. The XML in the name can be misleading as any data can be requested.

The advantage with **AJAX** is that it looks nice, giving a good user experience and there can be improvements in performance because only a part of the page is re-displayed instead of the whole page.

AJAX fits nicely with the use of jQuery and can be used with **PHP**. The **jQuery** library protects us from the complexities of different browsers because browsers implement the required functionality differently.

In this section we will be looking at how to use **AJAX** with **PHP**, in particular we can look at creating a page that retrieves data into a list from a database using **JSON**.

AJAX Operation

The diagram below illustrates the basic idea of how AJAX works. The AJAX engine essentially takes over the form submission request using JavaScript. The server receives the requests, does its processing, maybe extracting data from the database, and then returns the data to the browser where the AJAX engine updates part of the web page. This all happens in the background so that the browser can action other scripts while waiting for a response from the server.

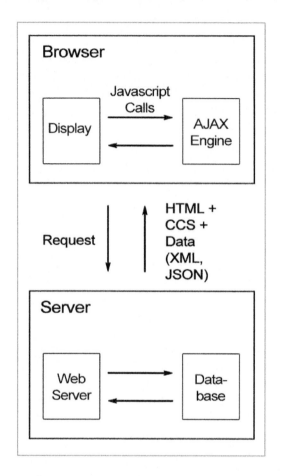

A simple AJAX example

The standard 'Hello World!' of **AJAX** using jQuery is shown below:

```
1.   <!DOCTYPE html>
2.   <html>
3.   <head>
4.   <meta charset="UTF-8" />
5.   <script
6.   src="https://ajax.googleapis.com/ajax/libs/jquery/3.4.1/jquery.min.j
     s"></script>
7.
8.   </head>
9.   <body>
10.
11.  <script type="text/javascript">
12.  $(document).ready(function(){
13.    $("#loadfile").click(function(){
14.      $("#div1").load("hello_world.txt");
15.    });
16.  });
17.  </script>
```

```
18.
19. <div id="div1">
20.       <h2>Click on the button to load the hello_world.txt file</h2>
21. </div>
22.
23. <br/>
24. <br/>
25.
26. <input type="button" id="loadfile" value="Load File" />
27.
28. </body>
29. </html>
```

Code File: 22_jquery/ajax01.html

This example uses a text file called "hello_world.txt" that contains any text you want and in this example is located in the same folder as the html page itself.

The jQuery should be familiar to you from previous examples. It uses the 'ready' function to check that the page has finished loading and then provides the click event to control the contents of div1.

When the button is clicked, the contents of the text file is loaded into div1 using .load

Note in this example the jQuery JavaScript file is remotely located on the google server.

As with other JQuery it uses callback functions, which is a function passed as a parameter to another function.

JSON

The above "Hello World!" example illustrates that we can read text files very easily from the server, but we need to be able to get formatted data from a database or other source so that we can display it in drop down lists or in data grids views on our web pages.

To do this we use a technology called **JSON**.

JSON stands for **J**ava**S**cript **O**bject **N**otation and is a method used for data exchange. The **JSON** format is based on JavaScript objects; it is plain text and can be read and created by most programming languages including **PHP**. The format consists of name / value pairs and is often used with **AJAX** where the JavaScript on the client computer is used to fetch and then decode and format the data.

An example of **JSON** that represents a company might be:

```
{
        "companyName": "The Software Distribution Company",
        "category": "Web Programming"
}
```

A more complex example might be:

```
{
        "companyName": "The Software Distribution Company",
        "category": "Web Programming",
        "address": {
                "firstLine": "45 Somewhere",
                "SecondLine": "The Big City",
                "postCode": "BA17 9AJ"
                },
}
```

PHP has the function **json_encode** that will encode the data values for you. Normally this data is in the form of an array, which we can easily write in PHP, or we can create an array dynamically using PHP database functions that we have used previously.

An example of encoding an array into a **JSON** call is:

```
1.  <?php
2.  $arr = array('name1' => John,
3.  'name2' => Paul,
4.  'name3' => George,
5.  'name4' => Ringo);
6.
7.  echo json_encode($arr);
8.  ?>
```

Code File: 22_jquery/json01.php

Upload the file to your web server and display the file in a browser.

The result will look something like this:

```
{"name1":"John","name2":"Paul","name3":"George","name4":"Ringo"}
```

NOTE: *You need PHP 5.2 or higher for the function **json_encode()**.*

A more useful example is:

```php
1.  <?php
2.
3.  $countries = array(
4.        array(
5.            "countryid" => "UK",
6.            "country" => "United Kingdom",
7.            "currency" => "GBP"
8.            ),
9.        array(
10.           "countryid" => "FR",
11.           "country" => "France",
12.           "currency" => "EUR"
13.           ),
14.       array(
15.           "countryid" => "GE",
16.           "country" => "Germany",
17.      "currency" => "EUR"
18.           )
19. );
20.
21. echo json_encode($countries);
22.
23. ?>
```

Code File: 22_jquery/json02.php

This example will output something like the following:

```
[
    {"countryid":"UK","country":"United Kingdom","currency":"GBP"},
    {"countryid":"FR","country":"France","currency":"EUR"},
    {"countryid":"GE","country":"Germany","currency":"EUR"}
]
```

This kind of **JSON** example would be used when we want to have a grid listing output on a web page, which we will see how to do later using **AJAX** calls.

We can create quite complex object representation of the real world using nested arrays.

```php
1.  <?php
2.
3.  $products = array(
4.        array(
5.            "id" => 2,
```

```
6.                 "name" => "Shirts",
7.            "price" => "19.99",
8.
9.            "sizes" => array (
10.                 "sizeL" => "4",
11.                 "sizeM" => "2",
12.                 "sizeS" => "1"
13.             )
14.
15.     ),
16.     array(
17.             "id" => "3",
18.             "name" => "Socks",
19.         "price" => "2.99",
20.
21.         "sizes" => array (
22.                 "sizeXL" => "5",
23.                 "sizeS" => "10"
24.             )
25.
26.     ),
27.     array(
28.             "id" => "4",
29.         "name" => "T Shirts",
30.             "price" => "1.99",
31.
32.         "sizes" => array (
33.                 "sizeL" => "3",
34.                 "sizeM" => "5"
35.             )
36.
37.     )
38. );
39.
40. echo json_encode($products);
41. ?>
```

Code File: 22_jquery/json03.php

This will gives an output similar to the following:

```
[{"id":2,"name":"Shirts","price":"19.99","sizes":{"sizeL":"4","sizeM"
:"2","sizeS":"1"}},{"id":"3","name":"Socks","price":"2.99","sizes":{"
sizeXL":"5","sizeS":"10"}},{"id":"4","name":"T
Shirts","price":"1.99","sizes":{"sizeL":"3","sizeM":"5"}}]
```

AJAX and PHP

In this section we want to take a **JSON** array and using **AJAX** and **PHP** display the data on a web page. We will be using **countries.php** as the source for the data so this file has to be located on your web server in the same folder as the html file that we are about to create.

First, create our example web page **ajax02.html** as follows:

```
1.  <!DOCTYPE html>
2.  <html>
3.  <head>
4.  <meta charset="UTF-8" />
5.  <title>AJAX and PHP</title>
6.  <script
7.  src="https://ajax.googleapis.com/ajax/libs/jquery/3.4.1/jquery.min.j
    s" type="text/javascript"></script>
8.
9.  </head>
10. <body>
11.
12. <input type="button" id="loadfile" value="Load File" />
13. <div id="result"></div>
14. </body>
15. </html>
```

Code File: 22_jquery/ajax02.html

Notice that we have an input button and a div where the result will be sent to.

Then we create the JavaScript to retrieve and display the data.

```
1.  <script type="text/javascript">
2.      $(document).ready(function(){
3.          //attach a jQuery live event to the button
4.          $("#loadfile").click(function(){
5.              $.getJSON('countries.php', function(data) {
6.                  //alert(data); //uncomment this for debug
7.                  //alert (data.country); //further debug
8.
9.                  $('#result').html(''); // Clear #result div
10.
11.                 fillSelect(data);    //Format the data and display
12.
13.              });
14.          });
15.      });
16.
17.  //Format the div and display the data in a table
18.  function fillSelect(data) {
19.      //alert(data);
20.
```

```
21.        var elm = "";
22.
23.        elm += '<table>';         //Start of table
24.        elm += '<tr>';
25.        elm += '<th>';
26.        elm += 'Country ID';
27.        elm += '</th>';
28.
29.        elm += '<th>';
30.        elm += 'Country';
31.        elm += '</th>';
32.
33.        elm += '<th>';
34.        elm += 'Currency';
35.        elm += '</th>';
36.        elm += '</tr>';
37.
38.        $.each(data, function(i, item) { // for each data element
39.             //alert(item.country);   //uncomment for debug
40.
41.             elm += '<tr>';
42.
43.             elm += '<td>';
44.             elm += item.countryid;
45.             elm += '</td>';
46.
47.             elm += '<td>';
48.             elm += item.country;
49.             elm += '</td>';
50.
51.             elm += '<td>';
52.             elm += item.currency;
53.             elm += '</td>';
54.
55.             elm += '</tr>';
56.
57.        });
58.
59.        elm += '</table>';         //End of table
60.
61.        $('#result').html(elm);
62.
63.  }
64.
65. </script>
```

The jQuery library has a full suite of **AJAX** methods that provide functions and methods to load data from the server without a browser page refresh.

The **AJAX** function that we are using here is **$.getJSON** that loads the JSON data from countries.php. function(data) is the call back function that is executed if the request is successful.

In the example, we take the retrieved data and process it using a loop.

Displaying the data in the #result div using JavaScript is very similar to the method that we use to display arrays in **PHP**. We process each row one row at a time using **$.each** to create the required HTML which in this case is a table that is output to the div.

The above technique can be used to construct any HTML element such as drop down lists, radio buttons and so on.

The complete example

```
1.  <!DOCTYPE html">
2.  <html>
3.  <head>
4.  <meta charset="UTF-8" />
5.  <title>AJAX and PHP</title>
6.  <script
7.  src="https://ajax.googleapis.com/ajax/libs/jquery/3.4.1/jquery.min.j
    s" type="text/javascript"></script>
8.
9.  <style type="text/css">
10. .body {font-family:Verdana, Arial, Helvetica, sans-serif;}
11. #result {margin-top:50px;margin-left:100px;}
12. </style>
13.
14. </head>
15. <body>
16.
17. <script type="text/javascript">
18.     $(document).ready(function(){
19.         //attach a jQuery live event to the button
20.         $("#loadfile").click(function(){
21.             $.getJSON('countries.php', function(data) {
22.                 //alert(data); //uncomment this for debug
23.                 //alert (data.country); //further debug
24.
25.                 $('#result').html(''); // Clear #result div
26.
27.                 fillSelect(data);    //Format the data and display
28.
29.             });
30.         });
31.     });
32.
33.     //Format the div and display the data in a table
34.     function fillSelect(data) {
35.         //alert(data);
36.
37.             var elm = "";
38.
```

```
39.            elm += '<table>';        //Start of table
40.            elm += '<tr>';
41.            elm += '<th>';
42.            elm += 'Country ID';
43.            elm += '</th>';
44.
45.            elm += '<th>';
46.            elm += 'Country';
47.            elm += '</th>';
48.
49.            elm += '<th>';
50.            elm += 'Currency';
51.            elm += '</th>';
52.            elm += '</tr>';
53.
54.        $.each(data, function(i, item) { // for each data element
55.            //alert(item.country);   //uncomment for debug
56.
57.            elm += '<tr>';
58.
59.            elm += '<td>';
60.            elm += item.countryid;
61.            elm += '</td>';
62.
63.            elm += '<td>';
64.            elm += item.country;
65.            elm += '</td>';
66.
67.            elm += '<td>';
68.            elm += item.currency;
69.            elm += '</td>';
70.
71.            elm += '</tr>';
72.
73.        });
74.
75.        elm += '</table>';        //End of table
76.
77.        $('#result').html(elm);
78.
79.    }
80.
81. </script>
82.
83. <input type="button" id="loadfile" value="Load File" />
84. <div id="result"></div>
85. </body>
86. </html>
```

Code File: 22_jquery/ajax03.html

Upload this file to your web server, together with **countries.php** and then display
the file **ajax03.html** in your web browser.

Converting JSON to JavaScript Arrays

There may be situations where you want to convert the JSON array to a standard JavaScript array so that you can manipulate it.

```
1.  var dataArray = jQuery.parseJSON(data);   //convert json to
    JavaScript arrary
```

where data is the array in JSON format.

What is Bootstrap?

Bootstrap is an open source framework of CSS, HTML and JavaScript files that we use to add functionality and layout to a web project.

So why are we looking at a CSS framework in a book on PHP? Well, it is super easy to add Bootstrap to a web page in one line of code and then create layouts and menus that look good and are responsive so they work well on a range of devices: mobile phones, tablets and desktop displays.

There are a number of similar frameworks available such as Pure by Yahoo and Foundation by Zurb but Bootstrap has become popular with very good documentation.

The latest version is 4, released in 2018, although you will still see many references to version 3.

Adding Bootstrap to a web page

(1) First create a new html page and start with an HTML 5 basic structure similar to the following:

```
1.  <!DOCTYPE html>
2.  <html>
3.  <head>
4.  <meta charset="UTF-8" />
5.  <title>Untitled Document</title>
6.  </head>
7.
8.  <body>
9.
10. </body>
11. </html>
```

Code File: 22_jquery/bootstrap01.html

(2) Go to https://getbootstrap.com/

(3) On the main page there should be a title "BootstrapCDN" where you will see the CSS stylesheet code. Copy and paste into the head of your web page.

This CSS gives the responsive layouts.

(4) There should also be a heading for the required JavaScript files that will consist of a number of links. Copy these links and place them on the web page just above the **</body>** tag. Note that these should be as far down the page as possible. These files provide functionality such as the responsive menu system. If you only need the layout features then you do not need to include these files.

Your web page will look something like the following:

```
1.  <!DOCTYPE html>
2.  <html>
3.  <head>
4.  <meta charset="UTF-8" />
5.  <title></title>
6.  <link rel="stylesheet"
7.      href="https://stackpath.bootstrapcdn.com/bootstrap/4.3.1/css/boo
    tstrap.min.css"
8.      integrity="sha384-
    ggOyR0iXCbMQv3Xipma34MD+dH/1fQ784/j6cY/iJTQUOhcWr7x9JvoRxT2MZw1T"
9.      crossorigin="anonymous">
10. </head>
11. <body>
12. <h2>Using Bootstrap</h2>
13.
14. <script src="https://code.jquery.com/jquery-3.3.1.slim.min.js"
15.     integrity="sha384-
    q8i/X+965Dz00rT7abK41JStQIAqVgRVzpbzo5smXKp4YfRvH+8abtTE1Pi6jizo"
16.     crossorigin="anonymous"></script>
17. <script src="https://cdnjs.cloudflare.com/ajax/libs/popper.js/1.14.7
    /umd/popper.min.js"
18.     integrity="sha384-
    UO2eT0CpHqdSJQ6hJty5KVphtPhzWj9WO1clHTMGa3JDZwrnQq4sF86dIHNDz0W1"
19.     crossorigin="anonymous"></script>
20. <script src="https://stackpath.bootstrapcdn.com/bootstrap/4.3.1/js/b
    ootstrap.min.js"
21.     integrity="sha384-
    JjSmVgyd0p3pXB1rRibZUAYoIIy6OrQ6VrjIEaFf/nJGzIxFDsf4x0xIM+B07jRM"
22.     crossorigin="anonymous"></script>
23.
24. </body>
25. </html>
```

Code File: 22_jquery/bootstrap02.html

(5) The next stage is to add in the layout. An easy way to do this is to look at the example layouts in source code and copy the html code over. In the following, I have copied out the code from the Jumbotron.

Columns in Bootstrap can be thought of as 12 individual columns that we can join together to suit the size requirements.

The example below shows three columns each made up using class="col-md-4".

```
1.  <div class="row">
2.
3.      <div class="col-md-4">
4.
5.      </div>
6.
7.      <div class="col-md-4">
8.
9.      </div>
10.
11.     <div class="col-md-4">
12.
13.     </div>
14.
15. </div>
```

The full code for the centre area is shown below:

```
1.  <div class="row">
2.    <div class="col-md-4">
3.      <h2>Heading 1</h2>
4.      <p>Donec id elit non mi porta gravida at eget metus. Fusce
5.          dapibus, tellus ac cursus commodo, tortor mauris condimentum
6.          nibh, ut fermentum massa justo sit amet risus.</p>
7.          <p><a class="btn btn-secondary"
                  href="#" role="button">View details</a></p>
8.    </div>
9.    <div class="col-md-4">
10.     <h2>Heading 2</h2>
11.     <p>Donec id elit non mi porta gravida at eget metus. Fusce
12.         dapibus, tellus ac cursus commodo,
13.         tortor mauris condimentum nibh, ut fermentum massa justo
14.         sit amet risus.</p>
15.         <p><a class="btn btn-secondary"
                  href="#" role="button">View details</a></p>
16.   </div>
17.   <div class="col-md-4">
18.     <h2>Heading 3</h2>
19.     <p>Donec sed odio dui. Cras justo odio, dapibus ac facilisis
20.         in, egestas eget quam. Vestibulum id ligula porta felis
21.         euismod semper.</p>
22.         <p><a class="btn btn-secondary"
                  href="#" role="button">View details</a></p>
23.   </div>
24. </div>
```

Code File: 22_jquery/bootstrap03.html

Summary

jQuery enables you to create web pages with added effects and interactions. The cross-browser support means you can be sure that they work on different browsers. jQuery is also the framework that provides cross-browser AJAX support. AJAX is the 'in thing' at the moment, because it creates web applications that look modern and responsive. The example that we have shown in this Chapter illustrates how to use data from a PHP script that can ultimately be derived from a database. We also illustrate the use of Bootstrap to create responsive HTML layouts.

Topics for Review

[1] List some of the uses of jQuery in PHP scripts.

[2] What is the purpose of $(document).ready(function() { }); ?

[3] What is the purpose of AJAX in PHP scripts?

[4] Explain what JSON can be used for.

23 - .htaccess and php.ini files

What is in this Chapter?

* Using an htaccess file.
* Creating an admin area with an .htpasswd file.
* The php.ini file.

You can do many things with .htaccess files including redirecting pages from one location to another. We use this particularly with 301 redirects to tell a web browser that the page has changed - it is used in situations where you move a page and you want Google to correctly understand that move.

NOTE: The .htaccess is very powerful and even the smallest error could mean that your web site will stop working. So make sure that you have a backup of the file when you make a change.

Since .htaccess is a hidden system file, you need to make sure that your FTP client is configured to show hidden files. This is usually an option in the program's preferences/options.

.htaccess files only work on Linux type web servers, not on Windows web servers.

When you create the .htaccess file, you will need to upload it to your web server to the folder where you want it to affect - quite often, this is the root of the web site, but it can be placed further down the directory tree in which case it will affect only those folders below it.

Things that can be done with an htaccess file

* Permanently redirect or temporarily redirect one URL to another - useful for informing search engines about files that have moved.

* Prevent browsers displaying a list of folders and files on your web site to improve your site security.

* Password protect a folder of a web site.

* Create a custom 404-error page.

To use an .htaccess file

(1) Create a new file called .htaccess on your local PC. Note that an htaccess file has a dot at the first character.

(2) For a Windows PC you may not be able to create a file with .htaccess, so create a text file with notepad or similar editor called htaccess.txt with the intention of uploading it to the server and then changing the file name on the server.

Examples of .htaccess files

301 is permanent redirect

If you have a web page that you have moved on your web site and are concerned that search engines and web sites may be still linking to the original location, then use the 301 redirect.

```
# Redirect old file path to new file path
Redirect 301 /oldpage.html http://www.yoursite.com/newpage.html
```

302 is temporary redirect

This method of redirect is used when you temporarily move a web page, but this is a rare occurrence.

```
# Redirect old file path to new file path - not normally used
Redirect 302 /oldpage.html http://www.yoursite.com/newpage.html
```

Defining a custom 404 error page

This is a useful feature to create a custom error message if a page does not exist on your server. If someone clicks on a link and that page is missing, the standard 404-error message is displayed. We can use this method to create a special web page on our site giving better information than the standard page.

```
# Custom 404 error page
ErrorDocument 404 /errordocs/error404.htm
```

Stop users displaying the directory listing of a web site

It is possible for users to view a list of web pages on your site. This is not normally something you want, especially if you have test pages and other pages you don't want normal users to see. This feature will prevent the display of a directory listing.

```
# Stop directory listings
IndexIgnore *
```

Stop users displaying the details of an htaccess file

This feature stops users viewing the .htaccess file itself, which again is useful for security reasons.

```
# Stop displaying of htaccess file
<Files .htaccess>
order allow,deny
deny from all
</Files>
```

Protect your admin area with an htaccess / htpasswd file

You may want to have a login system to protect an area of a web site. The htaccess / htpasswd system is a relatively simple way of doing this to pop up a login box. The method is **basic authentication** but is not considered a very secure method unless you are using https (SSL) connection, but is adequate for many purposes.

Create an .htaccess file

Go to **http://www.htaccesstools.com/htaccess-authentication/**

In the first box, enter in some optional text that will be displayed in the login box when the user accesses the area.

In the second box, you need to enter the file path name to a second file htpasswd file. The htpasswd file is where the list of users / passwords are to be located.

Click on the button, copy the text and place it into a text file. Name this file .htaccess and upload it to the folder that you want to protect. In this case, this would be the /admin/ folder.

Create the .htpasswd username / password file

Go to **http://www.htaccesstools.com/htpasswd-generator/**

In the first box, enter the username.

In the second box, enter the password.

Click the button, copy the text and place it into a text file. Name this file .htpasswd and upload it to a suitable location on your server. This can be anywhere on your server, but usually in a defined folder. The location is the same location as was entered in (1) above.

The folder as defined in (1) should now be protected by the username / password as defined in (2).

The php.ini file

The php.ini file is a special file for **PHP**. The php.ini file is where you define settings for your **PHP** site.

Usually, the server is already configured with standard settings for PHP that have been selected by your web-hosting administrator. Unless you specifically need to change one or more of the settings, there is no need to create or modify a php.ini file.

The type of things you would do with a php.ini file are:

* Modify the resource limits for such things as memory limits, execution time limits etc.
* Set the default error behaviour for **PHP** errors.
* Define logging.
* Define the modules that are available.
* Define the location of sessions on the server.

and many other configuration details.

Summary

This Chapter first looked at what you can do with an .htaccess file and then looked at the **php.ini** configuration file. Both of these subjects can help you make the most of a web server.

Topics for Review

[1] Can you use an .htaccess file on a Windows Server?

[2] List a few of the things you can do with an .htaccess file.

[3] Explain the purpose of the php.ini file.

24 - WordPress Plugins

What is in this Chapter?

* The structure of a WordPress plugin.
* Installing a plugin.
* Example of developing a simple plugin.

WordPress is a popular Blog and Content Management System (CMS) that can be programmed using Plugins and whose look and feel can be defined by Themes.

So you can use WordPress as the framework for your programming applications - you don't need to write a login system or an admin system, and you don't have to worry about upgrading WordPress for new versions of PHP because updates are managed automatically. You can also use the WordPress distribution system to make your application available to the public.

In this Chapter, we assume you have a WordPress Installation on a web server. You should make sure that WordPress is at the latest version.

Creating a Plugin

A Plugin is a PHP script or scripts that allow you to utilise the features of WordPress.

To create a Plugin you have to use specific WordPress calls and write particular code within the forms to make it work with WordPress. This section shows how to create a Plugin integrating it within the WordPress menu system.

Structure of WordPress Plugin

To write a Plugin you have to adhere to the WordPress recommended structure. You have to do this to make sure your Plugin works.

When you start to work with a Plugin, you should invent a folder name and a name for the Plugin that will be unique so it does not clash with other Plugins the users may install into their WordPress installation.

With my example, I am going to use **withinweb_keycodes** as the name of the Plugin and the prefix for all function names and variables names.

First version of the Plugin – plugin_01

Code File: 24_wordpress/plugin_01/

This Plugin will create a menu system in the WordPress admin area, it will create variables that the admin user can modify and it will create a set of admin pages where the admin user can manage the data.

* Create a new folder called **withinweb_keycodes**.
* In that folder, create a new file called **withinweb_keycodes.php**.
* This first script is an outline for creating menus and setting up some variables.

Go to the source code for the book, and under the folder for this Chapter, there is a folder called **plugin_01**. Copy the code from the file withinweb_keycodes.php.

Installing the Plugin

You install Plugins through the admin panel, and normally you do this with a file that is a zip file of your entire Plugin. In this example, we only have one file called **withinweb_keycodes.php**.

Using the folder **plugins_01** and the file called **withinweb_keycodes.php** we can try installing the Plugin.

* zip up the file.
* Log into your WordPress admin area and click on Plugins.
* Click on the Add New button at the top of the Plugins page.
* Click on Upload.
* Click on Browse and select the .zip file from your computer.
* Click on Install.

* Click on the Activate Plugin link.
* The Plugin should say that it was successfully installed.
* Go to the list of Plugins where you should see the newly installed activated Plugin.

Now you should now see a list of menus under the main menu of KeyCodes.

To deactivate and remove the Plugin:

* Go to the list of Plugins and click on the Deactivate link for the Plugin.
* Now that the Plugin is deactivated, click on Delete.
* Then click on the button that says 'Yes, delete these files'.

Explanation of the first version of the plugin

The Plugin **withinweb_keycodes.php** from the folder **plugins_01** should have worked correctly. We will now go through the code line by line.

Code File: 24_wordpress/plugin_01/

Plugin name

```
1.  /*
2.  Plugin Name: WithinWeb PHP-KeyCodes
3.  Plugin URI: http://www.withinweb.com/wp_phpkeycodes/
4.  Description: Sell software licence codes, key codes or PIN
            numbers using PayPal IPN.
5.  Author: Paul Gibbs
6.  Version: 1.0.0
7.  Author URI: http://www.withinweb.com/
8.  */
```

The first section shown above defines the Plugin and hence you need fill this out correctly. These comments always appear at the top of the Plugin file and are needed for correct activation.

Activation / deactivation hooks

The next two lines are hooks. WordPress provides you with a way to hook your code into the WordPress framework. The activation hook defines a function that is called on activation of the Plugin, in this example the function is **'withinweb_keycodes_install'** the details of which we will see shortly.

Similarly, the deactivation hook defines a function that is called on deactivation of the Plugin.

```
1.  register_activation_hook(__FILE__, 'withinweb_keycodes_install');
2.  register_deactivation_hook(__FILE__, 'withinweb_keycodes_deactivate'
    );
```

In both examples, the first parameter is the path to the main Plugin file that is **withinweb_keycodes.php** in this case. We can use the WordPress constant **__FILE__** that represents the file system path to the current .php file.

Menu definitions

The next line is:

```
1.  add_action( 'admin_menu', 'withinweb_keycodes_create_menu' );
```

The add_action function allows us to hook a function onto a specified action. So we are running the function **'withinweb_keycodes_create_menu'** for the hook **'admin_menu'** that runs after the basic panel structure is in place.

In our example, this is the **'withinweb_keycodes_create_menu'** function:

```
1.  function withinweb_keycodes_create_menu() {
2.
3.  //main menu
4.  add_menu_page( 'PHP-
    KeyCodes', 'KeyCodes', 'manage_options', __FILE__,
       'withinweb_keycodes_help_page');
5.
6.  //sub menu
7.  add_submenu_page(__FILE__, 'Setting for PHP-
    KeyCodes', 'Settings',
8.     'manage_options', __FILE__.'_settings',
       'withinweb_keycodes_settings_page' );
9.
10. add_submenu_page(__FILE__,
       'PHP-KeyCodes Sales', 'Sales', 'manage_options',
       __FILE__.'_sales', 'withinweb_keycodes_sales_page' );
11.
12. add_submenu_page(__FILE__,
       'Help with PHP-KeyCodes', 'Help', 'manage_options',
       __FILE__.'_help', 'withinweb_keycodes_help_page' );
```

```
13.
14. add_submenu_page(__FILE__,
        'About PHP-KeyCodes', 'About', 'manage_options',
        __FILE__.'_about', 'withinweb_keycodes_about_page' );
15.
16. add_submenu_page(__FILE__,
        'Uninstall PHP-KeyCodes', 'Uninstall', 'manage_options',
        __FILE__.'_uninstall','withinweb_keycodes_uninstall_page' );
17.
18. }
```

This defines the main menu link and a number of sub menu links.

The **add_menu_page** and the **add_submenu_page** have a number of parameters and you can see a full description in the WordPress documentation.

```
1.  <?php
2.  add_menu_page( $page_title, $menu_title, $capability, $menu_slug,
        $function, $icon_url, $position );
3.  ?>
```

* The first parameter is the title of the page: PHP-KeyCodes.
* The second parameter is the title of the menu: KeyCodes.
* The third parameter is to do with user roles. There are many of these and you will need to look them up in the WordPress documentation. In our example we use: manage_options.
* The fourth parameter is the menu slug that is the name used to refer to this menu.
* The last parameter is the function we will look at later.

The **add_submenu_page** is similar to the **add_menu_page**:

```
1.  <?php
2.  add_submenu_page( $parent_slug, $page_title, $menu_title,
        $capability, $menu_slug, $function );
3.  ?>
```

* The first parameter is the parent_slug and refers to the main menu as already defined.
* The second parameter is the title of the page.
* The third parameter is the title of the menu.
* The fourth parameter is the user role.
* The fourth parameter is the menu slug that is the name this menu is referred to.
* The fifth parameter is the function name.

The functions that are defined in the menus are as shown below:

```
1.  function withinweb_keycodes_settings_page() {
```

```
2.      if ( is_admin() )         //Check if admin user
3.         {
4.
5.         }
6.  }
7.
8.  function withinweb_keycodes_about_page() {
9.      if ( is_admin() )         //Check if admin user
10.        {
11.
12.        }
13. }
14.
15. function withinweb_keycodes_help_page() {
16.     if ( is_admin() )         //Check if admin user
17.        {
18.
19.        }
20. }
21.
22. function withinweb_keycodes_sales_page() {
23.     if ( is_admin() )         //Check if admin user
24.        {
25.
26.        }
27. }
28.
29. function withinweb_keycodes_uninstall_page() {
30.     if ( is_admin() )         //Check if admin user
31.        {
32.
33.        }
34. }
```

These don't do anything at the moment, but these are where we call the admin pages.

Installation function

The next part that we explain is the function that is run during installation and is called by the activation hook:

```
1.  function withinweb_keycodes_install() {
2.
3.  if ( get_option( 'withinweb_keycodes_op_array' ) === false )
4.     {
5.        $options_array['withinweb_keycodes_admin_email']
                  = 'admin@somewhere.com';
6.        $options_array['withinweb_keycodes_paypal_email'] = '';
7.        $options_array['withinweb_keycodes_cancel_url'] = '';
8.        $options_array['withinweb_keycodes_return_url'] = '';
9.        add_option( 'withinweb_keycodes_op_array', $options_array );
10.    }
```

```
11.
12. if ( get_option( 'withinweb_keycodes_environment_array' ) == false )
13.    {
14.    $environment_array['withinweb_keycodes_paypal_environment'] = '';
15.       add_option( 'withinweb_keycodes_environment_array',
                $environment_array );
16.    }
17.
18. }
```

In our example above, we are using this to create two variable arrays one called **'withinweb_keycodes_op_array'** and another called **'withinweb_keycodes_environment_array'** which we are going to use to store set up details.

We create the array names and then use the **add_option** function to add the name / value pair to the WordPress options database.

```
1.  add_option( 'withinweb_keycodes_op_array', $options_array );
```

We use this to create a new name called **withinweb_keycodes_op_array**.

We will be able to create an admin page to read and modify these settings later.

This method is the simplest way to create storage within the WordPress database.

This install script could include other installation functions such as creating custom tables.

Deactivation function

There is also a deactivation hook that calls the function **'withinweb_keycodes_deactivate'**. It is used for such things as clearing out variables, deleting custom tables and so on.

```
1.  function withinweb_keycodes_deactivate() {
2.
3.  }
```

Second Version of Plugin – plugin_02

Code File: 24_wordpress/plugin_02/

Admin functions

The next version of the plugin is from the source-code folder **plugin_02** that adds in the admin functions.

So first, we have to modify the following functions:

```
1.  function withinweb_keycodes_settings_page() {
2.      if ( is_admin() )         //Check if admin user
3.      {
4.         //we are in wp-admin
5.         require (plugin_dir_path(__FILE__) .'views/adminsettings.php')
   ;
6.      }
7.  }
8.
9.  function withinweb_keycodes_about_page() {
10.     if ( is_admin() )         //Check if admin user
11.     {
12.        //we are in wp-admin
13.        require (plugin_dir_path(__FILE__) .'views/adminabout.php');
14.     }
15. }
16.
17. function withinweb_keycodes_help_page() {
18.     if ( is_admin() )         //Check if admin user
19.     {
20.        //we are in wp-admin
21.        require (plugin_dir_path(__FILE__) .'views/adminhelp.php');
22.     }
23. }
24.
25. function withinweb_keycodes_sales_page() {
26.     if ( is_admin() )         //Check if admin user
27.     {
28.        //we are in wp-admin
29.        require (plugin_dir_path(__FILE__) .'views/adminsales.php');
30.     }
31. }
```

We have added in the reference to the admin file. So the settings page has the following added:

```
5.   require (plugin_dir_path(__FILE__) . 'views/adminsettings.php');
```

and similarly for the other functions.

We now create a new folder called **'views'** in our Plugin folder and then create a number of php files that match the above php file references.

So we create files called **adminabout.php**, **adminhelp.php**, **adminsales.php** and **adminsettings.php**

In each of these file we create some basic headings, so in the **adminabout.php** file we enter:

```
1.  <div class="wrap">
2.
3.    <h2>About the PHP-KeyCodes plugin</h2>
4.    <p>This plugin is used to sell pin codes, key codes, software licen
      ce codes using PayPal IPN system.</p>
5.
6.  </div>
```

and we add in similar text in the other files.

Testing the Plugin so far

We should test the Plugin so far, by first deactivating and deleting the Plugin and then installing the new Plugin.

zip up the contents of the folder to make the new zip file, then upload it by going to Install Plugin in the admin area.

This time when we click on the menu items, we should see the text for each admin page.

There is no need to go through the process of de-activating the plugin, deleting it and then re-activating the plugin, as we can upload all the files to the web server with ftp. However, sometimes it can be just as easy to go through the normal plugin installation method rather than using ftp if there are many changes to the plugin.

Third Version of Plugin – plugin_03

Code File: 24_wordpress/plugin_03/

Adding in the admin settings details

We are now going to modify the **adminsettings.php** page to add in the input text fields.

The **adminsettings.php** page becomes:

```
1.   <div class="wrap">
2.
3.   <h2>Settings for the PHP-KeyCodes plugin</h2>
4.   <p>This page provides you with the set up that is required to use th
     e KeyCodes system.</p>
5.   <?php
6.     if ( isset( $_GET['m'] ) && $_GET['m'] == '1' )
7.     {
8.     ?>
9.     <div id='message' class='updated fade'><p><strong>You have
           successfully updated your settings.</strong></p></div>
10.    <?php
11.      }
12.    ?>
13.
14.    <?php $options = get_option( 'withinweb_keycodes_op_array' ); ?>
15.    <?php $environment = get_option(
                 'withinweb_keycodes_environment_array' ); ?>
16.    <table class="form-table">
17.        <tbody>
18.          <tr class="form-field form-required">
19.           <th scope="row"><label for="ipn_callback">IPN Call Back URL
20.               <span class="description"></span></label></th>
21.              <td>
22.                 <?php echo $options['withinweb_keycodes_ipn_url']; ?>
23.              </td>
24.           </tr>
25.        </tbody>
26.    </table>
27.
28. <form method="post" action="admin-post.php">
29.   <input type="hidden" name="action"
                 value="withinweb_keycodes_environment" />
30.     <?php wp_nonce_field( 'withinweb_keycodes_op_verify',
                 'withinweb_keycodes_environment' ); ?>
31.
32.     <table class="form-table">
33.        <tbody>
34.          <tr class="form-field form-required">
35.           <th scope="row"><label for="paypal_server">PayPal environment
36.               <span class="description">(required)</span></label></th>
37.                 <td>
38.
```

```
39.                    <select id="environment" name="environment">
40.                       <option value="">Please select</option>
41.                       <option value="sandbox"
42.     <?php echo $environment['withinweb_keycodes_paypal_environment']
    == 'sandbox' ?
43.     'selected="selected"' : ''; ?>>Sandbox - Testing</option>
44.                   <option value="live" <?php echo
45.     $environment['withinweb_keycodes_paypal_environment']
        == 'live' ?
46.     'selected="selected"' : ''; ?>>Live - Production</option>
47.                   </select>
48.
49.                </td>
50.             </tr>
51.          </tbody>
52.       </table>
53.
54.     <p class="submit">
55.     <input type="submit" value="Save" class="button-primary"/>
56.     </p>
57.
58.  </form>
59.
60.  <p>
61.     <strong>PayPal Settings:</strong>
62.  </p>
63.  <form method="post" action="admin-post.php">
64.
65.     <input type="hidden" name="action"
           value="withinweb_keycodes_settings" />
66.     <?php wp_nonce_field( 'withinweb_keycodes_op_verify',
67.           'withinweb_keycodes_settings' ); ?>
68.
69.  <table class="form-table">
70.     <tbody>
71.        <tr class="form-field form-required">
72.        <th scope="row"><label for="admin_email_address">
           Admin email address
73.        <span class="description">(required)</span></label></th>
74.        <td><input type="text" value="<?php echo esc_html(
75.        $options['withinweb_keycodes_admin_email'] ); ?>"
           id="admin_email" name="admin_email" style="width:240px;" ></td>
76.        </tr>
77.
78.           <tr class="form-field form-required">
79.              <th scope="row"><label for="paypal_email_address">
              PayPal email address
80.              <span class="description">(required)</span></label></th>
81.              <td><input type="text" value="<?php echo esc_html(
82.              $options['withinweb_keycodes_paypal_email'] ); ?>"
                 id="paypal_email" name="paypal_email" style="width:240px;">
83.           </td>
84.           </tr>
85.
86.           <tr class="form-field form-required">
```

```
87.              <th scope="row"><label for="cancel_url">Cancel URL <span
88.                class="description">(required)</span></label></th>
89.              <td><input type="text" value="<?php echo esc_html(
                   $options['withinweb_keycodes_cancel_url'] ); ?>"
                   id="cancel_url" name="cancel_url"
                   style="width:360px;" ></td>
90.            </tr>
91.            <tr class="form-field form-required">
92.              <th scope="row"><label for="return_url">Return URL <span
93.                class="description">(required)</span></label></th>
94.              <td><input type="text" value="<?php echo esc_html(
95.        $options['withinweb_keycodes_return_url'] ); ?>" id="return_url"
96.              name="return_url"  style="width:360px;" ></td>
97.            </tr>
98.        </tbody>
99. </table>
100.
101.        <p class="submit">
102.          <input type="submit" value="Save" class="button-primary"/>
103.        </p>
104.
105.        </form>
106.
107.        </div>
```

We can break down each stage of the code as follows:

Message update code

The first part of the code is:

```
1.  <?php
2.  if ( isset( $_GET['m'] ) && $_GET['m'] == '1' )
3.  {
4.  ?>
5.  <div id='message' class='updated fade'><p><strong>You have successfu
    lly updated
6.       your settings.</strong></p></div>
7.  <?php
8.  }
9.  ?>
```

This displays a message when the data is updated and we will see how this works later.

Retrieving option values

```
1.  <?php $options = get_option( 'withinweb_keycodes_op_array' ); ?>
2.
3.  <?php $environment = get_option('withinweb_keycodes_environment_arra
    y' ); ?>
```

This is the code we use to retrieve the option values from the database, and then we retrieve each value from the array:

```
1.  <?php echo $options['withinweb_keycodes_ipn_url']; ?>
```

The form

To allow us to update data, we create a standard form:

```
1.  <form method="post" action="admin-post.php">
2.
3.  </form>
```

NOTE: *The action is always* ***'admin-post.php'***

The next two lines are important:

```
1.  <input type="hidden" name="action"
        value="withinweb_keycodes_environment" />
2.  <?php wp_nonce_field( 'withinweb_keycodes_op_verify',
        'withinweb_keycodes_environment' ); ?>
```

The first line is a hidden field. Its value **withinweb_keycodes_environment** when prefixed with **admin_post_** will match the add_action hook that we have already created:

```
1.  <?php
2.  add_action('admin_post_withinweb_keycodes_environment',
        'process_withinweb_keycodes_environment' );
3.  ?>
```

This action points to the function '**process_withinweb_keycodes_environment**' so when this form is posted, the function '**process_withinweb_keycodes_environment**' is called.

The next line (the **wp_nonce_field** line) is used as a security check that we will use in the process script to make sure it came from the correct location.

Testing so far

We can test our script so far by first deactivating and deleting the existing Plugin.

Zip up the new version by zipping the complete folder and upload the Plugin from the admin area.

When you install the Plugin, it should display the menu items as before but now when you go to the settings link it should show a form to allow the administrator to modify the settings data. Pressing Submit will have no effect because we have not done the coding for the submit button.

Processing the form data - plugin_04

Code File: 24_wordpress/plugin_04/

The process.php file

We now need to add in the necessary code to process the submit button which in this case will be saving the settings data.

First, create a new folder called **'scripts'** and create a new file in that folder called **'process.php'**

Modify the main file **withinweb_keycodes.php** by adding the following line - it can be placed near the bottom of the file before the closing ?> tag.

include('scripts/process.php');

The process.php file contains that actually code that does the processing – that is it contains the business logic of the script.

Copy the following code into process.php.

```
1.  <?php
2.  //-----------------------------------------------------------
3.  // Settings page
4.  function process_withinweb_keycodes_settings()
5.  {
6.      if ( !current_user_can( 'manage_options' ) )
7.      {
8.          wp_die( 'You are not allowed to be on this page.' );
9.      }
10.     // Check the nonce field
11.     if ( !check_admin_referer( 'withinweb_keycodes_op_verify',
12.            'withinweb_keycodes_settings' ) )
13.     {
14.         exit;
```

```php
15.   }
16.
17.   $options = get_option( 'withinweb_keycodes_op_array' );
18.
19.   if ( isset( $_POST['admin_email'] ) )
20.   {
21.    $options['withinweb_keycodes_admin_email'] = sanitize_text_field(
       $_POST['admin_email'] );
22.   }
23.   if ( isset( $_POST['paypal_email'] ) )
24.   {
25.   $options['withinweb_keycodes_paypal_email'] = sanitize_text_field(
       $_POST['paypal_email'] );
26.   }
27.   if ( isset( $_POST['cancel_url'] ) )
28.   {
29.    $options['withinweb_keycodes_cancel_url'] = sanitize_text_field(
30.    $_POST['cancel_url'] );
31.   }
32.   if ( isset( $_POST['return_url'] ) )
33.   {
34.    $options['withinweb_keycodes_return_url'] = sanitize_text_field(
35.    $_POST['return_url'] );
36.   }
37.   update_option( 'withinweb_keycodes_op_array', $options );
38.   wp_redirect(admin_url(
39.   'admin.php?page=withinweb_keycodes/withinweb_keycodes.php_settings
       &m=1' ) );
40.
41.   exit;
42. }
43. //-------------------------------------------------------------
44. //Environment settings
45. function process_withinweb_keycodes_environment()
46. {
47.   if ( !current_user_can( 'manage_options' ) )
48.   {
49.     wp_die( 'You are not allowed to be on this page.' );
50.   }
51.   // Check the nonce field
52.   if (!check_admin_referer( 'withinweb_keycodes_op_verify',
53.     'withinweb_keycodes_environment' ))
54.   {
55.     exit();
56.   }
57.   $options = get_option( 'withinweb_keycodes_environment_array' );
58.
59.   if ( isset( $_POST['environment'] ) )
60.   {
61.     $options['withinweb_keycodes_paypal_environment'] =
         sanitize_text_field($_POST['environment'] );
62.   }
63.   //echo($_POST['environment']);
64.
65.   update_option( 'withinweb_keycodes_environment_array', $options );
```

```
66.   wp_redirect(admin_url(
      'admin.php?page=withinweb_keycodes/withinweb_keycodes.php_settings
      &m=1' ) );
67.
68.   exit;
69. }
70. ?>
```

This is made up of two functions: **process_withinweb_keycodes_settings** and **process_withinweb_keycodes_environment** because we have two separate forms on the settings page. There was no particular reason why I choose to have two separate forms as I could have had just the one and updated the lot at the same time however, this does illustrate the technique.

If we look at the code for the function **process_withinweb_keycodes_settings,** the first part is:

```
1.  if ( !current_user_can( 'manage_options' ) )
2.  {
3.      wp_die( 'You are not allowed to be on this page.' );
4.  }
```

These above lines simply check the access level that this person must have.

The next lines are:

```
1.  // Check the nonce field
2.  if (!check_admin_referer( 'withinweb_keycodes_op_verify',
        'withinweb_keycodes_environment'))
3.  {
4.      exit();
5.  }
```

These check the nonce value and the two entries must match the values as set in the form otherwise the script will not continue.

```
1.  $options = get_option( 'withinweb_keycodes_op_array' );
```

The above line retrieves the settings as an array that we defined in the main page.

We can now get the posted values and save them back to the database.

```
1.  if ( isset( $_POST['admin_email'] ) )
2.  {
3.    $options['withinweb_keycodes_admin_email'] = sanitize_text_field(
          $_POST['admin_email'] );
4.  }
```

sanitize_text_field first filters out any odd characters that we don't want to save to the database and this is assigned to the $options array.

Saving the array back is done using the **update_option** function as shown below:

```
1.  update_option( 'withinweb_keycodes_op_array', $options );
2.  wp_redirect( admin_url(
      'admin.php?page=withinweb_keycodes/withinweb_keycodes.php_settings
      &m=1' ) );
3.  exit;
```

The **wp_redirect** line is a redirect back to the settings page so that the user is transferred back to the settings page. This is made up of:

admin.php?	where all processing originates
frompage=withinweb_keycodes/	the Plugin folder name
withinweb_keycodes.php	the main Plugin script name
_settings	the slug name for the page we want to go to as defined in the main script file
&m=1	indicates that the page has been updated

Adding in the process hooks

Before we can test the code, we have to add in some process hooks in the main withinweb_keycodes.php file.

The hooks use the **add_action** function to link the hook name with the function that will be called.

```
1.  //Create process hooks
2.  add_action( 'admin_post_withinweb_keycodes_settings',
        'process_withinweb_keycodes_settings' );
3.  add_action( 'admin_post_withinweb_keycodes_environment',
        'process_withinweb_keycodes_environment' );
4.  add_action( 'admin_post_withinweb_keycodes_createitem',
        'process_withinweb_keycodes_createitem' );
```

If we take the first line as an example:

```
1.  add_action( 'admin_post_withinweb_keycodes_settings',
2.          'process_withinweb_keycodes_settings' );
```

The function to be called is **'process_withinweb_keycodes_settings'**.

The hook name '**admin_post_withinweb_keycodes_settings**' is made up of **admin_post_** which represents the admin-post.php file that is being posted to, followed by **withinweb_keycodes_settings** which matches the hidden field we put into the adminsettings.php file.

So now, the process functions in process.php file are linked to the adminsettings.php file.

Testing the code

To test this version of the Plugin, deactivate and delete the previous of the Plugin and then zip the plugin_04.

Upload the zip file and then activate it.

You should be able to go to the settings page and then update the settings.

Summary

WordPress is one of many PHP applications that we can use as a Content Management System or blog system. This Chapter shows how to create a basic WordPress Plugin. With your knowledge of PHP, you can work with WordPress or any of the other similar applications, modify and change them to suit your requirements.

Topics for Review

[1] Study the WordPress official documentation on codex.wordpress.org in the Writing_a_Plugin section/

[2] Pay attention to Plugin_Development_Suggestions of the guide. If you don't follow the guidelines, WordPress will reject the plugin when you try to submit it to the catalogue.

[3] Create an account with WordPress so that you can submit your plugin.

[4] Understand the submit process to WordPress that uses svn.

This Appendix provides information on two additional areas important to web development: the first is creating a test web server and the second is working with the phpMyAdmin administrator interface.

There are a number of ways in which you can set up a test web server environment, but the method shown here using **UniformServer** I have found to be particularly useful and I hope you find it equally useful.

A web server test environment using UniformServer

When you are developing **PHP** files, it is useful to have a test environment on your local computer. It is even better to have an environment that you run from a portable USB stick and the "Uniform Server" is able to do that.

The blurb for Uniform Server says:

"The Uniform Server is a free lightweight WAMP server solution for Windows. Less than 24MB, modular design, includes the latest versions of Apache2, Perl5, PHP (switch between PHP56, PHP70, PHP71, PHP72, PHP73 or PHP74), MySQL5 or MariaDB5, phpMyAdmin or Adminer4. No installation required! No registry dust! Just unpack and fire up!"

Uniform Server web site is:

http://www.uniformserver.com/

Uniserver includes: **Apache2** web server, **MySQL** database system with **phpMyAdmin** interface and the **PHP** programming language.

This is called a WAMP server (**W**indows, **A**pache, **M**ySQL and **P**HP) and hence is intended for Windows computers, not Mac.

Installation is simply extracting the files and copying them to where you want to run them from, hence, there is no installation program and it will run in any location on your computer, although c:\program files or other similar Windows folders are not recommended because of permission issues.

Installing the files

Go to the web site:

http://www.uniformserver.com/

and download the latest version by clicking on the button. This will give you a single file of around 50Mbytes.

Copy or move the file onto your USB flash stick, and double click on it to extract all the files to your location. This will take at least 10 minutes, as there are a large number of small files.

The total space required is approximately 300Mbytes.

Once you have all the files extracted, you can move the folder where you want or just leave them where they are. A suitable folder name would be something like /uniformserver/ at the root of the flash drive, but it can be any name.

To run the application, double click on **UniController.exe** that will display a small pop up box. When this is minimised, an icon will also appear in the program tray.

You may see a display similar to the following:

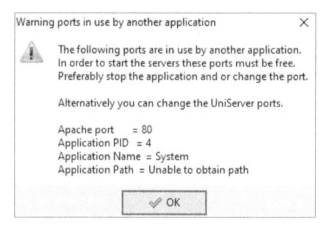

This means that you have another web server running on your computer. The easiest way to overcome this is to stop all other web servers. Run the 'Services' Application on your PC, find the services that are running a web service, right click on the name and select stop. These are the services that may be causing the issue:

World Wide Wide Publishing Services
SQL Server Reporting Services (SQLExpress)

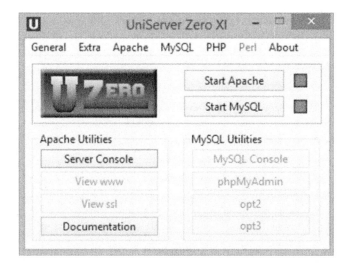

If you click on "Start Apache" and "Start MySQL", these applications will start up. Note that your PC will have to have a browser set as the default browser. This will usually be the case, but if not then it can be set in the Window "Default Program" control panel.

When you start MySQL, it will request for an admin password.

Your Windows Firewall control panel may pop up asking for a change in configuration, in which case you can just select the minimum setting to enable it to run on your local computer.

Once Apache and MySQL have started the red icons change to green.

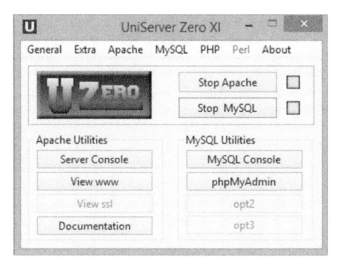

The location for your web files is in the folder www. There is already an index.php file in that location.

The web address will be **http://localhost/index.php** for this file. So, if you have a file called test.html in the www folder, then you can view it as
http://localhost/test.html

The Control Panel of UniformServer has configuration links. Note that you can only change the Apache settings after you stop the Apache server.

Using the web server

Now that you have the web server setup, you can create your website in the **www** folder that is accessed as a web site at http://localhost/

To access the MySQL database, you can use the web application **phpMyAdmin** accessed by http://localhost/phpmyadmin/

MySQL management using phpMyAdmin

phpMyAdmin is a web tool to manage all aspects of MySQL databases, tables and data. This is the most common way to manage MySQL and it will usually be available on most web hosting systems.

phpMyAdmin is used for:

* Creating databases and managing databases.
* Creating users to access those databases.
* Creating and managing tables in a database.
* Modifying data in tables.
* Running SQL commands against the tables.

Connecting to phpMyAdmin

phpMyAdmin is web based and hence you can use any modern web browser. **phpMyAdmin** comes in a number of different versions depending on the MySQL version it is connecting to and the facilities that you have may be slightly different depending on if you are using a hosting company or if you have installed it yourself on your local computer.

The example screenshots shown in this section may differ slightly to your version.

If you are using a hosting company for your web site, you will have some kind of control panel that you use to access **phpMyAdmin**. Log into your control panel and the find the **phpMyAdmin** icon.

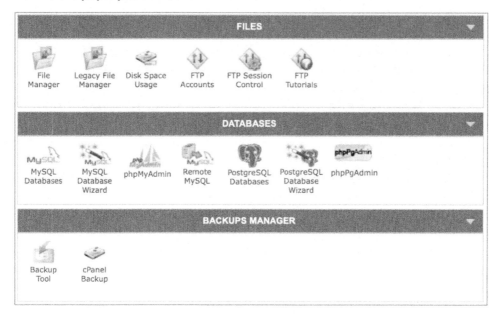

The above screenshot shows part of a typical **cPanel** display. Clicking on the **phpMyAdmin** icon will take you straight to the application, although some systems will ask for a username / password before you can access **phpMyAdmin**.

The **MySQL Databases** icon is where you create your database and users, while the **MySQL Wizard** is a useful utility that steps you through the process of creating a database and the required users.

The main display

The left hand side of **phpMyAdmin** consists of a list of the databases that are available to you. You may see some databases that are used by the system such as information_schema. You probably will not touch these and will not need to unless you have an advanced understanding of **MySQL**.

Creating a new database

Create database through the cPanel

cPanel allows you to create the database and to create the user as well. You will normally be given a link on your control panel to do this. When you click on the link, you will be taken to a page similar to the following:

Create a New Database

New Database: archiba8_

Create Database

Modify Databases

Check a Database: archiba8_phptutorials   Check the Database

Repair a Database: archiba8_phptutorials   Repair the Database

Current Databases

Search   Go

Enter in a name for your database and click on 'Create Database'.

Now you can create a user for the database.

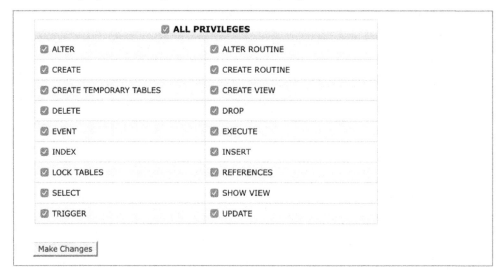

You must now create the user and password for the database by entering the values into the text boxes. You will need to write these down somewhere as these allow you to connect to the database by PHP scripts.

The last step is to add this user to a database, which you do by clicking on the 'Add' button.

This will display something similar to the following:

☑ ALL PRIVILEGES	
☑ ALTER	☑ ALTER ROUTINE
☑ CREATE	☑ CREATE ROUTINE
☑ CREATE TEMPORARY TABLES	☑ CREATE VIEW
☑ DELETE	☑ DROP
☑ EVENT	☑ EXECUTE
☑ INDEX	☑ INSERT
☑ LOCK TABLES	☑ REFERENCES
☑ SELECT	☑ SHOW VIEW
☑ TRIGGER	☑ UPDATE

Make Changes

It is this display where you add the permissions. You do not normally select 'All Privileges' as there are security implications. You should always select the minimum privileges that you can get away with. So for example, if you just want your web pages to display data rather than being able to update data you only need to choose **SELECT**.

Create database with phpMyAdmin

The other method of creating databases is with **phpMyAdmin**. You will need to do this if your database is on your local computer as in the example with using UniformServer as described in the previous section. The screenshot shown below illustrates how easy it is to create a database.

Click on the database tab and simply enter a database name and a collation - the collation defines the language sort order for results. I normally select **utf8_unicode_ci** being in the UK, but you choose the collation depending on your language.

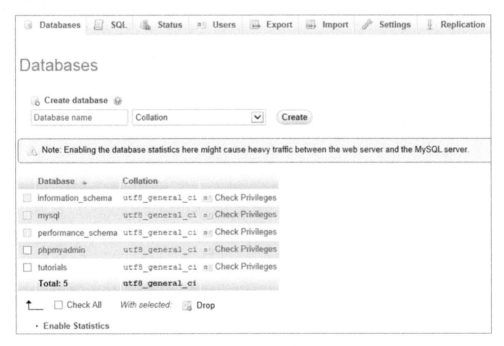

One you have created a database, you need to create a user with a password and the necessary privileges. The type of privileges that a user will need are SELECT, INSERT, UPDATE and DELETE to allow the underlying tables to be updated. You may also want the user to have CREATE privileges so that the user can create tables as well.

To create a user, enter this in the SQL script box:

```
1.  GRANT SELECT, INSERT, UPDATE, DELETE ON TUTORIALS.* TO
        'paul@localhost' IDENTIFIED BY 'paul123';
2.  FLUSH PRIVILEGES;
```

In the above example, TUTORIALS is the database name and the user name is 'paul' with a password of 'paul123'. It is assumed that the database host name is localhost.

In the following example, CREATE has been added to tables to be created:

```
1.  GRANT CREATE. SELECT, INSERT, UPDATE, DELETE ON TUTORIALS.* TO
        'paul'@'localhost' IDENTIFIED BY 'paul123';
2.  FLUSH PRIVILEGES;
```

Top menu display

The top tab menus provide you with the tools to manage your database and tables. The most commonly used will be the **Structure** tab and **SQL** tab. The **Structure** tab allows you to manage the columns and data types of the table while the **SQL** tab allows you to write SQL scripts and run them against each table.

Create your tables

Tables can be created within **phpMyAdmin** by defining column names and data types, or more commonly by running a **SQL** script.

Click on the database where you want to create the table. This will display a list of tables in that database similar to the following:

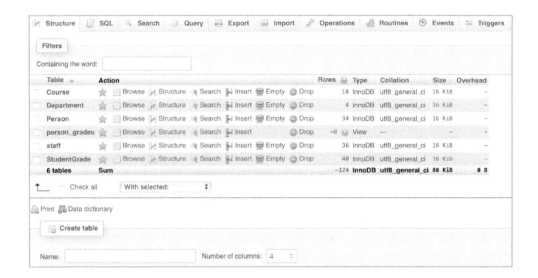

Note the top line of the display shows the current location.

You need to be careful to check this location or otherwise you may create a table in the wrong database.

In this example it is **Server: Uniform Server:3309 >> Database: tutorials**

The structure tab allows you to modify and view the structure of a table.

Suggested table example

As an example of creating a table, say we are creating a table with the following specification:

Suggested table name: **sales**

Suggested fields names: **RecID, CompanyName, DateOfPurchase, Quantity, Cost**

Define **Recid** as the primary key and define data types as appropriate.

RecID	INT	Auto-Number	Primary key
CompanyName	VARCHAR		

DateOfPurchase	VARCHAR
Quantity	INT
Cost	FLOAT

Each table you create has to have a primary key to identify uniquely each row. You can also set other columns to have unique values such as CompanyName.

Make sure you have clicked on the 'Structure' tab so you can modify and view the structure of a table.

Creating the table

Create a new table by typing in the table name and then entering the number of columns that the table will have. Once the table has been created, you can create new columns and define their names with data types.

So for example with the first column, the **RecID** has an integer (INT) data type and has to be the Primary key for the table. You set the Primary Key from the Index drop down list. **RecID** also has to be set as Auto-Number so that the record id is incremented each time a new record is created. This is done by ticking the A_I checkbox.

Adding records in the table

Now that we have created a table, we can create records.

To do this we first click on the database to list all the tables. Then click on the table name itself.

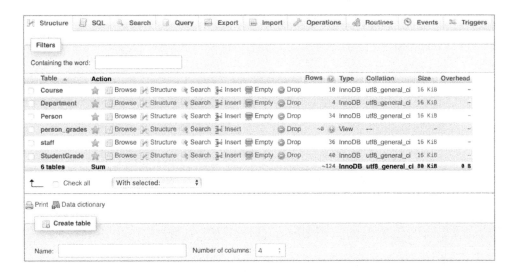

In the example screenshot above there is a table called **staff**. Click on the **Browse** link will display all the records in the table. The screenshot below illustrates the records in the table, if there are any.

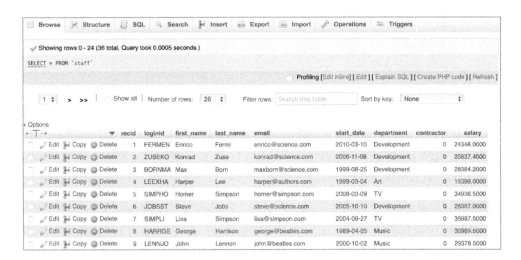

To add a new record, click on the **Insert** tab to display something similar to this screenshot below:

It is this display that allows you to enter into the **Value** field. Press the Go **button** to insert the data.

Running SQL scripts

One of the most common procedures that you use with **phpMyAdmin** is to run **SQL** scripts against the database and tables to query data from the table or to modify table structures.

In the **SQL** text box, if we enter:

```
1.  SELECT * FROM staff;
```

Then press the Go button, the SQL script will be run against that table.

NOTE: *A line of SQL is defined using the ; character at the end. If you are only entering in one line of SQL, then you do not need the ; character. However, if you are entering multiple lines, then you do need the ; character to separate the lines.*

Create tables with a SQL Script

Another common use of the SQL text box is to run management scripts such as creating tables.

An example of a create table SQL script is:

```
1.  CREATE TABLE Person (
2.       PersonID int NOT NULL AUTO_INCREMENT,
3.       LastName varchar(50) NOT NULL,
4.       FirstName varchar(50) NOT NULL,
5.       HireDate datetime NULL,
6.       EnrolmentDate datetime NULL,
7.  PRIMARY KEY (PersonID)
8.  );
```

Index

Printed in Great Britain
by Amazon